AFRICAN ELITE
THE BIG MEN OF A SMALL TOWN

Frontispiece:
The end of the railway lines awash on Gondo pier today

AFRICAN ELITE

THE BIG MEN OF A SMALL TOWN

JOAN VINCENT

COLUMBIA UNIVERSITY PRESS
NEW YORK & LONDON

Joan Vincent is Assistant Professor of Anthropology
at Barnard College.

FOR MY MOTHER
AND IN MEMORY OF MY FATHER

ISBN: 0-231-08332-7 *Paperback*
ISBN: 0-231-03353-2 *Clothbound*
Copyright © 1968, 1971 Columbia University Press

Library of Congress Catalog Card Number: 79-132691
Printed in the United States of America

Preface

The aim of my fieldwork in Teso, Uganda, in 1966–1967 was the study of a polyethnic community and involved district-level and community research into administrative history and the politics of agricultural development. Before selecting the trading center of Gondo for intensive research, I toured the southern and western parts of Teso District and consulted the Africana collection of Makerere University College Library to find a community that would satisfy my requirements. In essence these were that it should be ethnically heterogeneous but sufficiently small to permit study through traditional anthropological techniques of participant observation. During this period I visited Teso, and later Gondo fortnightly; began to acquire a smattering of Ateso; met Teso students and faculty at Makerere, researchers in neighboring districts and sister disciplines, and generally paved the way for entry into the field in August 1966.

After two weeks working in English and Ateso with the assistance of F. C. Odaet, a history student from Makerere, I met Washington Ekwaru of Ogera parish, who became my research assistant in Gondo. It quickly became apparent that we would have to use languages other than Ateso and English, and so I recruited a cohort of young co-workers, all Gondo residents with six to ten years' schooling in English, to transcribe taped conversations; collect data by means of questionnaires prepared in English, Ateso, and Lukenyi; and keep diaries. Schedules of inquiries arose out of the first six months' observation and were designed mainly to provide quantitative data, and to check biased or erroneous perceptions and guard against the personal element in daily participant observation.

[v]

On the whole, interethnic communication in Gondo was not difficult since many residents spoke both Ateso and other languages and were accustomed to shifting from one to another. For intensive interviews in matters felt to be of crucial importance or sensitivity, I was often fortunate to receive the help of visitors to Gondo, officials and civil servants fluent in English, who shared with me their usually fleeting visits to relatives.

Many residents gave me written texts, kept diaries and records of my design, and shared family documents with me—genealogies, burial lists, tax receipts, educational and military certificates, reports and letters of recommendation—personal papers of all description which were usually kept in the family bible inside a bag tied to the housepole or in the husband's box beneath his bed. At my request, Y. Elilu kept a written record of his court cases and discussed intricacies of evidence and judgment after each. Chiefs and ginnery officials permitted access to records as did firms in Soroti, Mbale, and Jinja which did business in Gondo. T. V. Kotecha gave me the use of rooms in an old ginnery bungalow.

While aiming at an intensive study of the parish over a calendar year, so important in an agricultural community, it was also necessary to set off these findings against the general background of the institutions and conditions of Serere and Teso as a whole. This entailed extensive use of archival material at sub-county headquarters in Kamod (court books, tax, birth, death and marriage registers); in Apapai dispensary; in Kamod and Ogelak schools; in Serere County headquarters (agricultural returns, census statistics); in Soroti (district records going back to 1907); in Entebbe (Uganda Government and Ministry of Agriculture archives); and in London (Foreign Office and Colonial Office archives at the Public Records Office). Although the parish chief allowed me to see his "returns" each month, no written records were kept at the parish level; those at the sub-county and county headquarters dated only from 1963 and only at Soroti were earlier documents preserved. Archival data on the historical development of Gondo and its administrative history were supplemented by interviews with its former chiefs.

Research was financed by a grant from the Ministry of Overseas Development of the United Kingdom and was carried out as a research fellow of the East African Institute of Social Research at Kampala. I received much practical help from staff and colleagues there, and in the departments of Sociology and Political Science at Makerere University College.

Parts of this work appeared in a dissertation presented at Columbia University where I was a Burgess Fellow in 1968. Conrad Arensberg, Robert Murphy, and Abraham Rosman of the Department of Anthropology shared the painful process by which a fieldwork experience became a doctoral dissertation. Raymond Apthorpe, David Barrett, George Bond, Abraham Rosman, Elliot Skinner, and Sharifa Zawawi were kind enough to read various chapters of this book in manuscript; its remaining deficiencies have slipped through their nets and are exclusively my catch. Miss Priscilla Pennell made the photographs presentable. A final word of appreciation must be expressed to the people of Gondo who tolerated my presence and allowed me, as a social anthropologist, to activate a status unfamiliar to them. I hope that I have nowhere betrayed their trust.

JOAN VINCENT

New York
September, 1969

Contents

Introduction

THE STUDY OF LOCAL-LEVEL POLITICS is becoming the meeting ground of social anthropology and political science in modern Africa. It is the arena in which the forces of the central government penetrate the social fabric, perhaps to encounter the indigenous resistance of local leadership. At the district level in Uganda there are five foci of leadership: the District Office where centrally appointed administrators serve short terms, touring, admonishing, encouraging, and homogenizing local areas; the District Council, a body of elected members who represent the interests of local constituencies in a legislative chamber; the chiefly hierarchy, an indigenous elite created out of the mission-educated whose spoils of office have, in the past, given them powers of patronage over the common man; the market economy, still largely in the hands of aliens; and, finally, the local community in which a few capable men rise above their fellows to provide leadership within its boundaries and a concerted front to the world outside. These men, the guardians and the political entrepreneurs of Gondo, a small polyethnic parish in Teso, are the subjects of this study. They form a strategic elite in this era when the goals of central government are to transform the countryside.

During the past decade, anthropologists have become increasingly interested in the political middleman—the inter-hierarchical office, as Gluckman puts it, of District Commissioner and village headman.[1] Studies of political brokers were pioneered by Wolf in Mexico and in southeast Asia by Geertz.[2] Between intercalary brokers such as these and the common man, informal, interstitial positions are filled by a spectrum of political actors. A chief may be a cultural broker, a gateman to another political arena by appointment, but within every

[1]

community there are those self-made men—those Big Men of Melanesian ethnography who are coming to light more and more in African studies as anthropologists drop their structural pose—who choose to operate in two political worlds and who become, therefore, increasingly significant when change and development are being engendered.

The Big Man has made his entry onto the ethnographic stage only during the past decade.[3] First stalking and rampaging in Melanesia, his presence has now been discerned—belatedly perhaps—behind the curtain of structuralism in Africa. His specter surely haunts Evans-Pritchard's description of the Nuer "bull" and he is well at home, as Worsley has shown, among the egalitarian Tallensi.[4] Schapera, as long ago as 1953, suggested the usefulness of studying the role of such a political operator; a suggestion Barth took up to good purpose in his study of political leadership among the Pathan of Swat.[5] There have, however, been no such studies of local leadership in polyethnic African communities.

That this is a gap which requires filling has become recognized with the changing needs of social scientists working in Africa. To the government official, the administrator, and the extension worker in Africa today—the agriculturist, the community developer, and the local administrative officer alike—Big Men are the linchpins of successful development projects. The "progressive farmer," "the influential," "the broker," "the gatekeeper"—by these and other terms the potentially cooperative role of the local leader is given recognition.

Because most studies of community power structures have been made in Western non-socialist societies, the economic basis of decision-making and power has been most evident; indeed, it has generally been assumed rather than determined. In Gondo at least three other possible bases for power were immediately apparent: dominant ethnic status, age differentiation, and political party influence. It was therefore even more striking to find that leadership in the polyethnic African setting was indeed related to the control by a few individuals of productivity and capital resources and their ability to limit the access of others to them. Community politics in Gondo revolved around agriculture, and since rural development is the prime target of most development programs, five-year plans, and external aid schemes in African countries, the characteristics of grassroots leadership in Gondo may well have more general implications. By pursuing traditional anthropological research procedures in a small community and through prolonged contact, intensive study, and observation of day-by-day behavior—watching, listening, checking, and testing—refinements of technique were possible that, it is hoped, will counter some of the criticisms made of studies of community power structure in the United States and Britain.[6] The account that follows is detailed and intensive. Days in the lives of a handful of people were watched and recorded, for it soon became apparent that action in the village, in reality, corresponded only tangentially with what was said to occur. The conscious model of the Gondo actor was an egalitarian myth that permitted leadership to pass unresented.

In Gondo, ethnicity was underscored and underplayed to an extent that was striking. Tribalism in Africa has been described by contemporary ethnographers as a cultural phenomenon in the countryside and a social force in newly formed urban centers. Here, I attempt, without inquiring into ethnicity as such, to assess its reality in social action. Again, a focus on choice—in this case, upon an individual's choice of ethnic status from among the many statuses at his disposal—brings out variations from time to time and from place to place. Ethnic status is at the disposal of an individual, and those whom he encounters, to stress or not to stress—and who is going to stress division in any form when cooperation and mutual trust are necessary for the maintenance of an agri-

[3]

cultural system upon which continuance in the community depends? This study reinforces the contention that land alone offers security in the present labor conditions of tropical Africa.[7]

I set out to analyze the way in which men rise to power in a polyethnic community. Communities such as Gondo, small trading centers and minor townships, are not as rare as the ethnographic literature might have us suppose, since they result from a movement of peoples that has long been extensive throughout the African continent and from efforts at modernization following upon colonial rule.[8]

Gondo is a small trading center situated in the savannaland of eastern Uganda, in Serere County, Teso District. As part of a developing peasant economy Teso is characterized by the cultivation of both subsistence and cash crops, in this case, cotton, and by a lack of labor migration on the part of its peoples. Culturally, the people of Teso have been described as Nilo-Hamites and have been seen to share the cattle complex of much of eastern Africa. In Gondo, cattle are less a part of both the cultural and marketing system than elsewhere in Teso, and fishing plays an important role in the economy. A cotton ginnery, established in 1912, seasonally attracts immigrant as well as local labor and is a most important source of cash in the community. For six months of the year, during the cotton-selling season, Gondo becomes a hustling contingent township before sinking back into the tranquility of the countryside. What is most important for our consideration here is that members of twenty different ethnic groups have been attracted to Gondo by its fertile soil, its cattle, its trading possibilities, its ginnery, and the rich potential of Lake Kyoga on the shores of which it lies, and have now remained there as permanent residents for three or four generations.

Since this is a study of political processes in the polyethnic community, and of leadership within it, I am concerned here not with the overall structure of the community and the inter-

[4]

dependence of its institutions but only with those aspects of its societal structure that set parameters to political actions. Structural and organizational elements are seen to be related through the choices made by individuals in pursuing alternative paths of action. This study of leadership, to adopt Mair's phrase, surveys the "room for maneuver" in a polyethnic community and plots the course by which a few individuals attain pre-eminence.[9]

In a community such as Gondo ethnicity is a likely building block in the societal structure, expressions of ethnic identity by certain individuals and groups providing a form of cultural adaptation to a microcosmopolitan environment. Since this environment is constantly in the process of change, the known history of the community and, for the individual, an awareness of the phases through which the development of the community has passed are an essential part of its contemporary social structure. An awareness of a range of choice extends backward over time as well as throughout the present society and beyond its boundaries. Differences in their perception of Gondo's past distinguish the older from the younger generations in their manipulation of areas of free choice in today's society.

Forces for conformity and opportunities for political entrepreneurship, social innovation, and individual advancement or spiralism determine the extent to which Gondo is today part of a society in which individuals differently find themselves in situations open to choice and manipulation. Spiralists are characteristically to be found in communities within which individual mobility is possible. They are the petty capitalists found in most country towns who are socially, economically, and geographically more mobile than their fellows—self-made men whose skill in maneuver brings them to a place on the narrow plateau of prestige within the community and permits them spatial mobility beyond its bounds. The essence of spiralism is captured in Bacon's observation

"On Great Place" when he writes: "All rising to great place is by a winding stair."[10] In Gondo the slow and tedious process of spiraling starts within the most fundamental field of operations existing in the rural parish: the politics of agriculture. Because Gondo is, as yet, a community in which the individual still depends largely for both social and economic status on his relation to land, differing opportunities for the control of land and labor play a large part in the pattern of political advancement within the community.

The manner in which such a community perdures when its members come from different ethnic backgrounds and operate, in some cases, for part of their lives in different cultures provides a case study of what Simmel saw as one of the great problems of sociology: how any society, conflict-ridden in a field of divisive forces, continues to exist. From the interrelated institutions that make up the societal structure, conflicts over those elements that bear upon political actions—ethnicity, land, women, and cattle—entail an inquiry into the actual leadership of Gondo parish at the time when fieldwork was carried out and an attempt to relate these findings and my own observations to the processes at work in the parish by which, over the course of time, only a few men rise to positions of power to lead the community and to represent its interests in the outside world. Since some of the findings that emerge from such an analysis may be relevant to the understanding of similar communities in Africa and elsewhere, a clarification of concepts is necessary at the outset. These are drawn from a widely accepted body of anthropological literature and are here related to provide an analysis of field behavior.

Structure, Network and Field

The parish is seen as possessing a structure which is made up of the network of social relations which links its members;

[6]

this is an open-ended network,[11] and the boundaries of the parish structure are externally determined, in this case, by the Teso District administration. Their delineation is arbitrary with respect to the internal structure of the community, having its meaning in the requisites of the external structure.

Varying degrees of incorporation into the community are permitted newcomers by members already in residence; the entry of each new individual is seen as bringing into being a field in which certain actors, brought together and defined by their interest in the outcome of the event, make decisions. A field is activity-determined. Actors relate to the situation in accordance with the values they recognize as being involved. A field of co-activity may constantly bring forward the same set of actors, in which case it may be said to be institutionalized. Institutional activities are governed by norms, expectations on the part of one member of the set regarding the actions of his co-activists. These norms are inculcated upon the occasion of almost any public gathering or ceremonial. The inspection of cattle at a bridewealth transfer or the parish meeting at which tax is assessed provide Gondo examples. A societal structure may then be defined as relationships between institutions within a society. A distinction between social and societal is useful since it serves to distinguish micro from macro level data.[12] The contrast between Gondo's former plural society and the plural social relations now maintained within the parish serves to exemplify this.

Status Set and Status Sequence

Each individual has at his command a status set, made up of statuses which he may or may not choose to activate in any given situation. Statuses are defined, and redefined, as field situations change. A status set Merton defines as "the complement of social statuses of an individual," and "statuses occurring with sufficient frequency as to be socially patterned" are designated as a status sequence.[13] The movement of an individual through a status sequence may be seen as an aspect of the socialization process (i.e., his enculturation) into the community. Elsewhere, Merton refers to statuses as being assigned by society and as positions in which individuals "find themselves," since he is concerned with their structural dimension.[14] Here, where I am interested in the problem of political activity within delineated social fields, my emphasis is on status adoption and rejection by individuals. The notion of status rejection is contained in Merton's analysis,[15] but that of adoption or activation draws more upon Goffman's idea of "the presentation of self" in everyday life.[16] While status sets adhere to the individual, status sequences are established in accordance with the structural limitations upon an individual's free manipulation and activation of the statuses within his status set. The life cycle of the individual exemplifies one such sequence; the process by which land is acquired in Gondo another such sequence. Further concepts which are part of this paradigm, such as visibility and observability (Merton),[17] incorporation and transaction (Barth),[18] dominant status, office and occupational niche, are made clear as the argument proceeds.

Structure and Organization

Since action in any community is not consistently in accord with the normative structure, Firth has found it useful to distinguish between structure and organization (cf. the *langue* and *parole* of de Saussure), and I adopt his definitions.

Structures, which may be either formal or informal, consist of "major patterns of relationship . . . which form a systematic arrangement and which as such serve to regulate further action along the same lines."[19] Organization, on the other hand, "refers to a field of social action which is identified in terms of pattern-sequence." Firth observes:

In the concept of social structure the qualities recognized are primarily those of persistence, continuity, form and pervasiveness through the social field. . . . The concept of organization has a complementary emphasis. It recognizes adaptation of behavior in respect of given ends, control of means in varying circumstances, which are set by changes in the external environment or by necessity to resolve conflict between structural principles. If structure implies order, organization implies a working towards order—though not necessarily the same order.[20]

Individual and Group

The adoption of such a framework as that outlined above is clearly useful for a study of individuals maneuvering to better their positions within the community. This micro concern is related to the macro level of structure by the perception that such maneuvering involves competition and conflict and, in the course of this process, brings about structural change.[21]

Action within a field situation brings about the alignment of individuals. When this is institutionalized, I use the term "group"; when the field is in the process of formation, the term "grouping" is adopted to convey the sense of process, of "coming into being." The structure of any society may be seen as made up of quasi-groups, and in this study I pursue that aspect of Ginsberg's definition not taken up by Mayer in his analysis of quasi-groups in complex societies:[22] "Aggregates or portions of the community which have no recognizable structure, but whose members have certain interests or modes of behavior in common, which may at any time lead them to form themselves into definite groups."[23] Such a usage allows for the analysis of group formation (which may be seen as interest groups contingent upon, and revolving around, issues) as an intervening dimension between the activation of statuses by individuals and the structural integration (by means of such mechanisms as overlapping memberships, cross-cutting ties and ecological relations) of the society.

Culture

Operating within this framework, the concept of culture is most usefully applied to learned behavior, one of its defining characteristics being persistence or continuity over time with a corollary emphasis on communication.[24] This permits me to conceptualize the microcosmopolitan culture of Gondo and to see part of the political process in the parish as involving the inculcation of that brand of behavior which is suited to the way of life of a polyethnic community as, for example, an underemphasis on ethnicity, an emphasis on neighborliness, and a high level of tolerance for diversity.

The social practice which I describe as the redefinition of ethnicity and in Gondo its understatement, emphasizes the perpetual existence of human choice within changing situations so that, even within the framework of ethnic categorization, there is ample room for maneuver. Situations of ethnic heterogeneity, sometimes called cultural pluralism, promote for attention one of the political building blocks of national integration in Africa. But delineation is frequently expressed in terms too rigid and too categorical to simulate reality. Ethnicity in operation is, like all else social, a tool in the hands of men; it is not a mystic force in itself; there is nothing sacrosanct about the African tribe. In Gondo's sixty years of recorded history, there are clearly times when ethnicity was politicized and there are times, perhaps more numerous, when it lies in no one's interest to admit ethnic distinctions into social and political encounters. Ethnicity is a mask of confrontation, and social life requires that confrontations be avoided wherever possible in everyday affairs.

[10]

INTRODUCTION

Tribal man, like his economic and political counterparts, is a man of straw in the study of contemporary African society; yet political scientists, agricultural developers, and even administrators who from their daily experience know better, seek to explain changing structures in terms of a tribal or cultural ethos. The political drama of developing Africa is largely set in the rural countryside where 80 per cent of its people live. Its cast includes depressed peasants, members of a small elite largely urbanized, and a somewhat larger entrepreneurial middle class. Other actors may well wait in the wings. The theme of the drama is the merging of all these into a participant citizenry, and it is through the playing out of these roles—rather than those of tribe or ethnic group—that the plot is revealed. Hence the units of this analysis are individuals, groups, and quasi-groups within perpetually changing social fields. Yet a cultural lag or a disciplinary hiatus places academic blinkers over the eyes of many social scientists newly arrived in Africa. They have inherited a wealth of structural studies of African societies in which anthropologists have presented them with finely drawn models. Some have taken models for realities. For these ethnographies, like the novels of Jane Austen, are miniatures etched with fine strokes on ivory: they are perfect in their detail while restrained in their purpose. A further aspect of this hiatus is revealed when dichotomies that sociology and anthropology are fast discarding—categorical distinctions between townsmen and tribesmen, rural and urban, tribal and western, traditional and modern—are taken up in such a way as to permit an interpretation of these earlier ethnographies as describing "traditional" society and, by ellipsis, as portraits of rural life in the contemporary scene. I hope this study of community leadership will dispel some of these notions, although its detail is petty, its individualization complete. In this, it may well permit the questioning of assumptions on which projected schemes of economic, administrative, and political development are based.

Note to the Reader

The Ateso orthography used in this study is in accord with Kiggen's *Ateso-English Dictionary* (1953). For words not included in this dictionary, such as clan names, I am following the spelling of W. Ekwaru. Clan prefixes are retained. A glossary appears in the appendix. To be consistent, the usage of the Uganda Government Press has been followed in rendering tribal names. This, at times, differs from the spelling adopted by ethnographers and others. Prefixes indicating person have been dropped in accordance with now standard anthropological procedure [Ganda for Baganda (pl.) and Muganda (sing.) ; Teso for Iteso (pl.) and Etesot/Atesot (sing., masc., and fem.)]. A distinction is still made, however, to indicate language and locality (Luganda, the language of the Ganda of Buganda; Ateso, the language of the Teso of Teso District).

ACTORS

In the text, every adult male in Gondo has been allocated a symbol and number indicating his ethnic status and his place of residence in one of the six wards in the parish.

The ethnic symbols are as follows:

T	Teso (Iteso)	D	Dama
N	Nyoro (Banyoro)		(Badama/Jopadhola)
A	Acholi	As	Asian
Kar	Karamojong	P	Pagero
	(Karimojong)		(Bachopi/Ipagero)
C	Kiga (Chiga)	S	Soga (Basoga)
Sw	Swahili	Kum	Kumam
Ar	Arab	Al	Alur
K	Kenyi	J	Luo (Lwo)
	(Bakenyi/Bakenye)	Sk	Sikh
G	Ganda (Baganda)	H	Hima (Bahima
L	Lango (Langi)		/Banyankole/
Lug	Lugbara		Nyankole/Ankole)

INTRODUCTION

The six wards are identified in the code as follows:

101-120 Aojabule   401-428 Adiding
201-229 Agologolo   501-563 Opucet
301-335 Kabola   601-6103 Township

Since this study traces the emergence of a strategic elite through competition for land and labor, a select list of the actors involved in the parish political arena is given below. The use of pseudonyms in no way affects credibility and the reader is invited, as he follows out the working of the plot, to predict which few individuals will emerge as the Big Men of the parish.

Kum 679	Abilu, George	K 418	Nakumusana, Kostant
T 109	Anyapo, Levi	T 217	Ocaet, Petero
T 625	Ebelu, George Henry	T 512	Ocen, Enosi
T 401	Ejau, Erinayo	T 114	Odera, Erieza
T 601	Elamu, Yokonia	T 606	Odico, Erismasi
N 639	Gawera, Eria	T 220	Odongo
T 611	Akora, Eria	T 203	Ogola, Martin
T 219	Aringa, Elija	J 692	Ogot, Anderea
P 224	Egimu s/o Mujwala	T 216	Okasu, Salimon
T 210	Ekweru, Yowana	T 201	Okello, Benefasio
T 402	Emenu,	Kum 682	Opolot, Daudi
	Nebukadnezar	T 302	Otieno,
S 333	Mugwerere, Salim		Charles Frederick
S 665	Sebwala, Mulisio	A 542	Otoo s/o Ejau
K 304	Mulojja s/o Musana	L 671	Oyat, James
K 312	Musana, Sabiti	As 699	Valji
P 632	Mukasa, Benefasio		

Documentation and case studies in the text are not restricted to these individuals.

For statistical purposes in certain aspects of the inquiry, a 20 per cent sample of the population, representative with respect to age, place of birth, ethnicity, and ward, was drawn up; in other cases, a random sample was used. Wherever possible, a saturation sample of the parishioners provided the raw data of the analysis.

To convert statistical data to the metric system: miles to kilometers multiply by 1.6093; square miles to square kilometers multiply by 2.5899; acres to hectares multiply by 0.405.

PART ONE

Gondo Society

TESO DISTRICT lies within the vast drainage system of Lakes Bisina and Kyoga and the Mpologoma River in eastern Uganda (Figure 1).[1] Its terrain is made up of low, gently rising promontories crisscrossed by a complex of swamps, streams, seasonal rivers, and lakes. The district lies at an average height of 3,500 feet m.s.l., and each isolated hill or granite outcrop that rises above the plain provides both temporal and spatial identification for the population. Swamps surround each stretch of higher land making each parish a virtual island, and movement beyond the parish—by bicycle, bus, or ferry— requires much more effort than communication within its boundaries. Relations beyond the parish thus entail economic costs.

Gondo parish covers some 9.2 square miles on the northern shore of the Serere peninsula in southwest Teso, the promontory at Gondo and the hill of Bululu, which juts southward 3 miles distant on the Kaberamaido shore opposite, forming the two lips of a bottleneck through which the waters of Lake Kojweri flow westward into Lake Kyoga and thence to the Victoria Nile. The parish lies 33° 15' east and 1° 37' north of the equator and is bounded by the lake to the north, a swamp to the east, and hills to the south and west (Figure 2). Only the hills of Gondo, which rise to 4,500 feet and are visible 75 miles away at Napak on the Karamoja boundary to the east, make Gondo a topographically distinctive parish. These hills provide a no man's land between the parishes of Gondo and Ogera, only the herdsmen beating the liminal slopes. The Forestry Department's Gondo Hill Reserve covers 4.09 square

← *A view across the parish*

FIGURE 1: MAP OF THE LAKE KYOGA REGION

miles but is undeveloped except for a small stand of conifers on the lower northeast face. Apart from forays into the lower foothills to cut saplings for house construction and for fuel, and the seasonal assertion of dominance by herdsmen burning the long grass to ensure a fresh season's growth, the hills belong to the baboon and monkey, the leopard and wild pig.

Below the hills an extensively cultivated plain stretches toward the east where a wide grass swamp marks the edge of habitation. This swamp is crossed by persistent streams during the dry months and fills in the wet season. A small hill, Kabola, lies at its western edge, and a weekly market is held at its foot, close to the roadside where the parishes of Kamod, Ogera, and Gondo meet. The swamp is crossed by an all-weather road along which buses and heavy trucks are able to forge most of the year; in the season of the heavy rains, schoolchildren set out at first light to walk to their classrooms in Kamod while bicycles and small vehicles wait until the

[18]

sun has hardened the surface, muddied by the night's storm, before taking to the road.

The soil of the parish shades from sandy loams along the lakeshore to brownish loams in the plain to infertile stony sands, derived from quartzite, covering the hills. Kabola swamp to the east contains black alluvial clays in which select patches are worked by potters from miles around. Throughout the parish, where the checkerboard of man-made gardens has not superimposed itself, the soil supports grassland and a scattering of trees. Bumps and mounds of past furrows cross empty grassy stretches, testifying to many seasons of long-established cultivation. Moist thicket supporting Combretum savanna dominates, with pockets of better soil where perennial crops can be cultivated. The ecological zone in which Gondo lies extends far beyond the boundaries of the parish; determined by the natural basin of Lake Kyoga itself, it covers a vast

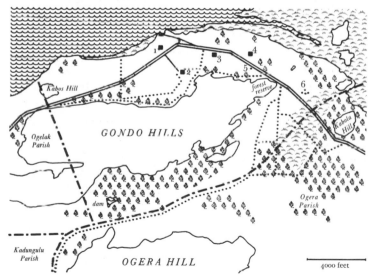

1 ginnery 2 bungalows 3 dukas 4 mosque 5 school 6 MoW camp

FIGURE 2: PHYSICAL FEATURES OF GONDO PARISH

region of central Uganda between the southern forest and the drier savanna lands of the north.

In Gondo, annual grass fires, cutting wood for fuel, and periodic clearing for cultivation leave little of the natural vegetative cover untouched. Pressure on land is not as great as in eastern Teso (in Bukedea, Ngora, and Kumi counties especially), and Gondo remains a frontier region (like Kaberamaido to the north) for the landless moving west. On the other side of Serere County resistance to this infiltration is beginning in anticipation of the carrying capacity of the land being reached, but no rumblings have yet reached Gondo. Nevertheless, natural erosion is severe both by the lakeshore and along the foothills, and land everywhere has to be worked carefully. The potential of Gondo is high, and settlers who have moved into the parish—especially Acholi from the north, Teso from eastern Kumi, and Luo from central Nyanza—are appreciative of the fertile soil and the great variety of crops that can be grown, and those twice a year.

The nutritional content of the diet is high. Millet, fish, and milk are available for most people much of the time; the government dispensary three miles away across the hills at Apapai records malaria, venereal diseases, and tuberculosis—but not malnutrition—as the chief ailments of the Gondo parishioner. There are many domesticated animals: cats, dogs, cattle, goats, a few sheep, and poultry (including turkey). The game in the hills is no longer hunted although an occasional hippopotamus may be shot by the lake. When this happens, its meat is ritually divided and held aloft in the direction of each surrounding hill in turn—Kabola, Ogera, Gondo, Kaweri, Alungar, Agule—a chant to the spirits of Gondo's visible world. Wild bird life in the parish is plentiful, colorful, and varied; each dawn chorus bears witness to the sufficiency of food resources in Gondo.

The water supply of the parish comes largely from the lake,

women and children fetching it in pots or *debes* (empty oil drums) either by headload or on the backs of bicycles. A borehole was drilled in the south of the parish where homes are as much as four miles from the lake, but it was allowed to fall into disrepair and is no longer used. Rain storage tanks beneath the gutters of the stone ginnery houses hold water for the first few weeks of the dry season, and a few villagers have orange bushes planted so that their leaves may channel rainwater into pots placed below. Lengths of rusty piping are similarly used. For the greater part of the dry season, however, no water is available except that from the lake, and the use of professional conveyors—male water-carriers on bicycles—raises its price accordingly.

Gondo experiences a bimodal rainfall with a total of slightly over forty inches a year. The first rains break in late March or April and continue until the beginning of June when the mid-season dry spell starts. The second rains, which begin in August and continue until September or October, are considered much less reliable than the first and the main crops are planted early in the year. The dry spell from November until March is very hot with dessicating winds from the east. During these months the temperature rises daily to over 90° F.; the average annual temperature is 72.5° F.

Communications

Gondo parish is crossed by an earth road running east-west between the shoreline and the hills. Its surface and its three culverts are kept in good repair by eight employees of the Ministry of Works who maintain a roadside camp at the Kabola end of the parish and a restrained antagonism for the parishioners, whom they consider to be inhospitable in the extreme. From this main road, tracks branch off to individual homesteads dispersed throughout the bush.

Four lakeshore landings are used by fishermen and travelers by canoe and ferry. That in the west is shared with the neighboring parish of Ogelak; the major landing (yet most under the eye of the Fisheries Officer and therefore shunned by those fishing without a license) is alongside the old quay which provides sheltered moorings on its westward side; two smaller landings to the east are approached by way of cleared channels through papyrus-fringed lagoons.

Gondo was chosen to be the commercial center of Teso in 1912 because of its excellent location for the export of cattle and cotton to the south and the import of manufactured goods into the north and east. Today its infrastructure is largely a relic of those glorious days when its port and township were thriving. While administrative development was spearheaded into Teso District through Kumi in the east, the territory was opened up economically by way of Lake Kyoga, on which a four-vessel flotilla operated until 1962, Gondo being one of nine ports served by it.[2] By 1966, however, the main line of communication in Teso ran between Mbale and Soroti through the three eastern counties. Serere County, which in the early days of the Kyoga system had been a major artery in a country-wide network of communications, became, with the introduction of rail transport in 1929, something of a backwater.

This is not to say, of course, that Gondo has become remote or is a "primitive isolate." On the contrary, there is far more communication between the community and the outside world than at any time in its history. The ubiquitous bicycle has shortened distances (there were 128 in the parish in 1966, 4 of them owned by women); and a daily bus service links Gondo with Serere, Mbale, and Jinja where connections can be made with buses traveling on to Kampala, the communications hub of Uganda as well as its seat of government. Not only can Gondo residents travel easily into surrounding areas;

the world comes to them daily in broadcasts over Radio Uganda and by way of the national press. During the cotton season from November to March in 1967, when there was more cash about, there were nine radios in the parish, five of them in shops. No newspapers are delivered to Gondo, but copies which seep in are widely circulated. These include English, Ateso, Luganda, Swahili, and Gujerati papers as well as mission newsletters and the Teso administration's newspaper, *Apupeta*.

Population

The population of Gondo parish in 1966, according to a field census, fell into twenty distinct ethnic categories and totaled 819. Of these, adult males numbered 278 and adult females 220. The surprisingly even sex ratio of 1:08 reflects the stable nature of the ginnery labor force and the integration of all ethnic groups into the settled life of the parish (Table 1). Age distribution and sex composition are, for our present purposes, most usefully related to the ethnicity of adult males. The seven females living alone in the parish are not included in field census material since the focus of this study is upon political activities and they, unlike some of the wives, play no part in the politics of the parish.

The 278 homesteads with male heads are distributed throughout the lowland plain. Different localities within the parish are given names which are generally recognized by all parishioners although, since a few of the older generation still call an area by a name given to it at an earlier period, some neighborhoods bear more than one name. In 1966 the parish was divided into six wards, and these I have related statistically to the ethnic composition of the parish. Each ward has a clearly defined character of its own, as described in Chapter 4. Ethnic categories are, for the most part, arrived

TABLE 1: AGE DISTRIBUTION AND SEX COMPOSITION RELATED TO ADULT MALE ETHNICITY

Age Categories of Males								Ethnicity of Homestead Head	Age Categories of Females							
8	7	6	5	4	3	2	1		1	2	3	4	5	6	7	8
		1						Sikh	1							
				1				Swahili			1					
					1			Kiga			1					
					1			Alur								
						1		Lugbara								
				1			3	Dama	3		1		1			
				2	2		1	Arab	5	1	2					
			1	1	1		2	Asian	1	1						
		3					4	Ganda	5		1	1	1			
		1		1	3		3	Karamojong			1	1				
		1	2	2	1	2	3	Hima	1	1	1	2				
			1	3	3	2	3	Kumam	3	3	3	2				
		1	1	4	2	2	14	Luo	16	3	3	2	3			
			4	1	4	1	1	Lango	3		2					
	1	1	3	2	2	3	7	Acholi	4	4	3	2	2			
1	1	1	4	2	5	4	12	Soga	16	5	2	2				
2		1	8	7	3	7	15	Pagero	15	6	6	1	8			
1		2	1	8	9	7	17	Nyoro	27	6	9	8				
2	2		5	11	6	17	24	Kenyi	18	17	9	6	4	1		
	2	7	16	21	21	24	39	Teso	50	29	22	21	9	2		
6	6	19	46	67	64	70	145		168	76	67	49	28	3		

Note: Age categorization can only be taken as approximate in many cases. Age category 8 refers to individuals in their eighties (i.e, estimated age 80–89); 7 to those in their seventies (70–79); etc.

at from the parish of origin (that is, the parish the respondent said he was born in) in conjunction with the tribal affiliation of his father. Gondo parishioners tend to identify themselves by parish or district of origin rather than by tribe, especially when they come—as many do—from the more heterogeneous regions immediately south of Lake Kyoga. Since I wanted to avoid singling out ethnicity as an object of interest during the field inquiry, this tabulation (Table 2) is the result of a year's indirect inquiry and observation; it does not represent any parishioner's mode of self-identification to a European questioner. In the end, some reconciliation and adjustment was called for on my part to arrive at a census of ethnicity comparable with that used in the Uganda census of 1959. (One of the local enumerators for that census, a parishioner, told me that he too had experienced some difficulty, being obliged at times to make somewhat arbitrary distinctions. Later I discovered from the Teso archives that the complexities and ambiguities of ethnic identification in Serere County as a whole had led to a spate of correspondence between the Teso District officers and the statisticians of the East African Statistical Bureau in Nairobi.)[3] By this taxonomy, members of 20 distinct ethnic groups are permanent, tax-paying residents of the parish. Such a high degree of ethnic heterogencity is not characteristic of Teso District as a whole, where all but 9 per cent of the population are Teso, but Serere County, according to the 1959 census, has a population falling into 27 distinct ethnic categories other than Teso.

Of the adult male homestead owners of Gondo, 36.10 per cent belong to Bantu-speaking groups.[4] These include Ganda, Kenyi, Kiga, Nyoro, and Soga (all from southern and western Uganda); a Swahili-speaking Ndereko from Tanzania; and two Swahili-speaking Arabs.[5] Members of most of these groups were present in Gondo long before the building of the port and ginnery in 1912.[6] A further 26.62 per cent of the popula-

TABLE 2: ETHNIC COMPOSITION RELATED TO LANGUAGE AND WARD

Citizenship	Language Family	Home District	Ethnicity	Lingua[a] Franca	No. of Adult Males	Percentage	Aoj	Ag	Kab	Ad	Op	Town
Ugandan	Eastern Nilotic[b]	Karamoja	Karamojong	T	5	35.26	1					4
		Teso	Teso	TG	93		18	21	2	4	21	27
	Sudanic	West Nile	Lugbara	LS	2							2
		Nile	Alur	LS	1						1	
		Acholi	Acholi	LS	11						8	3
	Nilotic	Lango	Lango	TLS	10	26.62				1	5	4
		K'do	Kumam	TS	9		1				1	7
Kenyan		Nyanza	Luo	LS	10						6	4
Ugandan		Ankole	Hima[e]	LG	8				1	1	3	3
			Pagero[d]	TG	23			7	5	5	3	3
		Bunyoro	Nyoro	SG	37				5		9	23
	Bantu	Buganda	Ganda	GS	4					1	1	2
		Kigezi	Kiga	GS	1							1
		Padhola	Dama[e]	LG	2	36.1					1	1
Tanzanian		Bukoba	Swahili	S	1						1	
Ugandan		Busoga	Soga	GS	13				2	2		9
			Kenyi	TG	42			1	20	14	3	4
	Afro-Asiatic	India	Arab	GS	2							2
			Sikh[f]	S	1							1
	Asiatic		Asian	S[g]	3	1.44						3
					278		20	29	35	28	63	103

a. Abbreviations are as follows: T Teso; S Swahili; G Luganda; L Luo. By lingua franca is meant the language to which a speaker is most likely to shift when he joins a polyethnic group.

b. Eastern Nilotic is Greenberg's term; Nilo-Hamitic is still widely used.

c. Hima in Teso are also called Banyankole. Relations between these and the Hema of Bunyoro are discussed by A. Southall, *Alur Society*, Cambridge, 1954. The characteristic predominantly milk diet was shared by some Hima and some Nyoro herdsmen in Gondo but not by all of either category.

d. See Chapter 6, fn. 2.

e. Jopadhola speak a Nilotic language belonging to the Luo group (B. Ogot, *History of the Southern Luo*, Vol. I, Nairobi, 1967; A. Southall, "The peopling of Africa—the linguistic and sociological evidence" in M. Posnansky (ed.), *Prelude to East African History*, London, 1966).

f. Gondo's Sikh (called Singasinga in Ateso) does not appear as an Asian in the parish records.

g. One Asian is fluent in Ateso, but this is exceptional.

tion are of Sudanic or Nilotic stock.[7] Acholi, Alur, Pagero, Kumam, and Lugbara, all from north and northwestern Uganda, came originally as labor migrants to the port and ginnery; Luo are recent immigrant fishermen from Central Nyanza in Kenya, attracted by the promise of Lake Kyoga's waters. The Teso, the "nationals" of the district, are an eastern Nilotic group speaking a language mutually intelligible to the Karamojong, Jie, Turkana, and Dodoth, peoples freqently referred to as "Nilo-Hamites."[8] They and the Karamojong form 35.26 per cent of the population. Into these three linguistic categories—Bantu, Nilotic and Sudanic, and Eastern Nilotic—fall 98.56 per cent of the population of Gondo. The remaining 1.44 per cent are Gujerati-speaking Asians, all but one born in East Africa.[9]

About 46.0 per cent of the parish were born there and, of the remainder, over 21 per cent have lived there for over twenty years. The regions from which the population came originally are shown in Figure 3. The pattern of movement between these "homelands" and the parish helps determine political status within the community.

Little in the general appearance of the 278 homesteads indicates from what part of Uganda, or elsewhere, their owners have come. Cultural homogeneity within the parish is striking, and categorization based on language and place of birth can only be misleading. The "languages of the hearth" spoken in two contrasted wards (the ethnically heterogeneous township and the predominantly Teso ward of Agologolo) give an indication of this. In a polyethnic community it is not surprising to find that most men command two or more languages which may be described as languages of commerce or administration; in Teso, these lingua franca are English, Swahili, Luganda, and Ateso, reflecting phases in the administrative history of the district. What is surprising in Gondo is to find so many polyglot women. It may be seen that there are only

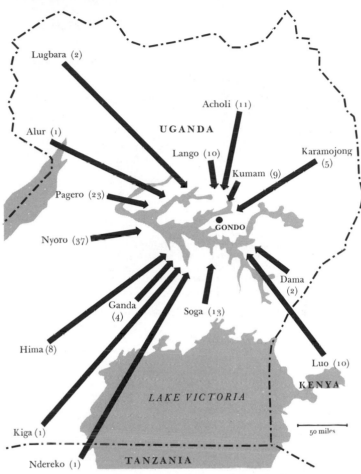

FIGURE 3: REGIONS FROM WHICH IMMIGRANTS COME TO GONDO

three homesteads in which only one language of the hearth is spoken and that, as might be expected, is Ateso (Table 3). Over 40 per cent of these homesteads are built upon mixed marriages.

Gondo is in many ways reminiscent of Hpalang in highland

[29]

TABLE 3: LANGUAGES OF AGOLOGOLO AND GONDO
TOWNSHIP HOMESTEADS

Ethnicity of Homestead Head	Languages of Agologolo Homesteads	
	Wives	*Husbands*
T	Ateso	Ateso, Swahili
T	Ateso	Ateso
T	Ateso	Ateso, Luganda, Swahili
T	Runyoro, Ateso	Ateso, Lukenyi
T	Ateso, Lukenyi	Ateso, Lukenyi, English
T	Ateso	Ateso, Swahili
T	Ateso	Ateso
T	Ateso	Ateso, Swahili
P	Ateso, Luchopi	Ateso, Luchopi, English
P	Ateso, Luchopi	Ateso, Luchopi
P	Ateso, Luchopi	Ateso, Luchopi
P	Ateso, Luchopi	Ateso, Luchopi
P	Ateso, Luchopi	Ateso, Luchopi, Luganda, English
P	Ateso, Luchopi	Ateso, Luchopi, Lukenyi
K	Lukenyi, Luganda	Ateso, Lukenyi, Luganda, Swahili

Ethnicity of Homestead Head	Languages of Township Homesteads	
	Wives	*Husbands*
T	1. Ateso 2. Ateso, Kumam 3. Ateso	Ateso, Swahili
T	Ateso, Kumam	Ateso, Swahili, Luganda
T	Ateso	Ateso
T	Ateso	Ateso, Swahili, English
T	Ateso	Ateso, Swahili
T	Ateso	Ateso, Swahili
T	Ateso, Kumam	Ateso, Kumam, Swahili
P	Luchopi	Luchopi, Ateso
Kum	1. Ateso, Kumam 2. Ateso, Kumam 3. Ateso, Kumam	Ateso, Kumam, Luganda, Swahili
N	Luchopi, Runyoro	Runyoro, Ateso, Swahili
S	Lusoga, Lukenyi	Lukenyi, Ateso, Lusoga, Swahili
S	Lusoga	Lusoga, Swahili, Ateso
K	Lukenyi, Lusoga	Lukenyi, Ateso, Swahili, English
J	Luo	Luo, Swahili, English
J	1. Luo 2. Luo 3. Luo	Luo, Ateso, Swahili
Sk	Somali, Swahili	Swahili, Gujerati

Burma, which is described by Leach as containing six sub-groups speaking distinct dialects. These did not loom large in ordinary everyday affairs and "the Hpalang community, despite its multiple linguistic factions, usually managed to act as if it were a culturally homogeneous entity."[10] The ease, in Gondo, of shifting from one language to another to accommodate or ostracize individuals joining a conversation group is a study in itself.

Such a population demonstrates the ineptness of a "cookie-cutter concept of culture."[11] Ethnographies make it apparent that the cultural backgrounds of Bantu-speaking peoples coming from the southern shores of Lake Kyoga are not so different from those of the Nilotes who descended on Gondo from the north. Since kinship and ethnic ideologies are functions of economic and political relations,[12] this is not surprising. Most of the Bantu speakers share a common history of conquest and overrule by Nyoro or Ganda at the end of the nineteenth century which weakened or wiped out many distinctive forms of social organization, such as blood brotherhood or age groupings, and imposed, with varying degrees of success, hierarchical forms of political organization. The Nilotes come from noncentralized societies; the Bantu speakers (apart from a few Nyoro from Hoima) from peripheral regions of centralized states where diminishing administrative returns resulted in their marginal incorporation. As a result, few hierarchically minded individuals come to Gondo. This makes an analogy with the moving frontier appropriate.

Moreover, the indigenous social structures of the immigrants are compatible. All reckon descent in the agnatic line, have joking relations with mothers' brothers, and practice mother-in-law avoidance. The basic domestic group in all is the elementary family; marriage is ideally polygynous and virilocal. There are no endogamous marriage rules. Bridewealth is a common contractual institution. Widow inheritance is common to all, and inheritance in general is patrilineal and restricted to males. The only structurally important cultural distinctions among the community at large relate to the different value that may be placed upon premarital chastity and different ways of institutionalizing extramarital sexual activities. On the whole, a lack of rigidity in both these matters encourages cross-ethnic liaisons. The political implications of this are discussed in Chapter 5.

On the whole, what differences remain are not a barrier to social interaction. The incremental development of the parish into a polyethnic community, and especially the establishment of a commercial frontier prior to any politicization of ethnicity by the administration (Chapter 3), fostered the growth of a community in which differences are tolerated, accepted, and welcomed as the natural order of things.

The prevalence of many British values and norms attached to labor and the use of money, education, language, religion, dress, and, to some extent, social behavior has had a general homogenizing effect. Most of the parishioners have been engaged in wage labor at some time in their lives, the majority of them within Gondo itself. Education is highly valued: 60 per cent of the males have had some primary school education through the missions, and nine, all in their early twenties, have received a year or two of secondary school education.

Religion

Statistics on "religion" in Gondo reflect the nature of an individual's schooling rather than his religious convictions. Since in Uganda religion has long been a basis for political factionalism,[13] an inquiry into both political and religious allegiances was a sensitive matter in Gondo in 1966. The figures shown in Table 4 can only be taken as approximate. They are based upon gradual familiarity over time with a large

TABLE 4: RELIGIOUS AFFILIATIONS OF ADULT MALES

| Ethnicity | Christian | | Muslim | Sikh and Hindu | Unaffiliated | TOTAL |
	Protestant	Catholic				
Karamojong					5	5
Teso	42	14	1		36	93
Lugbara		2				2
Alur		1				1
Acholi	4	2			5	11
Lango	3	3			4	10
Kumam	3	5			1	9
Luo	8		2			10
Hima	2	2	1		3	8
Pagero	1	9	3		10	23
Nyoro	6	10	7		14	37
Ganda	3		1			4
Kiga	1					1
Dama		2				2
Swahili			1			1
Soga		4	6		3	13
Kenyi	2	17	10		13	42
Arab			2			2
Sikh				1		1
Asian				3		3
TOTAL	75	70	34	4	95	278

proportion of the population and their family connections; upon the direct evidence of church attendance, especially at Easter and Christmas when religious affiliations are writ large as at no other time; upon indirect evidence (such as the diacritics of names); and on confidential communications. According to these figures it will be seen that two-thirds of the adult male population belong nominally to a universal religion: 52 per cent are Christian (about equally divided between Catholicism and the Native Anglican Church of Uganda) and 12 per cent Muslim. Most ethnic categories contain members of more than one denomination; some families have children in all three. Only with Muslims is religion the basis of anything more than an occasional social grouping and, with Muslims, Islam predominates over ethnicity or district of origin as a means of self and group definition. Although certain activities at times set Muslims apart from the population at large, religion is not, on the whole, a divisive force in Gondo and there are many other fields of co-activity in which membership is overlapping. The politics —or nonpolitics—of religion in Gondo is discussed in the following chapter.

For all the preceding census data, a fixed date was arrived at by balancing the influx of immigrant ginnery workers against the beginning of school terms when many children were away at the homes of kinsmen. Even so the extreme mobility of sectors of the population made the task difficult. The extent of this mobility for adult males was obtained by comparing tax registers over several years and then making inquiries among their neighbors and kin. There was no similar way of tracing the movements of women and children, and respondents' replies concerning the whereabouts and schooling of their children were frequently unreliable.

In the course of a thirty-month period (1965-1967), 18 persons were known to have died in the parish—13 men, 3 women, and 2 children. These figures reflect the selectivity of parishioners in the registration of deaths and my own inability to keep track of women and children. During this period 3 men returned to the parish from prison and took up their land again; 3 were sent to prison for periods of over six months; 11 returned from "town" or from staying with kin elsewhere for periods of over a year; and 53 men emigrated. Of these, 17 moved to Pingire or to Kaberamaido, either to fish or to acquire land for cultivation, and 15 returned to their "homelands" in Busoga, Bunyoro, Acholi, and Karamoja. One man, a Hima, was sent to the leprosarium at Ogino. Twelve men left Gondo for the urban centers of Soroti, Mbale, and Kampala; and one was said to have returned to India. Only one individual's destination was unknown to his neighbors. The reasons for this demographic instability and the nature of the structured flux that ensues will become clear in the course of this study.

Migrant Labor and the Ginnery

During the cotton ginning season between November and March, an erratic labor force enters the parish to work at the Kyere Cotton Company Ginnery. A breakdown of the 191 names on the muster roll for 1966/67 shows a hard core of Gondo residents (20.5 per cent) in regular employ while many others form part of a floating labor pool. The permanent component of the ginnery force is much higher than has been generally supposed; even more significant is the fact that over 35 per cent of the full-time local employees are Teso.[14] Acholi, Lango, and Nyoro make up most of the remainder. Poorly represented on the ginnery rolls are Kenyi and Pagero whose prime occupation within the parish is fishing. A large proportion of the remaining work force travel in daily from the neighboring parishes. Fewer than 30 males took up temporary residence in the ginnery lines for the season.

The ginnery muster roll is, in itself, somewhat misleading. Although it bears 191 names, there are only 80 jobs at the most to be filled each day, and two teams work five-hour shifts from seven in the morning until midday and from midday until five in the afternoon. There is also a small night squad. Each morning a line-up is held in the ginnery yard from which the day's workers are selected. The turnout is always adequate; most days a few men are turned away. In principle, the earliest to arrive are certain of employment, but the system is blatantly open to corruption and regular workers have an arrangement with the ginnery headman who, as the sole "Mswahili" in the parish, is immune to the force of moral ties grounded in ethnicity.

The minimum wage in January 1967 was 77 shillings per month, but few Gondo residents are at this point in the scale. Six of them earned over 190 shillings per month and the rest fall somewhere in between according to the type of job they are doing and the length of their service. The operation of the ginnery employment system ensures priorities and privileges for Gondo residents while allowing them plenty of free time, even during the height of the ginning season, to take part in the everyday activities of the parish.

Occupations and Income

Since an analysis of economic factors is going to play a large part in the study of prestige and privilege that follows, I will present here an economic profile of the Gondo population with respect to only two variables, occupation (Table 5) and "wealth," as measured by the graduated tax scale operating in Teso District (Table 6). So that comparisons may be made within several frameworks, these characteristics are related to ethnic and age criteria. It will become apparent that the property status of an individual depends primarily upon his position in the age cycle regardless of ethnicity.

Occupational categories were arrived at by listing the primary working activities of parishioners. As in most peasant economies, the majority of the residents pursued more than one occupation in the course of the seasonal round. The four-month ginnery employment is given priority since the wages earned make it two-thirds as profitable again as the growing of cotton for the average peasant. The only pursuit more rewarding is successful fishing. Since most subsistence

TABLE 5: PRIMARY OCCUPATIONS OF ADULT MALES BY AGE AND ETHNICITY

	Kar	T	Lug	Al	A	L	Kum	J	H	P	N	G	C	D	Sw	S	K	At	Sk	As	TOTAL	2	3	4	5	6	7	8
Cultivator	1	56			1	3	1			12	14		1	1		6	14	1			111	24	21	30	22	9	2	3
Ginner		15	1		8	5	2		1	1	8			1	1	1	1			3	49	8	15	12	12	2	2	
Fisherman		7		1	1	1	1		9	2	2						15				44	17	6	13	4	3		1
Herdsman	2	1						7		3	3							1			13	3	3	4	3	1	1	
Shopkeeper	2							1								1	7	1	1		11	5	3	3	1	1		
Porter		1			1	1	2					1									7	1	4	1	1			
Tailor		2					2														7	2	2	1		2	4	
Retired		3			1	1	1		1								3				8				2	2		2
Carpenter		2														2					4	2	1	1				
Boatbuilder																3					3	2	1					
Bicycle Repairer									2								1				3	2	1			1		
Butcher								1			1	1									2	1		1				
Potter										1											1		1					
Trader										1	1										1		1	1				
Fishmonger		1	1													2					2			1	1			
Dispenser																1					1			1				
Hotelkeeper									1												1	1						
Cook									1							1					1	1						
Cattle trader									1								1				1	1						
Diviner																1					1				1			
Nut seller																	1				1		1					
Schoolmaster		1																			1	1						
LMB inspector		2															2				2	1	1					
Fisheries officer		1															1				1	1	1					
Parish chief		1															1				1			1				
Bus driver		1							1												1	1			1			
TOTAL	5	93	2	1	11	10	9	10	8	23	37	4	1	2	1	13	42	2	1	3	278	70	64	67	46	19	6	6

TABLE 6: TAX STATUSES OF ADULT MALES BY AGE AND ETHNICITY

| | Tax in Shillings | | | | | | | | |
	50	60	80	100	150	200	600	Exempt	TOTAL
Ethnicity									
Karamojong	5								5
Teso	39	40	4	1	1	1		7	93
Lugbara	2								2
Alur	1								1
Acholi	3	5						1	11
Lango	9	1							10
Kumam	3	5	1						9
Luo	4	3	3						10
Hima	5	2	1						8
Pagero	6	15						2	23
Nyoro	15	16	3					3	37
Ganda	1	2	1						4
Kiga	1								1
Dama		2							2
Swahili			1						1
Soga	4	6			3				13
Kenyi	12	20	5	1				4	42
Arab		1	1						2
Sikh			1						1
Asian		1	1				1		3
TOTAL	110	119	24	2	4	1	1	17	278
Age									
20–29	35	29	4		2				70
30–39	31	27	2	1	2	1			64
40–49	15	40	8	1			1	2	67
50–59	23	16	5					2	46
60–69	5	7	5					2	19
70–79	1							5	6
80–89								6	6
TOTAL	110	119	24	2	4	1	1	17	278

crop agriculture is in the hands of women, the category of "male cultivators" indicates those who depend primarily on cotton for cash. Many of these also fish and own cattle. Over a third of the population is best described as cultivators (recognizing a distinction made by agriculturalists between cultivators and farmers); 16.2 per cent are fishermen; while the remaining quarter of the population not engaged in ginnery wage labor are in service occupations.

Graduated tax figures for Gondo parishioners are taken from the 1966 tax register. Over 80 per cent of the taxpayers fall into the two lowest brackets, paying under 60 shillings per annum, a reflection of the economic dimensions of homogeneity. Those in the next bracket, paying 80 shillings per annum, are mostly shopkeepers and fishermen while those paying over 100 shillings in tax are for the most part government-paid (or subsidized) individuals. An Asian mechanic at the ginnery has the highest taxable income in the parish. The political aspects of taxation in the community are discussed in Chapter 11; here it need only be noted that there is a strong element of subjectivity in assessing incomes. The tax of fishermen seems disproportionate to their actual earnings, while cattle are excluded from the inventory of taxable items.[15] Both facts represent political issues in the arena beyond the parish.

The Agricultural System of the Parish

Since most of Gondo's parishioners are peasant cultivators for at least eight months of the year, a description of the agricultural system provides a picture of the way of life for most of the community.[16] The agricultural calendar is shown in Figure 4. Although a fundamental distinction has been made between seed distributors and planters[17]—between millet and banana growers in the Gondo context—extensive contact between groups and long years of administrative control over

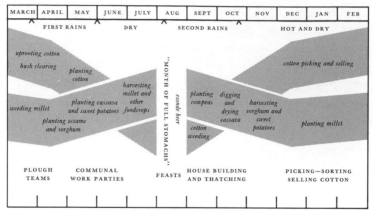

MARCH	APRIL	MAY	JUNE	JULY	AUG	SEPT	OCT	NOV	DEC	JAN	FEB

FIGURE 4: AGRICULTURAL CALENDAR

peasant agriculture have rendered these differences negligible. Crop and technological homogeneity prevail. Apart from various types of hoes, the only agricultural implement in use is an ox-drawn plough, of which there are thirty-nine in the parish as a whole. Millet, cassava, simsim, sweet potatoes, sorghum, and cowpeas are the main crops grown; only cotton, which was introduced into the parish in 1907, is grown exclusively for sale. Minor crops are exchanged and bartered between cultivators and at the local markets; a few are sold to shopkeepers in Gondo and Serere, but marketing facilities generally are poor.[18] Cotton marketing is rigidly controlled throughout Uganda; prices and the date on which selling may begin are announced early in November. The crop may be sold only at gazetted ginneries or cooperative growers' stores during a limited season which closes in March. One quarter of the annual cropping in Gondo, as elsewhere in Teso, is devoted to cotton, but the agricultural system has not developed around it: cotton growing has merely become an additional item.[19]

No marked division of labor distinguishes the sexes for most

[40]

agricultural tasks. Bush clearing is generally undertaken by men and the bulk of the weeding and bird-scaring by women and children, but no stigma is attached to either sex performing any task. Many operations are carried out by work parties and teams; their mobilization and structure, which have political significance, are described in Chapter 9.

The Historical Development of Gondo

Finally, the chronological table below outlines the history of Gondo within its relevant district and national context so that events referred to in the following chapters may more easily be placed in sequence.[20]

1896
Fort built by Kakunguru on Kaweri Island, 3½ miles offshore between Gondo and Bululu.

1898
Kirkpatrick, accompanied by Kakunguru, surveyed Lake Kyoga and reported on Gondo's mixed population.

1899
Serere County proclaimed.

1900
Year of famine.

1902
Kakunguru relieved of command in Teso, which becomes part of Mbale Collectorate with HQ at Kumi. Uganda police post at Serere; Bululu fort garrisoned by Nyoro.

1907
Poll tax 6/-.

1908
Ngora mission established by Kitching. First cotton crop; Indian traders at most centers.

1909
Poll tax ordinance proclaimed operative in Teso. TDA inaugurated. British East Africa Company (BEAC) agent arrives to find site

for ginnery. Teso exports cattle, hides, skins, groundnuts, simsim; imports native hoes, Amerikani cloth, beads, brass and iron ware, European provisions. Mulangira parish chief. Mwambazi Kenyi chief.

1910

Ploughing school opened at Kumi. Plague spreads westward from Nyoro at Kagwara. Wright, from Kampala, buying cotton in Gondo.

1911

Agricultural station opened at Kadungulu, 7 miles from Gondo. Makertich applies for, and Postlethwaite DC approves, plot of land at Gondo. Veterinary officer and stock inspector arrive. Bicycles introduced.

1912

Teso District established. BEAC and Bukedi (Uganda) Cotton Trading Company ginneries erected at Gondo with attendant stores; 14 semipermanent buildings; 4 house sites for Europeans. Yakobo appointed Ganda Agent. Cotton marketing restricted to Gondo, Sambwe, and Kagwara only in Serere County. Pier and trolley line built. Lake Kyoga steamers call every 5 days. 93 bicycles in Serere County. BEAC ox-drawn wagons cutting up road at Gondo; to be metalled. Two Europeans fined for assaulting Africans at Gondo. Town plan drawn up.

1913

Gondo township plans approved. Border-hovering by residents leads to big baraza in Gondo. Chiefs Mwambazi (K) and Kijanjaro (P) acting for Namionjo (N) sent to recall them. Visit by ADC and chiefs to Kaweri Island, pop. 21. Projected removal of Asian Bazaar. Gondo made cotton seed distribution center for district. Mulangira applies to have Nyoro removed from Gondo.

1914

District HQ moved from Kumi to Soroti. Port built at Lalle in Soroti County.

1915

KAR recruitment challenged by Europeans at ginnery. Public works carried out; pier completed; telegraph line started Gondo-Mbale. Rinderpest.

1916

Compulsory cotton acreage ½ acre. Mulangira dismissed; Egadu appointed. Mwambazi recovers 28 out of 57 Kenyi from Busoga. Agricultural station moved to Soroti.

1917

Outbreak of cerebro-spinal meningitis in Gondo; 29 deaths. Roads flooded. Post office in use. Weekly steamer visits. Township clearing supervised by ADC at cost of 150/-. Currency notes introduced at ginnery.

1918

Famine; 2,131 deaths in sub-county. Four Asians at BEAC arrested for theft of 6000/-. Township Headman, Zakaria Kada (G) appointed. Death of postmaster from influenza epidemic. Suggestion that P.O. should be at Soroti.

1919

Tax 19/-. Food shortage; supplies commandeered by administration and Asians forced to sell at "equitable prices." Ex-KAR employed as ginnery askaris.

1920

Telegraph installed at Soroti. Agricultural station moved to Serere.

1921

Temple-Perkins DC. Poor labor relations at ginneries.

1922

Police post established at Gondo. Abolition of Agents. Pier extended and heightened. Poor cotton season. Exports 1,844; imports 1,030 tons.

1923

Dispensary opened at Serere. *Kasanvu* abolished. Imports 1,750; exports 4,573 tons.

1924

Kenyi merged in local administration. Uganda Labor Department set up for voluntary recruitment. Yafesi Ikuret parish chief. District Native Council of Chiefs established. Imports 2,166; exports 3,471 tons.

1925

Ateso adopted in primary schools. Acholi and Lugbara brought in groups of 20–30 to ginneries.

1926

Captain Phillips DC. Office of Township Headman abolished. Parish reunified. Measles epidemic (2–3% mortality).

1927

Famine. Trade poor. Ginnery labor problems. European of Gondo kills Kamod woman with car. Mikieri Oguti parish chief.

1928

Famine. 3,323 fed for 12 weeks in Gondo. Captain Mackenzie D C. Kasilo County carved out of Serere. Oil press built for crushing simsim.

1929

New pay scale for chiefs based on tax collection. Railway reached Soroti. Plague in Gondo introduced from Lango; ferry curtailed.

1930

Lalle steamers curtailed; ferries reopened. Bad cotton season. European at ginnery made Hon. Member of Legislative Council.

1932

Rinderpest epidemic. Steamer now fortnightly as at Lalle.

1933

Kennedy D C. District Native Council revived.

1934

Husbands granaries replace communal granaries. Abolition of labor for chiefs (luwalo). Elections of village chiefs introduced. Central government inquiry into ginning conditions.

1937

Teso local government system introduced.

1938

Food shortage. Mrs. Makertich discouraged from returning to Gondo.

1939

Commercial fisheries and crocodile outfit at Gondo. Forest Reserve demarcated. Kaberamaido becomes part of Teso District.

1941

New sub-county H Q built at Gondo. Good cotton crop.

1942

Amalgamation of counties into 4 wartime divisions.

1944

Famine.

GONDO SOCIETY

1945

Sub-county headquarters moved from Gondo to Kamod.

1946

District reorganized into seven counties.

1954

Ginnery damaged by fire (1 Lango killed).

1956

Kabos (Makertich) Estate reverted to the Crown. Cooperative farm planned but so overpopulated it proved impracticable. Gondo market gutted by fire.

1957

Outboard engine introduced on fishing craft at Gondo. Chiefs dealt with ginnery labor strike.

1958

First direct elections to Legislative Council. Obwangor returned for Teso.

1961

National elections held; J. O. Anyoti elected for Teso West.

1962

Lake Kyoga steamer service discontinued. National pre-independence elections held; Anyoti re-elected.

1963

Independence of Uganda. Office of village chief abolished.

1966

Kabaka of Buganda ousted. Mr. Milton Obote becomes President of Uganda. State of Emergency declared throughout Uganda during which all public meetings are banned.

Political Institutions

THE PARISH OF GONDO came into being in 1902 when the lands that the Ganda had conquered in southwestern Teso became part of the Mbale Collectorate. The first administrative reference to it, by the district officer stationed at Kumi, concerns 280 bags of cottonseed from Entebbe which were transported across Lake Kyoga on a Nyoro chief's canoes to reach Gondo on June 4, 1909.[1] At that time Gondo was a frontier post between Buganda and the developing east. Today it is a political backwater.

The political community is encapsulated within three hierarchies of external politics. These have grown up over time. Earliest was the bureaucracy of Teso District administration inaugurated in 1909, by which governmental authority in Gondo came to be exercised by a parish chief. The historical development of this office and its current functioning serves to distinguish the Teso variety of chief from an intercalary office holder who serves elsewhere in Africa as a political hinge between people and government. Next, the council system of Teso local government was introduced in 1937 to balance the growing powers of the appointed chiefs with a system of elective representation (modeled upon that of England and Wales) in which a parish council is elected to form its lowest tier. Most recently, in 1958, Gondo became part of a constituency for the election of a national representative to the Uganda Legislative Council, later the National Assembly.

These three external political systems provide institutional parameters to political action within Gondo parish, but political action is also institutionalized within the community in

← *The sub-county chief addressing the parish tax meeting*

ways not recognized by outside authorities. Indeed, for all but exceptional men, the parish is virtually a closed political arena since the politics of land and labor within Gondo do not bring the kind of prestige that carries a man far beyond its boundaries. In Gondo, unlike some other Teso parishes, the maintenance and bridging of discontinuities between the local and district level of politics has not yet been achieved. This is, in part, attributable to its polyethnic character.

The Administrative Hierarchy

Parish boundaries are determined by the requirements of local administration, about three hundred adult males being considered most suitable for control by one official, a parish chief, who is an appointed, salaried local government officer with administrative and judicial functions. Gondo has, for most of its history, been a small parish by Teso standards, its size reflecting administrative concern for what is believed to be its distinctive problem, an ethnically heterogeneous population.[2]

Teso District, administered from Soroti, contains eight counties, of which Serere is the oldest. Serere Township, fifteen miles from Gondo, contains the county headquarters from which jurisdiction is maintained over eight sub-counties, of which Bugondo is one. Bugondo in turn contains the seven parishes of Ogelak, Gondo, Ogera, Agule, Kamod, Atirir, and Ongoto.

The area over which the Gondo parish chief rules has changed during the past sixty years. The parish has always been within the sub-county of Bugondo within the county of Serere, except for the years 1928 to 1932 when a short-lived, small county of Kasilo was created. By and large, the history of this area has been one of shifting amalgamations of administrative units designed to maintain populations at sizes chiefs might find manageable. Thus, as the population of Gondo and its surrounding parishes fluctuated, so boundaries changed. Yet, within these flexible boundaries, the structural unit that is today's Gondo parish has remained the same, permitting a focus on locality that is very useful in tracing the nature and extent of political and social change. We can note five changes in the external relations of Gondo between 1902 and the present.

Prior to 1912, the three villages of Gondo, Ogelak, and Ogera formed one parish under chief Mulangira. Between 1912 and 1925, the parish consisted of the villages of Gondo, Kabola, and Ogelak (Obukito) and excluded an area two miles in radius around Gondo pier which was designated a separate township with its own chief. After 1925, the township was submerged, with its headman, into Gondo parish. The parish population was then 1,426, the number of taxpayers in the trading center only 258. This unit, made up of Gondo, Kabola, and Ogelak, lasted until 1940 when, under wartime exigencies, the parishes of Ogera and Gondo were amalgamated. Village chiefs were crucial to the successful administration of this large unit under an overworked parish chief, and the final change in Gondo's administration came in 1963, the year following Uganda's independence, when the office of village chief was abolished. The large parish of Gondo was thereupon made into three parishes—Gondo, Ogera, and Ogelak—each under a separate parish chief.

The British officer who administered Teso from 1913 until 1916 has described the introduction of the pyramidal hierarchy of territorial offices that is the present administrative system of Teso:[3]

After the Nubi mutiny something had to be found for the brilliant Muganda leader Semei Kakunguru. . . . Accordingly, Kakunguru and his followers were told to go and occupy Bukedi. The warlike Lango barred the way to the northwest so Kakunguru

swept through the less hardy Teso. . . . When the British administration took over the country it also took over Kakunguru's system.
His leading followers were absorbed as Government Agents, and
continued to administer the local natives. . . . At the same time an
effort was made to commence building up a Native Administration
by the selection and appointment of leading local natives as Chiefs
and headmen.

In making these appointments the Buganda hierarchy of *ssaza*
(county), *gombolola* (sub-county), *muluka* (parish) and *muton-
gole* (sub-parish or village) was adhered to. Not that this was un-
natural—the Baganda presented to our administrators of his days
the picture of a well organized and efficient system of indigenous
government. . . . It was almost inevitable that their system should
be adopted; unfortunately it was not adapted to local conditions.

The hierarchical system imposed upon Teso—as much a
British as a Ganda creation, since its main feature, the fixed
hierarchy of parish, sub-county and county, was as alien to
the Ganda as to the Teso[4]—was still the most efficient arm of
political organization in Teso in 1966. It remains almost
solely responsible for the collection of revenue, the dissemination of national and local government information, and the
maintenance of law and order.

The parish chief, the administration's representative living
within the community and a potential political broker for the
parish in its wider political setting, does not perform this role
in Gondo. His office is one of clientship, not of traditional
leadership. In the early days chiefs chosen by Kakunguru
were, indeed, men of local significance, able to command a
following, extort taxes, and muster labor. Many were retained
by the British as client chiefs, sanctioned by the force of
Ganda and British guns and obliged to operate within two
distinct, tangentially related, arenas. The dual identity of
Oluga, the Teso leader responsible for "letting in the Ganda"
and known to them only as Mulangira, captures the spirit of
his operations within two contrasting political structures.

During the first years of their administration, British officers painstakingly disengaged such chiefs from their political bases, attempting to make them solely dependent on—and, so ran the argument, loyal to—the district bureaucracy.

The establishment of colonial administration in Teso has been described as if there were little resistance to the British, their Ganda agents, or their Teso client chiefs.[5] Administrative officers considered their first task to be the establishment of law and order and, to make its enforcement viable, the collection of taxes. At the grass-roots level, the tax collector was the parish chief who was given 5 per cent of all he collected. There were also, of course, other perquisites to chiefly office, not least among them the power to select the labor force from among the residents of the parish he ruled.

In the early days, the duties of the parish chief were multifarious. Besides being answerable to touring district officers for the conduct of those under his jurisdiction, he also had to send children to be educated at the mission schools; to grow a large garden of cotton and see that his parishioners did the same; and to ensure that an adequate number of men and women turned out for labor. He was responsible for the maintenance of roads, rest camps, and administrative headquarters within his parish and was held personally responsible for any failure of his parishioners to buy ploughs, grow cotton, and pay taxes.

Since the exercise of such authority was bound to cause enmity, chiefs were equipped with guns (a maximum of twelve each), and some also hired, on their own initiative, small bands of retainers. The realities of the chief's position were not appreciated by the British. When first recommending that chiefs be armed, the Provincial Commissioner observed that "if the chiefs are to be able to obtain power over and maintain order among the people they must be allowed to have sufficient guns for the purpose of over-awing anyone who may be truculent. . . . Should a chief misbehave at any time, the allowance of guns could be reduced and, I believe, the loss of prestige would be felt."[6] Local chiefs, more concerned with loss of life than loss of prestige, behaved. The chiefs' methods were harsh, and necessarily so or they would not have survived. Two outstanding convictions of chiefs in 1909 and 1912 for killing parishioners reflect the proximity of their parishes to district headquarters rather than the rarity of the incidents. Official brutality was unusual neither then nor in 1966, although fatal beatings of parishioners tend at present to fetch manslaughter rather than murder charges. Chiefs expect to be feared rather than respected. Their headquarters, homes, and wives have all been, at times, subject to reprisals by aggrieved parishioners. In 1967 every chief interviewed who had held office in Gondo recalled constant fears of incendiarism and violence. Even during my short time in the field, I recorded cases elsewhere in Serere County of court buildings being burned down and parish chiefs being assaulted. One sub-county chief expressed a fear that he would be transferred to a place where his headquarters would be far from a main thoroughfare, and the chief of one parish frequently asked if I could buy a secondhand shot gun for him in Kampala. Open unrest expressed elsewhere in Teso over the amount of "official land" held by chiefs has not yet reached Serere or Gondo where land is still plentiful, but with rising taxation and falling cotton prices the parish chief is nevertheless an open target for criticism of the government whose servant he is.

Today the parish chief is neither a local man nor the holder of traditional Teso authority. He is neither a conservative force in a community of his fellows nor an intermediary between the parish and the wider political arena. He is wholly an outsider, mistrusted and disliked. Basic to the nature of his office in Gondo is a lack of interdependence between ruler and subject and an absence of checks on the abuse of power. Any checks upon the parish chief come largely from above since he fears the displeasure of his superiors, and this has to be weighed against fears of violence from below. Unlike traditional chiefs, client chiefs need have no fear of rivals and little need to consult with influential men in the parish. Yet some compromise has to be reached with men powerful in community affairs who, by their very existence, form a strategic elite between the people and their government-appointed chief.

The parish chief is an executive officer backed by the strength of the law. The nearest he comes to performing services for the community are, perhaps, his recognition of a newcomer to the parish by "walking the bounds" of land newly granted to the settler by the ward headman and his duty of speaking on behalf of a poor parishioner at the annual tax assessment meeting. In Gondo, both performances frequently go by default. Parishioners have secure tenure of land without the recognition of the parish chief and I learned of no occasion on which has he used a veto power. Two political fields overlap at such a time. When a man has resided for one year in the parish he becomes a taxpaying resident of that administrative unit; his acceptance by the community may take considerably longer and may not occur at all.

As an adjudicator, the parish chief operates at a level above the neighborhood moots of the Big Men and elders and below the sub-county level. There is no court house in the parish, and most cases are settled either at the moots or in the higher court. Although responsible for the actual collection of taxes in the parish, the chief acts as little more than a messenger boy for the sub-county chief who, when taxes come in slowly, appears on the scene himself. Receipts are issued by a clerk at sub-county headquarters where the tax registers are kept. It is not unknown for groups of parish chiefs to get together to harass defaulters; the Gondo chief was placed on probation for such activities in 1967 but was subsequently reinstated.

The parish chief no longer obtains either power or prestige through the size of his parish, the material advantages of office, his monthly salary, or the above average number of wives he is able to acquire. These and the contacts between parishes that he is able to make during his period of tenure are primarily a form of investment for the day when he may retire to his natal parish to play there the part of Big Man.

The Representative Council System

The taxpayers of Gondo parish form a political community, not only because they are contained within a common administrative unit under a parish chief but also in another sense; they are all eligible to compete for political office within the parish since the administrative hierarchy is paralleled by a representative political structure.

The British introduced a representative form of political organization in 1937 largely to counter the growing powers of appointed chiefs, their unrepresentativeness, and their abuse of authority. It was intended to give voice to the peasants against their chiefly exploiters. At the base of the pyramid system of councils was to be the parish council, which was envisaged as consisting of the parish chief as chairman with his two or three village chiefs as official members. The unofficial members would consist of two clan elders along with three other villagers elected at a village meeting where every adult male had a vote. In addition to these official and elected members, there was to be a Muslim, and a Protestant and Catholic parishioner chosen by the missions. By this count, the parish council would contain no fewer than eleven members. From the parish council one member for every 150 taxpayers would be elected to a sub-county council; from there one member for each 750 taxpayers would be sent to a county council. Each county council, in turn, would send one elected member for every 1,500 taxpayers to a district council which met at Soroti under the chairmanship of the District Commissioner. This district council, as a legislative body, laid down district by-laws which were then enforced by the chiefs.[7]

In principle, an individual's election to his parish council might be his first step on a path leading to significant political office. In a parish such as Gondo with only a few taxpayers, there was, however, little chance for the elected member who was sent up to the sub-county level to advance any further, since, in all but exceptional cases, a District Councillor came from the largest parish in his constituency.[8] For a parish like Gondo the parish council has remained, since its inception, limited in scope; parish councils are of interest to us not because they provide a steppingstone into wider political arenas or because they permit the voice of the parish to be carried upward to the district level, but because they make visible competition for prestige within the parish itself. The institution feeds back into the parish political arena since prestige is gained from being elected to it, although office seldom carries the incumbent far beyond the parish level. There is, in effect, from the parochial point of view, no dissipation of political energies into wider political arenas.

The Gondo parish council of 1966 was described to me by one of its councillors, Charles Frederick Otieno.

There are three members, Erismasi Odico, Levi Anyapo and myself. No, there are four; I have forgotten Enosi Ocen. Ocact, the parish chief, is Chairman. We are chosen by the people of the parish who collect together for this purpose. In the past, a council lasted three years; this time it has been going for five years. The last election was in March 1961. You go and stand behind the one you choose to be a councillor. Women are welcome to vote but normally they don't turn up.

Our purpose is to settle land disputes and to look into all the everyday problems concerning the common man. We are not concerned with crime or taxes; they are the job of the parish chief. We don't usually meet in the dry season only in the planting season. between March and May, for that is when land disputes arise. We don't really do anything very useful because if we pass judgement in a case, and the accused is defeated, the parish chief always encourages him to appeal to the sub-county chief. This hinders our progress. We settle cases; then we hear they are still going on at the next level. We can't do anything about it because we don't want to push ourselves ahead and annoy the administrators. This is common to all the parishes I know about.

This parish council, which might be expected to be the major political institution in the parish, is, in Gondo, relatively unimportant. Since the chief is always an alien, elected elders might be invaluable as parish leaders were they indeed the "true representatives of the peasants, deriving their authority from Teso social organization of pre-administration days," as F. R. Kennedy, the District Commissioner who introduced the system, believed.[9] In Gondo such "clan elders" as exist operate outside of the parish council and apart from any formal political institution. This is not surprising, for Kennedy read into the Teso clan system a governmental significance that never existed, failing to distinguish between familial and political authority. The political office of "clan elder" (apolon k'ateker) is as alien to the parishioners as their bureaucratic client chiefs. Not one of the four men on the council today was born in the parish and only one, Ocen, belongs to a leading Gondo family. All but Ocen are political entrepreneurs who see council activity as yet another platform on which they may stand to further their political interests.

The only other account that we have of Teso parish councils suggests that in this respect Gondo is not unique. Writing of Usuku councillors who usually tend to be "clan elders," Burke suggests that they are individuals lacking in traditional authority, merely important or wealthy men, or in a few cases, friends of the parish chief. Their authority and influence is based not on clan leadership but on locality. These men have become, in effect, area headmen or sub-chiefs, who regard themselves as an integral, though unofficial, part of the chiefly hierarchy. They exercise authority over all the Teso residents in their areas. "The importance of these little known petty chiefs cannot be over-emphasized," Burke suggests. "They are the real link between government and people."[10]

The Usuku parish leaders described by Burke differ significantly from those in Gondo and its neighboring parishes. First, in Gondo, Ogera, and Ogelak, the roles of clan elder and parish councillor rarely coincide. Secondly, ward headmen are elected by, and have authority over, all the residents in their neighborhoods, regardless of tribal origin. Both Nyoro and Kenyi have been elected to office in Gondo. Thirdly, ward headmen are very far from considering themselves to be petty chiefs or part of the administration as in Usuku but, on the contrary, are seen to represent the people against the parish chief and the administration at large. Most important, there is an intermediary between the ward headmen and the parish chief, who is known in western Serere as the *emorimor*, a community leader or coordinator."[11] This important office will be discussed in some detail at the end of this chapter.

The Party Political Arena

Not only is the Gondo parishioner a taxpayer in an administrative structure and a voter in the District representative system, he is also a political constituent in the nationwide electoral system in operation in the Republic of Uganda.

Direct elections to the Uganda Legislative Council were first held in 1958, and Gondo parishioners—men and women alike —were mobilized by chiefs as part of a Teso District constituency. Cuthbert Obwangor, an early member of the Uganda

National Congress (UNC), which, as the direct descendant of the Uganda Federation of African Farmers, enjoyed some success in eastern Serere County and in which some of Gondo's Big Men were actively engaged, was returned with an overwhelming majority. The next elections, held in March 1961, saw the Uganda Peoples Congress (UPC) campaigning in Gondo, its candidate, J. O. Anyoti, defeating M. Etatao of the Democratic Party (DP), a Soroti man, by a 5,965 majority. Of 25,647 registered voters, 68 per cent cast their ballots in this West Teso constituency. This was a lower poll than in other parts of Teso, where the attitude and efficiency of the chiefs were again important factors in the mobilization of the electorate.[12] Women also played an active role in Teso electoral politics,[13] and a well-organized women's arm of the UPC was still in evidence in Gondo in 1966. That there is no strong youth wing reflects the gerontocratic nature of politics in Teso, for which Gondo may, in this respect, provide a case study.

Anyoti stood for re-election in the crucial pre-independence elections of April 1962, which confirmed the strength of UPC in the West Teso constituency. He defeated Emmanuel Otala (DP) by a majority of 2,635 votes, 41.7 per cent of the constituency casting their ballots. Otala, a favorite-son candidate in Gondo since he is a member of the local Icaak clan, is a Catholic and an Education Officer working at Mbale. He attributed his defeat not to his religion or party, but to his belonging to one of the poorer and less influential clans in the parish. Nevertheless, his political identity and participation, as a Teso Catholic DP member in a parish in which most Catholics are non-Teso, has done much to avert superimposed or overlapping cleavages between Catholics and Protestants, DP and UPC, Teso and non-Teso, in Gondo parish.

Throughout Uganda as a whole the UPC government has gained increasing support since 1962 when it commanded only

35 seats in the National Assembly. By June 1964 this number had risen to 58 and by January 1966 to 75, which gave the party the necessary two-thirds majority to amend the Constitution. The gradual accumulation /of strength by the UPC has had repercussions throughout the lower levels of political activity, most markedly in the District Council. National elections due to be held some time before April 1967 were postponed, and this established a precedent for all conciliar politics throughout Teso.

Interrelationships between the Three External Institutions

Although the intricate relationships that exist, mostly at an informal level, between the three political structures external to the parish cannot here be discussed in the detail they merit, their nature serves to highlight the extent to which Gondo parishioners are put at a disadvantage by their distance from the ultimate sources of political power in the nation-state. Three types of interrelationship may be distinguished: overlapping memberships between institutions, ecological relationships, and cross-cutting social ties between individuals.

In earlier times Chiefs were also *ex officio* members of the elected District Council as they still are of lower councils. Today Anyoti, the UPC National Assemblyman, is Chairman of Teso District Council, and its recent polarization, each elected member declaring allegiance to either the UPC or the DP, has led to party political ideology playing a role similar to that of regional factionalism in former days. Since the underlying economic causes of cleavage between north and south still exist, it is not likely to replace this factionalism, as recent quarrels over Land Board appointments show, and the position may well be aggravated by the fact that the few remaining DP politicians come from the southern counties.[14] Ecological relationships sustain the interrelation of the three political hierarchies into a larger system. Although the tie that formerly existed between the District Commissioner and the District Council lapsed in 1963, it has recently been restored, the Commissioner having been given supervisory powers over the finances of the Council in particular. He also maintains a watching brief over the lower councils. Thus the civil servant office of Commissioner is articulated with both the local representative councils and the Ministry of Regional Administration headed by its UPC cabinet member. Finally, numerous cross-cutting ties operate between individuals and link institutions. Family connections between District Councillors and chiefs are intricate, and political interests are shared. A recent development has been the "kicking upstairs" of an opposition member by appointing him parish chief or road headman; this interpretation accepts a current Teso evaluation that salaried, pensionable appointments are more valuable than elected positions carrying allowances, while recognizing the diminishing political powers of chiefly office.

No formal pattern emerges of mobility from one political institution to another: an individual operates within them one by one as the occasion arises. For the Gondo parishioner, the opportunity seldom occurs. As the representative of a small parish, it is extremely unlikely that the Gondo councillor elected to the sub-county level will rise any higher in the hierarchy and that his voice will carry very far. Many Aojabule residents align with Ogera parish in their social activities partly because a former District Councillor resides there, to whom doors are still open in Soroti. Emmanuel Otala (also a former District Councillor) might serve Gondo parishioners well, but, as we saw, he failed to win election as Democratic Party candidate within the wider constituency. Also, as an Education Officer posted out of the district to Mbale, he is somewhat inaccessible. After his retirement, when he returns to Gondo and becomes established there, he may well serve as the political broker the parish now lacks. However, at the moment, there is a common belief that the UPC, as the party in power since 1964, has rewarded those who supported them. In such vein parishioners account for Gondo being a political backwater.

The Community Political Structure

The parish political community encapsulated within these three external structures differs from them in that its form is not hierarchical. Although the parish chief is officially answerable for what goes on in the parish, most of its day-by-day administration lies in the hands of five ward headmen (*apolon ka ateker* in Ateso; *omukulu wekika* in Lukenyi) chosen from among the residents by the parish at large—or by a small proportion of them—at the prompting of the parish chief. The 1963 elections, held on the neutral ground opposite the shops, were simply organized, with supporters lining up behind their nominees for each of the five wards. In this manner visible support was given to Yokani Elamu (T 601), Township and Adiding; Sabiti Musana (K 312), Kabola; Yowana Ekweru (T 210), Agologolo; Ramoni Ekwaru (T 104), Aojabule; and Enosi Ocen (T 512), Opucct. From among their number they chose Ocen to be *emorimor* or coordinator.

Ward headmen are in daily contact with most of the people, visiting their homes and sharing their beer (which is seen to be their sole "payment"), unlike the parish chief who is most frequently encountered in public places such as the ginnery, duka, or school courtyard. Even for the annual census for which the chief is responsible, information is gathered by each headman going round his ward and then reporting back to the chief's homestead where the final compilation is made. In their daily contact when there is news to disseminate, headmen operate in different ways: some call meetings of all their ward members, others go round from homestead to homestead. In cases of trouble in the parish the ward headman is immediately fetched and, indeed, he spends most of his mornings going from place to place, on foot, settling disputes and hearing grievances. The parish chief, on the other hand, cycles from point to point with only fleeting contact with those parishioners he is not seeking out. The office of ward headman is a time-consuming one for which the individual must offer himself; he cannot be drafted by either the parish chief or the people. Ward headmen are generally cultivators from families well established in Gondo since they must rely on dependents to further their cultivation while they themselves are engaged on community affairs. Businessmen and newcomers would have neither time for the all-consuming office nor support. Nevertheless, to offer oneself as a candidate for headmanship is clearly one way of staking a claim to community-wide recognition.

Ward headmen are responsible for all in their neighborhoods regardless of age, race, or ethnicity. Formerly certain groups of ginnery immigrants had their own leadership to some degree, but with their integration into the community and their diminishing numbers in proportion to other ginnery workers (perhaps also because their jobs are secure), this is no longer the case although the names of former representatives are still known. Thus Acholi recall the leadership (1928–1945) of Anderea Oyat (the father of A 670); of Gingorio (1945–1957); and, since 1957, of Otoo (A 542). Similarly the Lango refer to Amuno (1926–1948), Oddi (1948–1954), and Opuno (L 546) in this fashion. Today the chief approaches both Acholi and Lango through the headmen of the wards in which they reside. Only the Luo, on some occasions, seem to accentuate ethnic separateness; this may be due to the complications involved in some still being Kenyan citizens and paying taxes outside of the parish. All those in Gondo, however, are resident taxpayers, and any ethnic institutions in which they are involved have their origins in the neighboring parish of Ogelak where the Luo are more numerous, having their own school (which some Teso children attend), sectarian church (Legia Maria), and cooperative fishing groups. The Luo residents of Gondo are less communalistic than those of Ogelak, one even being the current secretary of the cotton growers cooperative which serves the three parishes.

Although the parish political structure contains no hierarchy of offices, when confronted with the need to take joint action in the face of an external threat, a centralized structure seems to have emerged *de novo*.[15] Vertical authority relations are a feature of both Ganda and European political structures in which authority is conceptually equated with height or elevation. In an acephelous society, on the other hand, authority is conceived as horizontally structured, "the resultant of ongoing interaction between individuals."[16] Thus, in Gondo, the office of emorimor or coordinator, which I referred to previously, is not seen as a rung in the ladder of authority above which is the office of parish chief, but rather is it a position within a horizontal community power structure, made up of clan elders and ward headmen, which may be articulated with the bureaucracy if the contingency arises. This power of articulation lies not at the discretion of a "superior" chief, as was made abundantly clear in Gondo in 1966, but with the community whose coordinator the emorimor is. A distinction between authority as institutionalized power and authority as prestige,[17] bestowed and withdrawn by the community, contributes to an understanding of the cohort-type politics that exists in Gondo.[18]

A crisis situation in the relationship of the chief and the emorimor in Gondo in January 1967 illustrates both the nature of the authority and the sanctions that exist. Dissatisfied with the cooperation he was receiving from the emorimor, the chief dismissed him as a ward headman on the grounds that he had not paid his tax. The emorimor was not sorry to accept this indirect discharge from his obligations to the community since he had fallen into poverty as his time was given up more and more to the affairs of the parish. The ward headmen proceeded to elect another of their fellows emorimor, the chief agreeing to pay a small increment to the new man.

In their choice of emorimor ward headmen recognize established prestige in the community and an ability to "speak up for" the community to outsiders. Of one former village (*erony*) chief who became emorimor it was said, "Once he worked for the government, now he works for us." Although his office is informal and unrecognized by the administration, the emorimor is certainly the most powerful man in the parish ex officio. Parish chiefs articulate their roles with the office in different ways: the Ogera chief pays a small salary and his load is made correspondingly lighter; the Gondo chief, as we saw, took a hard line and received little cooperation from the parish at large.

The dialectic in the office of emorimor brings the community and the administration closer together while keeping them apart. In his executive aspect the emorimor mobilizes groups to carry out communal tasks within the parish; in his judicial aspect his performance prevents community quarrels falling into the hands of outsiders. In this respect, perhaps, Gondo might be described as a political community maintaining "law within and war without."

3

Land and Labor:
The Historical Dimension

THE UGANDA PROTECTORATE'S POLICIES toward the introduction of cash crops, the control of land and labor resources, and its internal and external economic interests shaped the development and structure of Gondo as a polyethnic community. In general, a distinction was recognized between the peasant economies of the south and east—mainly the coffee- and cotton-producing areas of Buganda, Busoga, and Teso— and the labor-supplying regions of the north—West Nile, Acholi, and, in earlier times, Lango. Regions in western Uganda were seen as intermediate in this respect. At different times the labor-recruiting policies of the central government shifted in emphasis within both districts and regions, but the widely accepted colonial view of Uganda as an "undeveloped estate" was always, to some extent, contradicted by administrative policies aimed at making each district into a self-sufficient entity.[1] Nowhere was this more apparent than in Teso.

Incompatability between the goals of the administration and the aims of those subject to it also helped to shape Gondo parish. For most parishioners administrative penetration into the local community had a horizontal rather than a vertical dimension. Changes taking place in Gondo were measured against those within other communities making up the wider social universe of its residents—communities not only in

← *A herd passing through the ginnery yard, its right of way assured (the ginnery office serves as the parish Post Office; Dudumaki is the trade name of an insecticide used on cotton)*

[67]

Serere and Kaberamaido and neighboring Teso counties but in Busoga and Lango and other districts as well. District administrative policies toward other towns and villages within this network, toward emigrants even further afield, and toward the African laboring class generally were as relevant to the formation of the Gondo parishioner's political awareness and to issues of group identity, leadership, and political action as changes taking place within the parish itself. In Teso generally societal forces conditioned the nature and extent of administrative change to a marked degree.

Two contrasting phases mark Gondo's development between 1912 and 1966. In its initial growth the community acquired its polyethnic character as, first, a port; later, two ginneries and, ultimately, a township were established there. Schemes for its development as a major industrial and commercial center for eastern Uganda were then allowed to lapse as rail communication replaced the Lake Kyoga transport system in the plans of the central government so that a second phase, from 1926 until the present, has been characterized by economic decline.

Plans to establish a port at Gondo were first broached after Kirkpatrick's survey of Lake Kyoga in 1898, and by 1913 a township had grown up around it large enough to be recognized in the Uganda Gazette of that year. Its population consisted of 5,000 Africans, many of them temporary laborers conscripted for the building of the port and ginneries, 10 Asians, and 8 Europeans. Soroti, later to become the district headquarters, had at that time 4,000 African, 3 Asian, and no European residents. The administration of Gondo was, as we have seen, shared by a township headman who was responsible for an area within a two-mile radius of the pier and a parish chief in charge of an area covering the present Gondo and Ogelak parishes.[2]

The records of the administration and the recollections of

[68]

Gondo's former chiefs and contemporary residents suggest that the political relations of the parish and township were largely labor relations.[3] Two forms of compulsory labor recruitment were available to the administration at that time: *luwalo,* one month's compulsory, unpaid labor for the upkeep of local roads and public works, and *kasanvu,* a form of labor taxation imposed by the central government throughout Uganda and involving forced migration to tasks for which the worker was paid at a wage below the market rate.[4] Although it was intended that luwalo corvée labor be used with discretion, most chiefs made of it a personal labor force, and its manipulation soon became one of the most visible sources of their prestige. It was nevertheless preferable to kasanvu for the peasant who wanted to fulfill his obligations without leaving his parish. In neighboring Busoga, where cash payment for head porterage was as widely adopted by commercial enterprises as in Serere, taxpayers were allowed to commutate kasanvu into cash payments, but this arrangement was not permitted in Teso until 1919. Both forms of labor were extensively used in Gondo to meet the needs of head porterage, road work, the building of the ginneries, offices, and pier, and the single track railway leading to it, as well as for regular municipal labor. From the start the township headman and the parish chief were obliged to compete for control over the resident taxpayers whom they were required to muster for these many labor demands at the cost of their own administrative offices. Furthermore, when the owners with their ginneries in operation later experienced difficulty in obtaining workers, kasanvu labor was frequently provided by the chief to make up deficiencies.

Although some of this labor was paid, the line between voluntary and coerced labor was finely drawn, and the only recourse open to peasants seeking to avoid the double demands of parish chief and township headman was to move away. Some Teso moved out of the township to settle in Agologolo ward to the east; others moved even further away across the lake to Kaberamaido where they not only escaped the arduous labor demands of Teso administrators but also paid lower taxes. Gondo chiefs—Teso, Kenyi, and Nyoro— were periodically sent to bring back defecting "followers." Not until late in 1913 did the administration finally concede the need to "even out labor obligations for the natives in the immediate neighborhood" of Gondo township, justifying their concession with the observation that the places of those who had moved away were being taken by "a large number of aliens of doubtful character, none of them subject to the control of chiefs." As one visiting district officer observed in 1913, "these centers seem to possess a peculiar charm for many native rascals."⁵ It appeared to the administration that conditions grew even worse after 1914 when the Ganda agent was withdrawn. Mass departures for Lango spread disease, completely disorganized the regulation of labor, and, most heinous of all in official eyes, necessitated large-scale alterations in the tax registers.

Labor demands were not the only extortions suffered by the Gondo parishioner at this time. Cotton growing was enforced to meet the requirements of the Poll Tax Ordinances proclaimed in Teso in 1909, and already by November 1916 the compulsory acreage per man had been increased to half an acre. In Gondo, Chief Oluga was dismissed for being unable to enforce cash crop cultivation. The tax, which had been 6 shillings per male in 1907, reached 15 shillings by 1919, and increased fourfold in the next half century. Ginnery and plantation labor held no prospects for the Gondo peasant already overburdened by competing labor demands and enforced cotton production which permitted little time for the cultivation of essential foodcrops. The famine of 1918–1919, when 2,131 persons died in Bugondo sub-county alone, suggests that the Gondo peasant was, indeed, unable to maintain a balanced input of labor largely because cotton proved labor intensive at the very time when subsistence requirements were heaviest. Gondo parishioners recall the living dead being thrown into public graves. Ultimately the administration intervened to provide famine relief and control food prices, both actions setting precedents for later intervention into the peasant agricultural cycle and the market economy.[6]

Among the negative effects of this extensive drain on the manpower resources of the Gondo community was an obligatory weakening of reliance on kin and neighbors and an impoverishment of the subsistence economy; its positive results included the consolidation of a laboring class of Africans unmindful of ethnic distinctions in the light of their shared burdens.

From the beginning it was the rate at which Gondo grew even more than the mushrooming of its population around the port and ginneries that patterned social relations there. Commercial frontiers had outpaced those of the administration so that, to all outward appearances, district officers moved in to protect the Africans against exploitation by commercial interests. Paternally playing a watchdog role with regard to African development, the administrators constantly alerted each other to the peasants' oppressors—cotton-buying Asians, clever but unscrupulous Ganda ("smarter than the unsophisticated Teso"), alien traders of all descriptions, European employers, and, not least, the client chiefs of their own creation.[7]

The volatile situation developing around the port and ginneries bred inevitable conflict. Apart from the ravaging competition for labor among ginneries, Asian traders, and the Works Department; between parish chief and township headman; between Protestant catechist and Catholic priest; between demands for cash and demands for subsistence, certain hostilities which might be variously interpreted in class or ethnic terms were also apparent. Sporadic incidents of European and Asian homes being destroyed by arson, frequent thefts from Ganda and Asian merchants, and assaults against Teso chiefs, as well as widespread violence arising from drunkenness, prostitution, and crime, led the district administration, belatedly, to organize the orderly development of a respectable township around Gondo's commercial sinks.[8]

An Inspector of Sleeping Sickness and the Medical Officer from Mbale were dispatched to inaugurate this project since, at this time, a close connection was perceived between health and labor problems throughout the Protectorate. After inoculation campaigns had been carried out on Kaweri Island and in Gondo, an area around the pier was surveyed and the first planned township in Uganda began to take shape on the drawing board. The high-level correspondence that ensued between July 1912, when the plan was first presented, and its final acceptance fifteen months later indicates the importance attached to Gondo as a port through which northern and eastern Uganda were to be opened up. Parishioners and townsfolk alike could hardly fail to be aware of their position athwart the fulcrum of an expanding colonial territory. The flow of traffic through Gondo was impressive—traders, missionaries, administrative officers, big game hunters, visiting Americans, army recruiters, schoolteachers, catechists, nurses, veterinary officials, the first motor vehicle in December 1912, as well as heavy machinery, books, trunks, mail, money orders, and telegrams. Moreover, township development was under the eye of the highest authorities in the Protectorate. In October 1913, final plans were "approved verbally and provisionally by the Governor at an interview at Government House, at which the Chief Secretary, the Principal Medical Officer, the Director of Agriculture and the Land Officer were present" and within a few years the Gondo town plan became the blueprint for urban development throughout eastern and northern Uganda.[9]

In October 1912, the anonymous contributor of "Bukedi Notes" to the *Uganda Herald* described Gondo in the following words:

Bugondo is being looked upon as "Kibuga," or the Kampala of Bukedi. I have heard the Natives term it such. The life, activity and progress of the place is astonishing in so short a time. Over 1,000 Bakedi have worked as porters for the two ginning Firms, and earned enough to pay their poll tax. The British East African Corporation Ltd. are employing labor on a large scale; and Mr. Lord (the chief engineer of BEAC Ltd.) has daily applicants who voluntarily offer their services.[10]

This rapid expansion of the commercial frontier led the Acting District Commissioner to recommend the policing of Gondo as early as November 1912 and his memorandum to the Provincial Commissioner conveys a vivid impression of the growing pains of the developing multiracial township.[11] Gondo is, he says,

a rapidly growing place . . . already the chief commercial center in the district. . . . The business premises (uninhabited at night) consist at present of two ginneries with stores and auxiliary buildings, an Agriculture Department store, one private store, and an Indian bazaar of ten shops. There are ten or more Europeans living there in temporary buildings and the number of both business premises and residential houses will be considerably increased when the settlement of the plan of the port now in course of preparation admits of the granting of applications for plots. Several business firms may be expected to have representatives always living at Bugondo. The Lake Chioga steamer boat serves the port at least four times per month and the presence of police is necessary on such occasions.

I have received many complaints of theft. The natives on Lake Chioga are a mixed and difficult character and the business carried on at Bugondo brings in and attracts subordinates, Indians and natives, who go to increase the number of people who are known by experience to make work for the police. I regret also I have to say that the conduct of some Europeans living in or passing through Bugondo has given rise to difficult cases with natives and I regard it as necessary that the Government police should be in evidence there.

In 1916 Egadu, the father of Gondo's present parish chief, was appointed to succeed Oluga because, according to the Serere touring books, Gondo township "with its cosmopolitan population requires a strong and energetic chief capable of dealing with Europeans and Asiatics as well as natives."[12]

Gondo developed into a racially segregated township within a plural society not in response to cultural differences but as a result of enforced government regulations. The principles on which these were based were still being set forth in 1947.[13]

Segregation of the African population from the Asian is desirable from both sides. From the Asian point of view, as from the Europeans, it is desirable to have a haven of refuge from the African, where one can live in one's own manner—out of sight and out of hearing. Even inside a Township, it is considered desirable for Europeans to have an appreciable gap around their houses in which no African housing (apart from personal servants) is allowed.

The habits of the two races differ, and also their resistance to such diseases as malaria, and fly-borne disease. . . .

Owing to their late arrival on the scene, the first task of the town planners in Gondo was to relocate persons already settled around the port and ginnery. This involved a gradual clearing of African huts and banana shambas (an indication of the well-established Bantu presence) from an area within a two-mile radius of the pier. The 1912 Township Plan that they attempted to implement reflected both an overly optimistic anticipation of the economic development of Teso in general and Gondo in particular and something of the political philosophy of the alien administration with respect to its African subjects.[14] Areas were set aside for European bun-

galows, Asian quarters, and "European and Asian housing"
(Figure 5). (The first are the stone houses still standing in
Gondo in 1966, the Asian quarters are the line of present
dukas, but no other permanent housing was ever erected.)
Apart from these racial distinctions, segregation was on the
basis of occupational categories. Thus the Swahili lines of the
Public Works Department were set at the edge of the municipal boundary, close to the mosque around which clus-
stered Muslim African dwellings. African porters in the
steamer service and the labor force of the Bukedi (Uganda)
Trading Company ginnery were located behind the market,
and African servants, along with the British East African
Corporation ginnery labor, were strung along the road leading
to Kadungulu. Where Eria's hotel now stands at the crossroads, a police post was established and the huts of migrant
squatters sprang up seasonally behind it where today's ginnery
lines are to be found. Although the Church Missionary

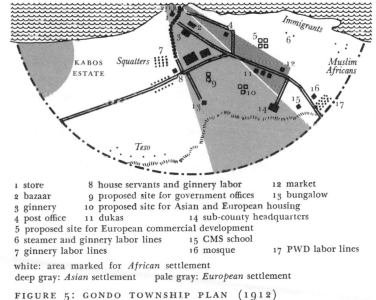

1 store	8 house servants and ginnery labor	12 market
2 bazaar	9 proposed site for government offices	13 bungalow
3 ginnery	10 proposed site for Asian and European housing	
4 post office	11 dukas	14 sub-county headquarters
5 proposed site for European commercial development		
6 steamer and ginnery labor lines	15 CMS school	
7 ginnery labor lines	16 mosque	17 PWD labor lines

white: area marked for *African* settlement
deep gray: *Asian* settlement   pale gray: *European* settlement

FIGURE 5: GONDO TOWNSHIP PLAN (1912)

Society school appears never to have been more than a mud and wattle building, the present NAC school-cum-church still stands on the same site. The government offices, trading plots, and European commercial buildings contained in the plan did not leave the drawing board although an Asian bazaar and a post office were erected as proposed. The 76-acre Kabos estate on the shore of Lake Kyoga in the west of the parish was the property of a British employee of the PWD who, after a short spell of government service in western Uganda, set up as a "Commission Agent, Buyer of Livestock and Produce" in Gondo. After his death in 1924, the Teso administration discouraged his widow and daughters from staying on there.

Beyond the township boundaries no attempt was made to order the population spatially, homes beyond the two-mile limit being recognized as part of a distinct jurisdiction, the parish, until 1925. Within the township Africans were viewed, first, in economic terms as discrete task forces—ginnery, port, PWD, house servants—and, secondly, politically as resident aliens in a predominantly Teso environment. Although there was some correspondence between tribal identity and occupational pursuits, no recognition was given to tribal groups as such: those within the two-mile limit were considered townsmen and contrasted with the Teso peasant occupying his homestead and working his land beyond the township boundary. There was no official acknowledgment of the Teso in the town or the non-Teso settler in the countryside.

Even in a general context, social realities blurred the administrative distinction between the Teso population and aliens, the Serere County census of 1911 showing a category of "resident" cutting across both sectors. Two breeds of alien were differentiated: "resident aliens" including Kenyi, "Badope," Soga, and Nyoro under chiefs; and a "floating alien native population" which also included Soga and Nyoro as well as Ganda, Gweri, Gisu, Nyuli, Kavirondo, Swahili, and

Masai.[15] Thus of the three largest Bantu categories, the Nyoro and Soga were considered permanent residents along with Kenyi and Teso and only the Ganda were viewed wholly as aliens, being perceived for the most part as administrators employed by the government in much the same way as were the colonial officers themselves. Ganda had their own schools and churches throughout Serere, forming a discrete elite among Africans.[16]

The people of Gondo, regardless of ethnicity, were obliged to operate in two political arenas, town and parish, recognizing two authorities. Yet, for the most part, the distinction was more honored in the breach than in the observance. Teso homesteads lay within the municipal boundaries from the days before the township was created and, although residents in the immediate vicinity of European homes were evicted, most maintained social and economic links with homesteads throughout the parish in a manner that rendered the boundary socially unreal. That the township zone was in no way isolated from the surrounding countryside affected the character of its development. In time the presence of Teso living within the municipal boundaries undermined the allotment of functional areas to various occupational groups, since Teso landowners were frequently willing to lend land and sponsor new settlers regardless of administrative niceties. Gondo's open spaces, designed as buffer zones between different categories of resident, were short-lived since the Teso parishioner was not prepared to recognize his own exclusiveness when he could gain more by operating within the municipal context than as a "tribesman" under a parish chief.

Nor was it in the interests of the commercial class in Gondo to assist the administration in delimiting labor supplies and discouraging the migration of Teso to town. That sense of community versus government, "we" against "they," commonly found in rural areas was shared by most Gondo residents regardless of race. Ginnery officials frequently intervened to restrain the brutality of the chief when he was on ginnery land or to prevent the catechist's forcible seizure of children for schooling. On one occasion in 1915 Europeans at the ginnery even defended interests they shared with the Africans by taking the law into their own hands and resisting central government officers. A recruiting vessel of the King's African Rifles (KAR) had called at Gondo, and the ginnery residents were evidently obliged to intervene to prevent the shanghaiing of their African workers. Boarding the vessel, three Europeans released the Gondo men; for this trespass they were subsequently brought to court and heavily fined.[17]

In spite of discrepancies such as these between planned segregation and its actual operation, by their very manner of laying down rules for township development, primarily out of concern for the healthfulness of the area for European residents, the administration accentuated cultural pluralism in Gondo in two ways. First, they adopted a plan with segregated residential areas and, secondly, they enforced Protectorate regulations limiting the nature and extent of non-African settlement and land ownership in rural areas. The plural society that emerged, a society in which the union of differing racial elements was not voluntary but was imposed by the colonial power and by the force of economic circumstance,[18] was characteristic of the Protectorate as a whole, Gondo exemplifying in microcosm the relations crystallized by the establishment of the cotton industry throughout the territory.[19] In sanctioning the political supremacy of a European minority, in accepting ethnic ranking, and in advocating residential segregation, the Teso administration gave visible expression to an ideology of cultural pluralism which they shared with the white commercial class and which brought about covert ethnic politicization on the part of the Africans with whom they were in contact.

The three main features of a plural society are generally understood to be, first, polyethnicity; secondly, residential segregation; and, thirdly, commercial intercourse. A medley of peoples, as Furnivall puts it, each group holding by its own religion, culture, and language, its own ideas and ways, live side by side, but separately within the same political unit. At the heart of the plural society lies commercial intercourse, members of the different sections meeting as individuals only in the marketplace, buying and selling,[20] but a further characteristic of the plural society, and a complementary one, is the imposition of an ideology of racial superiority around which all else is structured.[21] Cultural pluralism becomes politically relevant only when differential access to positions of differing advantage is institutionalized in ethnic terms. The mere existence of social and cultural categories in the population is not enough to account for political cleavages; it is the process of politicizing ethnicity and the ideology that validates it that distinguishes a plural society. Thus, although the organizational reality of social interaction in Gondo differed from the model plural society (many cross-cutting ties existing between groups aligned against each other in commercial or political spheres), nevertheless, in the sense that there was a dominant ideology of European supremacy and segregation backed by legal sanctions and force, this phase in Gondo's development may be seen to contrast sharply with the type of pluralistic relations that came into being later.

Until the completion of Gondo township in 1917, parishioners and townsfolk alike were constantly swept into the affairs of the district that was fast emerging around Soroti and the Uganda Protectorate that Entebbe was molding into shape. Two hundred men planted grass beneath the trees in Gondo under the supervision of an Assistant District Commissioner. Sub-county headquarters were set up opposite the market, and a bicycle runner carried mail twice weekly to

Soroti district headquarters. In 1924, 76 Asian traders and 16 Europeans lived permanently in the township; 30 Africans were in full-time ginnery employment; 21 worked with the Uganda Railways; 9 were in the ferry service; 12 were in administration; 5 were builders; the Steamer Service employed 20; and a further 87 served in the Public Works Department. The total African population of the parish (which included Ogelak in 1924) was 1,426 and that of the township 1,132.[22]

The events that brought about the economic decline of Gondo had their beginnings as early as 1914 when the district headquarters was moved from Kumi to Soroti and construction begun on Lalle port, seven miles to the east, to eliminate the long trek of head porters from Gondo. In the years that followed, the imports and exports of Lalle grew as those of Gondo declined until the death knell for both port and township at Gondo was sounded in 1929 when the railhead finally reached Soroti. In 1912 Gondo was the largest municipality in Teso with an estimated population of over five thousand. By the middle of the century fifteen minor townships in the surrounding district were all larger than Gondo. The Lake Kyoga steamer service lingered on until 1962, calling at Gondo, but by that date most of the Serere cotton had been sent by rail for many years. In 1966 bales were sent from the Kyere Cotton Company at Gondo to the railhead at Soroti whence they traveled directly to Mombasa for shipment overseas. Ultimately Gondo suffered the final indignity of being gazetted a trading center rather than a township.

Yet the decline of the municipality was as gradual as its growth had been rapid, and this very gradualism was a factor in determining the character of the polyethnic community. In 1911, as we have seen, the population of Gondo, like that of Serere as a whole, was largely made up of Teso and Bantu from the southern shores of Lake Kyoga. This situation began to alter gradually after 1918, the war years having changed the character of both the administration and the African labor force. Personnel of both were returning from the wars, and the District Commissioner, one of five "captains" who held office between 1919 and 1931, feeling that many of the men who had served with the KAR could not be expected to "return to their old status," set up a procedure whereby returning soldiers were given jobs as foremen, night watchmen, or askaris in the ginneries of the district.[23] Most of those who came to Gondo were of Nilotic stock and thus began the trickle of labor migration from the north that became an established flow by 1924 when the Uganda Labour Department set up a voluntary labor recruitment scheme to encourage wage migration from the north and west.[24] Shortly afterward recruitment was put in the hands of an official organizer who saw to it that labor was steered toward the magnet areas closest to the homelands of the migrants, and so there grew up something of an Acholi and Lango monopoly on ginnery labor in Gondo that is still evident today.

Employers throughout Teso, from the early twenties on, complained of labor shortages wherever cotton was grown, and the district administration saw it as part of its duty to remedy matters. By 1926, however, in Gondo the office of township headman had been abolished, and the parish chief had had restored to him his original responsibilities over all the residents of the area regardless of race or permanence of settlement. The ginneries had become more autonomous in the local setting, restricted in their practices only by national industrial regulations and international labor agreements. As the ginneries became more and more autonomous and the interest of district officials more remote, concern with Gondo's polyethnicity subsided, and townsmen, regardless of tribe, were able to sink back stolidly into the countryside. In this they were aided by a fortuitous action on the part of the

[81]

central government, which, in 1934, ordered an inquiry into conditions prevailing in the cotton industry. Finding labor conditions to be poor, pressure was placed on ginners under the Masters and Servants Ordinance to improve the housing and diet of employees along with their conditions and hours of work.[25] In Gondo, perhaps to avoid having to make drastic changes, the ginnery managements offered grants of land to their immigrant workers. These were avidly taken up by the northern laborers, and so to the mixture of Teso and Bantu homesteads in the east of the town was added a mixture of Teso and Nilotic homesteads in the west. Since ginnery labor occupied, at most, six months of the year, and since agriculture was largely in the hands of women anyway, there had developed in Gondo by the late thirties the polyethnic peasant society that is to be found there today.

Settlement patterns have changed little during the past generation as the following chapter will show and, without doubt, the most important legacy of the past has been the fact that the Township Plan of 1912 never became, in effect, anything more than a blueprint. The complex of interethnic relations established around the port and ginneries never developed into the patchwork of racial and tribal enclaves common elsewhere in colonial Africa. Yet a knowledge of this past pluralistic society informs the contemporary political situation. If societal structure sets parameters to political action, change comes about through organizational deviations over time. Gondo history is not only contained in the archives of Soroti, Entebbe, and London but is part of the living memory and experience of those who are political actors in the contemporary scene. Hence, another part of that same legacy, and intertwined with the ideology of ethnic pluralism, is that common front which the residents of the community, regardless of occupation or ethnicity, offered to outsiders. As Beattie found in Bunyoro—and as is characteristic of peasant society the world over—the State is something external, even oppressive; the community, even in its diversity, provides the intimate and familiar context of everyday village life.[26]

Today, little of the past remains written on the Gondo landscape. The Makertich house at Kabos is an empty shell, cotton plants rising above its empty windows; the water tank of the bazaar squats in the corner of a ploughed field; only a slab of concrete, cracking as weeds pierce its surface, remains of the old market gutted by fire in 1956. A grove of mango trees, militarily spaced, marks the site of the former headquarters, moved to Kamod eight miles away in 1945. The single line track running down to the pier ends in six inches of water. A solitary ginnery operates for part of the year while the outhouses of the other provide accommodation for ginnery workers and immigrant townsmen. There is no longer a telegraph office or a police post; no longer tennis courts or even a football field. There is no incinerator, no garbage pit, no water pipes. There is no school or church at the crossroads as the Catholic mission once planned; a grass-thatched mud and wattle schoolhouse serves the Protestants of the community as both. Above the rickety table that serves occasionally as an altar stands the text: *Edeke des amina kadini teker kere murokoli* ("Let it be trumpeted abroad that God loves all his people"). The planned development of a stone-built township with its squares and avenues did not materialize. By 1966 only an increasing ethnic heterogeneity from periphery to core distinguished the erstwhile township within the rural parish. Patterns reflecting the artificial restrictions on the movements of peoples prescribed in ethnic terms in the colonial township had been wholly blurred.

Ecology and Community

THE MODERN AFRICAN URBAN COMMUNITY is usually better conceived of as a single field of social relations than as an entity made up of separate ethnic communities. Yet, in the case of Gondo where good archives provide information on population movement and growth has been to a large extent natural rather than forced, the social relations established within the boundaries of the parish may well be described in ecological terms as the adaptation of peoples to an environment over time. At the end of the last century the settlement of each ethnic group in Gondo was discrete, being dependent upon livelihood. Kenyi and Pagero fishermen favored the lakeshore, while Teso with their herds preferred to establish homesteads in the lee of the hills. Nyoro, principally traders and occasionally herders, settled between the two. After the establishment of the ginneries in 1912, the acquisition of land by immigrants led to interstitial settlement between the four original ecologically spaced groups, expansion within the parish being limited by the lake to the north, the marshy swamps of Kabola to the east, and the hills to the south and west. As population density increased, the social field became more and more enmeshed so that, today, it is certainly possible to see in Gondo parish one field of social interaction. But to see it only in this way would be to obscure past ecological processes which have explanatory importance for social relations. It is as necessary to understand how such relations came about as to note that they exist.

Gondo parish appears at first sight to be a kind of cultural hodgepodge on the shores of Lake Kyoga. An ecological de-

← *The Nyoro cycle repairer*

scription of it brings some preliminary order. Moreover, although the settlement pattern is not the same as the interactional systems within a community, it is a cultural expression of these; and the location of homesteads both reflects and affects the ways in which inhabitants act together.[1] Although a full discussion here of the twenty ethnic groups permanently resident in the community and the multiple facets of their relations with the land and with each other is impossible, the sketch that follows is designed to serve as a descriptive introduction to the processes by which individuals and groups leave their "ecological niches" and, to follow the analogy, through ecosystemic change, are able to exploit other environments.

Three major ecological zones, which cut across and link neighborhoods, provide the outer shell for transactional relations in the parish: the flat woodland savanna, the lakeshore, and the hills (Figure 6). The activities of man overlap the

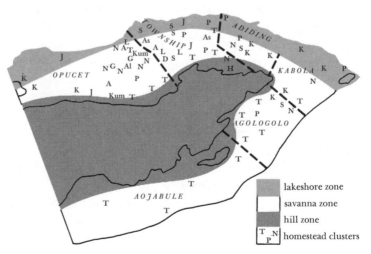

FIGURE 6: SETTLEMENT IN GONDO PARISH, 1966, SHOWING WARDS AND ECOLOGICAL ZONES

boundaries of all three zones. On the dry-swamp, grassy lake-shore, the fisherman comes in contact with the cattle herders and the buyers of his fish. At the foot of the hill slopes, herder and cultivator have conflicting interests in the grasslands. In the savanna between, all have their homes and cultivate their crops.

Within the three zones, six neighborhoods or wards may be distinguished. In Aojabule and Agologolo, lying to the east and south of the Gondo hills, reliance is primarily upon cattle and subsistence agriculture. Along the lakeshore, the fishing neighborhoods of Kabola and Adiding are separated from the land in the lee of the hill by the road from Kadun-gulu to Serere, with its ribbon of small shops, the mosque and the "church," stone-built stores or *dukas*, and, at the crossroads, a conglomeration of ambitious mud and wattle huts which convert themselves into shopfronts—entrepreneurial commer-cial enterprise on the doorstep of the ginnery—the oldest and best established of them, now a complex of sleeping rooms, being Eria's eating house or hotel. Between the hill and the pier lie the one remaining ginnery, a set of concrete cabins erected as ginnery lines, and the homes of former ginnery workers, which are set among the marchlands of old estab-lished families whose own homesteads line the foot of the hill; these are linked by a path that winds round to Agologolo and Aojabule, and separated by it from immediate contact with the brash crowded development below. Here homesteads are smaller than elsewhere in the parish but are, nevertheless, remnants of the same settlement pattern. This is the area of the old township which, in the height of its glory, was "Kibuga" or "Kampala" to the people of Gondo. To the west of the township is the neighborhood of Opucet where, again, a line of core homesteads skirts the hill, looking down upon the homes of immigrant residents and then to the lakeshore where the fishermen are settled.

[87]

"Town"

Members of different ethnic groups are not scattered at random throughout these six wards (Figure 6). The most densely settled part, and the most heterogeneous, is the former township. Today this is the heart of the parish wrapped around the ginnery and the dukas and the small shops which lie between. Behind the ginnery lies an open stretch of ground which narrows to form the base of the low grassy bank which is all that remains of Gondo pier. Nearby the small modern stone house of the Fisheries Officer, built in 1966, stands on an acre of land. The dukas and shops provide meeting places for the members of different ethnic groups, and most popular is the Gondo Hotel which has an open space swept before it where, under the tree at one corner, a gaming board (*bao*) is set up. A day rarely passes without its use by a casual bunch of time-killing parishioners. This hotel is the terminus for buses from Jinja making an overnight stop before their return run via Kadungulu and Kagwara on the following day.

Only in the township has land been bought and sold and that only four times. This is the most ethnically heterogeneous neighborhood, members of eighteen out of the twenty ethnic groups represented in the parish being permanently resident here. With respect to occupation, 35 per cent of its inhabitants are traders or in service occupations connected with trade. Tailors, porters, butchers, small shopkeepers, and latrine cleaners predominate. A further 24 per cent of the township residents work full shifts at the ginnery regularly every cotton season, a characteristic not shared by the rest of the parish whose salaried employment is much more casual.

A narrow reach of the old township fronts the lake, and there two Luo fishermen and one Ssesse Islander (hence a "Ganda") have their homes. Although the Kenyi dominate the fishing of the parish as a whole, none live in the township, apart from two landless young men (affines of a Nyoro) who work as porters at the dukas. Near the hill, within the township, the Teso ward headman, Elamu (T 601), a large landowner compared with others in this neighborhood, seasonally hires out his ox-plough team to his neighbors for cash, a practice less common in the rest of the parish where a reciprocal ploughing system operates. There are also in the township three of the parish's seven women living alone.

The township soil is productive, but considerable fragmentation of holdings has taken place over the years. Near the foothills the daily trek of cattle up into the hills has caused severe erosion. Herds wind their way toward the slopes in the early morning and descend to the lake only an hour or so before sunset. Although there are only two large herds within the township, one belonging to a Pagero (P 632) and the other to a retired Hima herdsman (H 696), most of the cattle from the eastern zones of the parish also traverse the township foothills each day. And, to the constant likelihood of cattle damaging growing crops is added, periodically, the raids of monkeys and baboons from the hills.

In the township proper 37 per cent of the men have no land; 3 per cent borrow land annually; 25 per cent have below 2.5 units of land, the bare minimum estimated for subsistence needs; and 30 per cent have between 2.0 and 5.0 units. Only 4 per cent have over 5.1 units, which constitute an average holding in the outer wards of the parish.[2]

Opucet

Although ecological criteria delimit the "town" ward to 102 homesteads, Gondo township as demarcated by the administration in 1912 included within its two-mile radius a ward on either side of the ginnery. The crescent to the west I have called Opucet, after the crest of the Gondo hills which looks down on it. For administrative purposes this is included within the same ward as the township under one headman. The neighborhood to the east is Adiding, today a separate ward.

Opucet is, in many ways, an extension of the township proper, especially within the triangle contained by the road to Kadungulu, the track to the ginnery owners' bungalows, and the path to the home of a prominent Acholi (A 542) who worked at the ginnery until his retirement in 1964. Within this triangle are the homes of twenty-two Nyoro, Ganda, and Acholi former ginnery workers. The land itself once belonged to the ginnery but was opened up to employees in 1936. This policy was encouraged by the administration's drive to make employers give better wages and living conditions to ginnery workers, measures intended to reduce the excessively large muster rolls, the maintenance of which encouraged roving, discontented groups of seasonally homeless unemployed. Elsewhere in the district this policy effectively encouraged Teso to enter wage employment; in Gondo it served to give land rights to men of other districts.

There is less conflict over land and fewer boundary disputes in Opucet than in most other neighborhoods. This is partly because land grants were made to ginnery workers at a time when there was still sufficient free land to make fairly large grants; partly because the holdings are usually inherited by only one heir from the home district so that fragmentation does not occur; and partly because the Teso landholdings under the hill are untouched by the arrangement and are still, on the whole, adequate. Twenty-one of the homesteads in Opucet, or one-third of the total, are Teso. These all lie in the curve of the foothills and are predominantly in, or contiguous to, the land of the Icaak clan. Before the arrival of the Icaak, however, almost the whole of Opucet and Kabos to the west was the land of Omukule Okello, the Big Man of the parish at the turn of the century. During his office as chief under the Ganda his Igoria clansmen moved away to the east to settle in Aojabule and Agologolo where they were able to escape the heavy labor demands of the town.

The rest of the families in Opucet border the road to Kadungulu, most of them with little land. They are in service trades—Ganda tinkers, Soga carpenters, Nyoro diviners. The Kumam, Lango, and Pagero elements living there are affines of Teso residents, there being no barrier to marriages between these ethnic groups and the tendency being for recent immigrants from Kaweri Island and Kaberamaido to settle here in the west, nearest the direction of their coming. There are no large herds of cattle in the Opucet crescent and, hence, no Hima since it is only those with large herds who consider it worthwhile to employ migrant Hima. There has been less movement away from the hills than in the east and south of the parish because, although the foothills are just as badly eroded, animals are less troublesome than in the other wards.

The western end of the narrow strip of Opucet which lies along the lakeshore is newly settled. It was formerly the Kabos estate owned by the European trader, Makertich. After his death Kenyi and, later, Luo fishermen from Ogelak parish gradually moved onto the land. Today part of it belongs to a family of Nyoro cattle traders with five homesteads and two large herds. Two other herds, Luo-owned, are tended by Hima. The soil in the lakeside area is poor, much of it salt marsh and swamp for part of the year, so that there is little prospect for extensive cultivation, and the fifteen remaining homes in Opucet belong to ginnery workers who choose to live near their place of work even though this limits their access to land. All these men were on the muster roll at the ginnery for the entire year.

Adiding

The third ward within the boundaries of the former township is a neighborhood known as Adiding, which contains members of seven ethnic groups in twenty-eight homesteads. It forms a distinct zone and is the original strip of shoreline where early Teso and Kenyi encounters took place and where their interdependence grew, the Kenyi coming ashore at first only to barter fish and reedware and to bury their dead. The lagoon-cum-papyrus swamp shoreline is favored by the Kenyi, who, unlike the Luo, do not venture far into the open lake. Theirs is the specialist fishing of dugout canoe, trap, and line in still water. Almost half the homesteads in Adiding are Kenyi.

The second element in the composition of Adiding is allegiance to Islam. This came about through a combination of circumstances. First, the earliest generation of Kenyi to settle in Adiding after being driven off their papyrus islands by tax-collecting chiefs was Muslim. Later, when the administration gave permission for the establishment of permanent lines for Swahili employees of the Public Works Department at the two-mile boundary of the Township, at the edge of Adiding, these workers were also Muslim. The first mosque was built in 1918, and the white stone mosque with its Qu'ran school which stands on the same site today provides the focal point of this neighborhood, serving as a gathering place for Muslims in the way that beer parties do for the rest of the community.

A Hima herdsman looks after the second largest herd in the parish, that of a Kenyi, Nakumusana (K 418), who was appointed sub-chief for his tribe throughout Serere County in 1912 and who served in this capacity until 1924 when ethnic representation was abolished. Adiding was also the initial niche of Pagero families driven off Kaweri Island; some remain there while others, for social rather than economic reasons, migrate to Agologolo, a predominantly Teso ward.

Adiding remains primarily a neighborhood of fishermen. Those who are not fishermen are itinerant traders, fishmongers, groundnut sellers, dealers in cloth, cycle repairers, and the like. Land is fairly evenly, if meagrely, distributed. The inhabitants, being abstemious Muslims, have no recourse to communal work parties, common throughout the rest of the parish, since these are rewarded with millet beer. Moreover, few homestead heads are adequately polygamous for household labor requirements. This lack is aggravated by a trend toward Catholicism among the younger Kenyi. There are fewer granaries per homestead in Adiding than in any other ward outside of the township although a granary for each wife, as well as a husband's granary for famine relief, was formerly compulsory by district by-law. Much food is purchased from the dukas with cash earned through fishing and trade.

Kabola

Three wards lie beyond the limits of the township of 1912. Kabola, to the east of Adiding along the lakeshore, contains thirty-five homesteads, twenty of which belong to the second generation overflow of the original Kenyi settlers. The homes of all three Kenyi core lineages stretch from Adiding into Kabola. Pagero and Nyoro fishermen are also resident in this ward. Soga homesteads, those of a Muslim follower of Kakunguru (S 333) and his children, lie close to the mosque. A Hima looks after the cattle of Kenyi fisherman-turned-trader, Sharif Musa (K 315), who has acquired two shops, one in Kabola on the road to Kamod and the other a duka in the township that he rents during the cotton season.

Kabola has much unoccupied, uncultivated land, especially to the east at the foot of Kabola hill, but the neighborhood also has the largest number of children per homestead in the parish. Some land is swampy, but there could be more intensive cultivation if the Kenyi landholders were not primarily interested in fishing. There is no movement of Teso cultivators into the area apart from a former PWD foreman, Otieno (T 302), who obtained land next to his roadside camp. Some land belongs to Teso who live across the road in Agologolo.

Agologolo

Agologolo, the largest predominantly Teso neighborhood, both numerically and in cultivatable acres, lies to the east of the Gondo hills. All Pagero and Kenyi living there are affinally related to the Teso families. Indeed, there is no one in Agologolo who is not in some way related by kinship links that extend over four generations. Although in the thirties migration took place from Adiding into Agologolo (it was said that "sickness" and the raiding of hippopotami along the lakeshore drove people out), Adiding is generally accounted the more fertile, and in recent years there has been some movement back. Migration to neighboring Ogera parish also occurred as opportunities for inheritance arose. There were two main reasons for this: the acquisition of a large tract of Agologolo land for the government-appointed parish chief; and the increasing menace of baboons, wild pigs, and monkeys which were formerly exterminated by game-loving resident Europeans or by district officers empowered to organize a "traditional" Teso communal hunt. Such a hunt was apparently an annual event in 1912 but was banned by the administration shortly afterward.

While the loss of land to government is not resented as elsewhere in Teso, it nevertheless limits expansion within Agologolo. The cohesion of the younger members of the Ilale patrigroup has led to overfragmentation in the north, and most supplement their incomes from the marginal land by fishing, pot making, and regular ginnery employment. A couple of young men have in their time migrated to Kaberamaido to claim land from their mothers' brothers but chose to return to Agologolo, prepared to supplement their cotton incomes with other occupational activities. All ward members are primarily cultivators; three have large herds which they look after themselves in the "traditional" Teso manner taking turn and turn about without any payment being involved.

Aojabule

The last of the six wards to be described is Aojabule, which lies on the far side of the hill from the township. This neighborhood contains only twenty homesteads, of which eighteen are Teso, mostly an overflow of the Igoria patrigroup from Agologolo and peripheral clans which have their foci in Ogera parish. The administration included Aojabule in Gondo parish mainly because Ogera was already too large for the parish chief to collect taxes efficiently, and nearly all the families living there are related to those in contiguous Ogera wards where their direct political interests lie. Two non-Teso live in Aojabule, a Karamojong who is the former herder and a Kumam who is the present herder of a large Teso landowner resident in Ogera with over one hundred head of cattle. The Karamojong was given land in Aojabule upon his retirement in 1963.

The Process of Establishing Man-Land Relations in the Parish

There are four kinds of man-land relationships in Gondo (Table 7). First, there are the landholders who may acquire land in any of four ways: by inheritance from a kinsman; by gift of a kinsman, usually father or mother's brothers; by gift of a sponsor; or by purchase.

Secondly, there are the land users, who "borrow" land sea-

[95]

TABLE 7: LAND USE IN GONDO PARISH

A Ethnic Group	B Number in Parish	C Land-Holders	D Land Users	E Hired Workers	F Non-users of Land	G Units Held	H Average Holding
T	92	78	7	3	4	511.5	6.6
K	42	35	3		4	202.0	5.7
P	23	20			3	95.0	4.5
N	37	27	3	3	4	164.5	6.3
S	13	5	6	1	2	35.0	7.0
G	4	4				17.5	4.3
A	10	9	1		1	52.0	5.7
L	10	7	2	1		27.0	3.8
Kum	9	6	2	1		45.0	5.0
Kar	5	2			3	10.5	5.25
Other	5	1	1		3	5.5	5.5
Sw	1	1				7.5	7.5
Ar	2		2			6.0	3.0
As	4				4		
H	8		3		5	4.0	4.0
J	11	9		1	1	42.0	4.6
TOTAL	278	204	30	10	34		

sonally, paying as token rent produce from the gardens or a pot or two of millet beer. (Landholders with too little land may also rent gardens and plots in this manner.) Client-patron relations often grow out of such borrowing, which may, under certain circumstances, carry the newcomer who wishes much further into the community. This arrangement represents an intermediate stage within the community; for the individual it is a limbo status within a sequence. A newcomer who hopes to reside permanently in the parish borrows land until he has lived there long enough for his sponsor to feel that his good neighborliness has been demonstrated to those around him. The *rite de passage* of "walking the bounds" in the presence of the sponsor, his neighbors, and often the parish chief marks a change of status from land user to landholder.[3] The two Kumam borrowers shown in Table 7 exemplify this kind of relationship and will probably be given these gardens in the near future. One, George Abilu (Kum 679), is a young man who has built a small shop opposite the ginnery gates. Through his friendship with a fellow Kumam married into a Teso family in Aojabule, he and his brother have been allowed to open several gardens there since land is still plentiful. In most cases, however, the amount of land borrowed is very small. The three Soga boatbuilders, for example, each borrow one small plot on which their wives grow cassava and cowpeas. Sometimes ginnery workers and herders acquire small plots close to their homestead on which to grow vegetables in a similar manner.

Thirdly, a small group of hired laborers, locally known as porters, work only on the land of others. They are usually transients and few in number at any one time. Poor men with land of their own but without women also choose, sometimes, to work for cash on the land of others. There is no stigma attached to laboring on the land as there is with porterage for the ginnery or shops.

Finally, there is a very small group of non-users of land. Most of these individuals (12 per cent of the total population) have kin or affines with land on whom they can rely so that they are not wholly dependent on the cash economy. Such landed connections sharply divide the shopkeepers of the parish; Kenyi and Soga shopkeepers belong to landholding groups while Asians and the Luo dispenser have no such ties. The wives of the Soga and Kenyi shopkeepers engage in work parties, especially at harvesttime, and this wifely participation is one reason they are not considered outsiders in the community as are Hima and Asians. The sharing of labor on the land is the most basic of community experiences. "Soil-brotherhood," to use Redfield's term,[4] is the crux of the distinction between "we" and "they" in Gondo's peasant community and more important to social interaction within the community than ethnicity. The Nyoro who possesses land is a fellow-villager; the Teso without land is not. Land ownership and the establishment of a homestead and a family make for community. Because it is tied to the land, development within the parish is shaped by a homogeneous way of life which overshadows the heterogeneity of ethnic origins. The latter is an accident of birth; the former a design for living.

Part of this design can be unraveled by looking more closely at those who have no land. It is by virtue of their chosen occupations that they are without. Most of them are full-time, unmarried ginnery employees who live in the ginnery lines and have sufficient cash to buy food. Some will later acquire land and wives in the parish. Those Nyoro, Karamojong, and Hima without land all follow traditional ethnic specialization as herders and so buy food from the profits of their milk sales. Should any of these men change their occupational status, they will acquire land. With respect to status sequence, they will shift from being non-users of land to being land borrowers and ultimately owners. This was the case, for example, with the Karamojong herdsman (Kar 120) in Aojabule who formerly worked for a large Teso landowner. Upon retirement as a herdsman, he was given land by his former employer. Later, after the death of his employer, he inherited one of his wives and a portion of his land.

To purchase land—as Opolot (Kum 682), Ogot (J 692), and Odico (T 606) did—might seem to set a group of incomers apart from other landowners. Under the circumstances of the purchases, however, this was not the case. Fellow-feeling was reinforced with members of the community, who commiserated with the purchaser that he had had to buy land which had been alienated by outsiders, the ginnery in the first two cases, a Ganda "prostitute" in the case of Odico. In a sense, their purchases were looked upon as restoring the *status quo ante*. These men and their wives were seen to work on the land and were heard to express the Gondo creed that the land would never again be sold. No permanent resident in Gondo has ever sold land voluntarily. Fragmentation occurs solely through gift and inheritance.

There is no shortage of land in Gondo. Not only does double cropping reduce the acreage required for subsistence, but opportunities of cash employment and chances of success at fishing both lessen the importance of the actual quantity of land. Indeed, part of the value of land lies in giving some of it away. A landowner may even give away some of his land in one place and, on occasion, rent gardens elsewhere in the parish. All the large core-family holdings are fragmented. Most of the 204 owners were given their land by settlers already in residence as they became their dependents, consanguineal or affinal kinsmen, retired employees, or friends. To sponsor a newcomer by lending and then giving him land is one way of acquiring prestige in the eyes of neighbors. Sometimes a newcomer will be given land between that of two sponsors; sometimes he will be given a corner of his sponsor's own land. In return the sponsor acquires a good neighbor, someone he can count on in times of need, and a member of his support group in his future agricultural transactions, as a later discussion of Agologolo sponsorship will show.

The land pattern is informative, and the history and nature of settlement in Gondo may be read from its contemporary design. Throughout Gondo, men who are sponsored are given land at the edge of a holding. This means that the land of individuals who have been given the blessing of those whose land borders theirs—individuals of achieved rather than ascribed position—lies between the landholdings from which the gainers of ascribed statuses have been rewarded. The land of the sponsored settler becomes a buffer zone between the two core holdings, and disruptive quarrels between men with inherited, inalienable rights in land are thereby averted.

In the diagram, condition A gives way to condition B, thus:

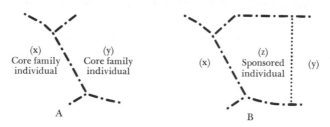

The acquisition of land by (z) is the joint grace of (x) and (y) personally—a matter of their choice, since either could have refused the newcomer the recognition of landowning status when his sponsor put him forward. Thus, in Agologolo, a Kenyi (K 222) and two Yaiyeru (P 228 and P 229) act as buffers between the land of the Yachwa and the land of the Imodoi. To the north, Ekweru (T 210) Ilale and Ocomu (T 218) Imodoi, on the other hand, constantly quarrel over attempts to extend land rights by ploughing over their common boundary. Moreover, Ocoto (P 223) may be seen as a pawn in their struggle, as will be shown in Chapter 10. Sponsorship underlies both the integration of newcomers into the parish and the movement of residents within the community. The receipt of land by an individual in a neighborhood away from his natal holding is the most visible indicator of his placing friendship or occupational ties above those of ethnicity. Thus, a member of Ilale core family of Agologolo (T 609) moved to live on land near the ginnery next to a friend who had sponsored him. In this chapter I began the ordering of the personnel of the community strictly within their Gondo context, setting aside the nature of cultural origins. One basis of differentiation, as we have seen, lies in the ways in which individuals come into the parish, and the ways in which they themselves are related to the unfolding process of landholding and to patterns of social interaction within neighborhoods. To become integrated within the community an individual must relinquish home-based or familial ties and choose to establish new transactional patterns by activating other statuses.

Our structural analysis of land has shown in the community two related themes: first, the setting aside of ethnic status as a dominant basis for social interaction, and secondly, the importance of changing statuses in relation to land in the community. Since it is the ownership of land that indicates true membership in the community, it is an essential status for a political entrepreneur. Yet prestige is earned by cultivation of a large acreage rather than simply by its ownership. To command a labor force (whether it be of wives, dependents, clients, neighbors, or porters) by which a larger than average number of gardens and plots can be worked is a virtual guarantee of recognition. A balance has to be maintained, however, for a man must not appear to rise at the expense of his fellows, and giving away land is also a desirable and praiseworthy act. Just as capital assets have to be visible to the community at large, so land must be seen to be used either in cultivation or in patronage.

The emergence of a representative elite in Gondo comes about by the manipulation of social statuses other than ethnicity. As the most important among these is an individual's land-working status, a logical projection of potential community leaders can be made on the basis of land ownership. The seventeen largest landowners in Gondo parish all have over eight acres of land (Table 8). They belong to five

AFRICAN ELITE

TABLE 8: OWNERS OF THE LARGEST LANDHOLDINGS

Code Number	Name	Units of Land	Neighbor-hood	Resident Status	Aged over 40 Years	Poly-gamous
T 109	Anyapo	14.5	Aojabule	O	x	x
T 302	Otieno	12.0	Kabola	O		x
T 402	Emenu	11.5	Adiding	C	x	x
T 116	Eliedu	11.5	Aojabule	C	x	
J 692	Ogot	10.5	Town	O		x
N 328	Katunda	10.5	Kabola	O		
S 333	Mugwerere	10.5	Kabola	O	x	
P 527	Asilo	10.5	Opucet	C		
N 331	Mukasa	10.0	Kabola	O		
T 104	Ekwaru	9.5	Aojabule	C	x	x
T 105	Enjutu	9.5	Aojabule	C		
T 216	Okasu	9.5	Agologolo	C	x	
P 632	Mukasa	9.5	Town	C	x	
T 606	Odico	9.5	Town	O		x
T 114	Odera	8.5	Aojabule	C	x	x
T 217	Ocaet	8.0	Agologolo	O		x
T 203	Ogola	7.5	Agologolo	C		x

Note: C = member of core family; O = office incumbent

ethnic categories: Teso, Pagero, Nyoro, Luo, and Soga. There is no tendency toward the monopolization of land by any one dominant ethnic group; if there were, Kenyi would figure more prominently and Luo would be unplaced. The social characteristics of each landowner are presented according to a categorization of residence developed in the following chapter, in which it may be seen that nine of the landowners were born in the parish and belong to core families while eight joined the community as adult office incumbents.

It is not unusual in peasant societies for a distinction to be made between those who work the land and those who do not,

[102]

and there are cases where this alone may be sufficient to account for the stratification of the society.[5] In Gondo, however, land is no more likely to be the sole determinant of elite status than is ethnicity. Land acts as a common denominator. All are equal who share the land of the parish. Thus, our inquiry into what sets certain individuals above others must be pursued further.

Kinship, Marriage, and Property Relations

BOTH THE INTERNAL STRUCTURING and the external relations of Teso domestic groups facilitate social integration, individual incorporation, and mobility in the polyethnic community. The Teso, who together with Kenyi and Pagero form the host group of the parish, account for one-third of the population. Partly by virtue of their original rights in the land and first occupancy of the littoral, but even more because administrative legitimacy was accorded to the Teso way of life throughout the district—including willy-nilly polyethnic Gondo—the Teso form a dominant social group. My account is based upon a close analysis of Teso patterns of kinship and marriage extant in Agologolo ward in 1966 and a comparison with the adjacent ward of Omongolem in Ogera parish. Nothing observed in Serere, Soroti, or Ngora counties would lead me to modify this account, nor is it contradicted by any published observations of Lawrence, Wright, or Burke, but without further fieldwork one could not assume it fitted Teso social patterns beyond western Serere.[1]

It is perhaps surprising that structural incorporation comes about in Gondo partly through an elaboration of integrative principles which existed before the community came into being. Such persistence might be expected in a homogenous, centralized society; modern Bunyoro, for example, has been described as retaining many of the segmentary characteristics of a clan and lineage system in its contemporary political set-up.[2] Where the indigenous peoples have an acephalous

← *A Teso homestead*

societal structure, however, as in Teso, administrative measures and, specifically, the imposition of a hierarchy of alien
chiefs might have been expected to breach continuity. That
this did not happen in Teso was partly due to influential administrators, especially F. R. Kennedy, who made a somewhat
unreal effort to establish a system of indirect rule by "dis-
interring" and "resurrecting" the "traditional" modes of Teso
social organization which existed before Kakunguru's conquest. Ganda pacification was believed to have destroyed
much of the social fabric, including an age-grade system and
the authority of clan elders. Official recognition of elders and
the creation of a conciliar structure within which they were
supposedly representative gave legitimacy to a gerontocratic
model of Teso societal organization in Gondo, in spite of the
fact that the Teso were neither predominant numerically nor
the sole indigenous element in the population. The conciliar
effort, like the effort to homogenize landholding practices
within the district, was, in effect, an administrative thumb
thrust into a wall of custom long breached by economic development.[3] Modern sustenance of the system served to protect
the interests of those with dominant status, reinforcing the
hold of elders over younger men who might otherwise have
followed alternative paths, as was the case elsewhere.[4]

Although no ideological design for living was imposed upon
the polyethnic Gondo community by either the administration
or the Teso themselves, the Teso blueprint of kinship and
marriage proved an eminently suitable vehicle, first, for the
absorption of alien peoples and, secondly, for the integration
of a settled agricultural community without the development
of ethnic stratification in a way, for example, that the hierarchical Ganda structure was not.[5] As we saw in the last chapter,
land, along with the opportunity to obtain land, was one of
the most important factors determining relations between
members of different ethnic groups in Gondo. In a rapidly

developing society, land provides an element of security in changing times; and to immigrants, many of whom left their homelands because of the lack of opportunity to obtain cash and sufficient land for their needs, the fertile gardens of Gondo were recompense enough or reason enough for being absorbed into a polyethnic society. The power of the elders was also enhanced by their control of land, which became a commodity sought by sons and immigrants alike. As we shall see, there is competition in the community between sons and sponsors of immigrant settlers which, as land becomes scarcer in Kaberamaido and Serere, "traditional" patterns of dispersion and acquisition fail to solve.

Groups and Categories

There are seven basic units of personnel organization among the Teso. Four extend through the wider community having in common interests in property rights. These are:

(1) *etogo*
The children of one mother, the minimal residential unit.

(2) *ere*
The elementary family of a man, his wives, and children.

(3) *ekek*
A small, localized segment of a patrilineage larger than an extended family but of varying structure, sometimes three generations deep, but usually consisting of two or three brothers and their children. Among the Kumam, a similar group has been termed a patrigroup.[6]

(4) *ateker$_1$*
A contingent lineage group, larger than the *ekek*, which is dispersed over an area of some two hundred square miles and which meets collectively on ritual occasions.

Kinship idiom is also used to categorize perceived relationships beyond the wider community:

(5) *ateker*$_2$
A clan.

(6) *eisenere*
A dialect grouping. There are four of these in Teso District.

(7) *ateker*$_3$
The Teso as a whole, the tribe.

Although non-Teso are fitted into the social organization at the kinship level, they cannot fit into the categories. The few Kumam and Karamojong who share Teso clan names are not incorporated on this common basis into Gondo society; neither are individual Teso from other eisenere who similarly share clan names. At the level of the kinship group the Teso system facilitates integration; the conceptual categorical dimension accentuates distinctions. [Although we must pass over the categories of clan, dialect grouping, and tribe in our concern with community integration in Gondo, these categories may be extremely relevant to wider political loyalties outside of the parish and can, under certain circumstances, be a source of conflict within. That between the north (Iseera) and south (Ngoratok), referred to earlier, has repercussions at the local level in Ogera. In Gondo, there are few Ngoratok immigrants and no hostility has developed.] Residence patterns within Gondo are affected by development processes within the kin-based groups—etogo, ere and ekek—not by clan, dialect, and tribal affiliations. A description of the house-property complex and the development of the domestic group makes this clear.[7]

House-Property Complex

Teso reckon descent in the agnatic line, the basic residential grouping being the elementary family of a man, his wife or wives, and children; the key to familial organization is the house-property complex, a social institution well suited to a

[108]

society practicing interethnic marriage. Teso marriage is, ideally, polygamous and virilocal; in actual fact, both of these features are functions of the relative positions of the groups contracting the marriage.

The homestead is occupied by an elementary family and consists of a sleeping hut, kitchen, and granary for each wife and her children. If there are many wives, two may occasionally share a kitchen, but this is seen as a likely cause of quarrels and is avoided wherever possible. The separate spatial identity of the house of each wife serves to maintain a continuing awareness of relations with other patrigroups or ethnic groups while, at the same time, the inclusion of the house within a bounded homestead reinforces the commonality of interests. Organization along the lines of the house-property complex places no barriers in the path of a Teso wishing to take wives from other ethnic groups in the way that organization along the lines of an extended family grouping might, for example.

All land belongs to the husband, who divides it into gardens and plots distributed among his wives, the first wife having a larger holding. The cotton grown in each garden is the property of that household, and each wife keeps her cash profits in a tin buried under the floor of her hut. A wife can never refuse her husband money, although she might argue about its use. Cash for seeds comes from the household, but usually the husband has the final word about what is to be planted in each field. Generally all wives grow the same crops, by his choice, and compete as to who can produce the most. Fish is either caught for the *etogo* or purchased with cash by the wife cooking that day. The garden produce of each wife pays for clothes and school fees for her children. A son is allotted the use of land in his mother's gardens by his father, and these fields may belong to him after he marries. When a daughter is married, the cattle received are considered the joint property of her natal *etogo*, of her father and mother; milk and any calves produced belong to that household, not to the homestead at large. In spite of this degree of house independence within the homestead, the husband is the sole entrepreneur, his wives and children forming part of his support group in the agricultural politics of the parish.

Social Capital and the Domestic Group

The Teso domestic group, like any other, maintains, replenishes, and transmits the social capital from generation to generation,[8] but in a society which practices marriage between individuals of different ethnic groups, the social capital which is handed down across the generations over time acquires a character all its own, distinct from that of any of the cultural heritages of its components. Hence the recognition that Gondo is indeed a community—"a basic unit of organization and transmission . . . a structured social field of interindividual relationships unfolding over time"[9]—which might be described, for want of a better expression, as microcosmopolitan.

An individual's initial social identity is acquired within his natal family. When the moral system of any one family, into which a child is enculturated and socialized, does not differ significantly from that of any others, members of such family groups will not see themselves as very different kinds of people. The basic social identity of an individual born in Gondo relates to his birth in a polyethnic community where peoples of different ethnic backgrounds share a common cultural heritage. The Gondo-born pride themselves on their nontribal ethos if such considerations are forced upon them, claiming that the distinctive character of their community lies in the very fact that it is, indeed, made up of individuals from many backgrounds. They live together harmoniously and find it a better place for this very fact.

A second corollary of the dynamics of the domestic group

in a community where interethnic marriage is practiced is that the process of internal development itself brings about movement across ethnic boundaries. Residence patterns are not only the crystallization at a given time of the development process within the internal domestic system: they are also the crystallization of that external politico-jural, cross-ethnic development process, synthetically called incorporation, assimilation, or integration. Since the domestic group exists not in a vacuum but within the immediate context of a neighborhood, a politico-jural domain, every individual is simultaneously an actor in both domestic and politico-jural domains, a role in one being partly defined by norms prevailing in the other. In a community where marriage occurs between members of different ethnic groups, the cross-ethnic relationships established through marriage are thus extended to the neighborhood context of those involved. The various mechanisms maintaining Teso values of good neighborliness also serve, therefore, to maintain harmonious relations between members of different ethnic groups. Such marriages serve to break down discrete ethnic neighborhoods and, in social interaction, emphasis comes to be placed on affinal and neighborly status rather than on ethnicity. The integration of Gondo as a microcosmopolitan community which results from a high degree of marriage between such groups cannot be presented in detail for the whole parish since relations go back over four generations and involve more than two-thirds of its residents. In the next chapter Agologolo neighborhood provides a microscopic view of the highly involuted process involved.

The extent to which the domestic organization of different ethnic groups in the parish conforms to the Teso model, both in its developmental and synchronic aspects, may be judged by comparing the composition of their residential groups (Figure 7). The large extended family grouping which emerges at phase four of the Teso development cycle (and which then

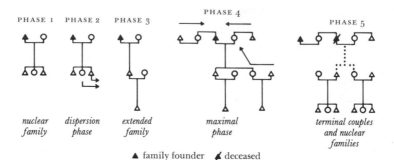

PHASE 1   PHASE 2   PHASE 3   PHASE 4   PHASE 5

nuclear family   *dispersion phase*   *extended family*   *maximal phase*   *terminal couples and nuclear families*

▲ family founder   ✗ deceased

FIGURE 7: RESIDENTIAL GROUP COMPOSITION IN DYNAMIC AND STATIC PERSPECTIVE

PATTERN 1966

Homestead composition	Ethnicity																		
	T	K	P	N	S	G	A	L	Kum	Kar	H	J	Sw	Ar	As	Lug	Al	C	D	TOTAL
1m+5w+c	1																			1
1m+4w+c	2										1									3
1m+3w+c	4							1												5
1m+2w+c	7	3	2	2		1								1						16
1m+1w+c	20	13	8	14	10		3	2	1		3	3		1	2				1	81
1m+1w (initial)	13	12	5	1		5		3	1		1									41
1m+1w (terminal)	14	4	4	3	1	1	3	1	1		1	1	4	1					1	40
1m+c		1		2	1															4
1m	32	9	4	15	2	1		7	3		3	4	1		2	2	1	1		87
TOTAL	93	42	23	37	13	4	11	10	9	5	8	10	1	2	4	2	1	1	2	278

Note: m stands for man; w stands for woman; c stands for child/children.

A couple in the *initial* phase have not borne children; a couple at the *terminal* phase have adult children away from home.

This table does not necessarily reflect *marital* co-residence.

divides into several residential groups in the next phase) appears in the overall community structure in the same proportion as it does within the Teso sub-category. The Teso domestic group development process appears to correlate with that of other homestead groups throughout the community, regardless of ethnicity, due to Teso marital imperialism toward other ethnic groups. Single men not yet set up in domestic homesteads account for 31 per cent of the total population of the parish. Individuals of all ethnic groups integrated by ties of kinship and affinity account for over 60 per cent.

The close similarity of residence composition is most marked among the three indigenous groups of Teso, Kenyi, and Pagero. Historical and ecological factors account for the ambiguous position of the Nyoro. The actual process by which the Teso model becomes applied throughout the community —from the indigenous groups to those most numerously related to them (as, for example, the Kenyi to the Nyoro or the Teso to the Kumam), and then partially to other ethnic groups according to the length of time since their arrival in the parish, but not at all to the outsiders (Asians and Hima)— will be made apparent when we explore the political aspects of the core social matrix.

More than similarities in residential group composition are apparent from this tabulation, for the importance of polygamy in allying individuals of different ethnic groups also emerges. In all, 13.4 per cent of all marriages in the parish are polygamous. Of those of Teso males, only 26 of the 39 women involved are Teso, others being Pagero, Kenyi, Kumam, and Soga. For two of the three Kenyi, polygamy reflects the acceptance of Teso prestige values over the teachings of the Catholic church. The third is a Kenyi Muslim. The two Pagero each have one Kenyi and one Pagero wife. Both Nyoro polygamists are married to Nyoro women from outside the parish. The Ganda has one Nyoro and one Ganda wife. The three wives of the Kumam consist of a Teso, a Kumam, and a Pagero. The Luo man with four wives has one Lango wife while the other three are all Luo. (Luo place a strong emphasis on premarital chastity in women.) All these men are nominally Christian, but they place the political and economic advantages of polygamy above religion. All nine men having more than two wives are men of prestige in the community. Six of them are among the largest landowners in the parish:

Erimasi Odico (T 606), Nebukadnezar Emenu (T 402), George Henry Ebelu (T 625), Charles Frederick Otieno (T 302), Ocaet (T 217), and Levi Anyapo (T 109). The remaining three are Daudi Opolot (Kum 682), Anderea Ogot (J 692), and Yowana Ekweru (T 210).

A status syndrome involving marital status, occupation, and permanency in the parish is indicated by the unmarried status of most Lango, Lugbara, Alur, Kiga, Karamojong, and Hima. Most of these are either wage laborers or herdsmen. The proportion of single to married Teso males is almost identical with the proportion of single men to the total male population, indicating the lack of Teso dominance by virtue of ethnicity. Conversely, members of other ethnic groups are as well established in permanent domesticity as the Teso in Gondo. This has not been the case generally in urban African communities with a dominant host group and suggests that Gondo may be more usefully described in other than ethnic terms.

Kinship and Locality

Where members of the same extended family choose to settle contiguously, there is a spatial representation of the patrigroup (*ekek*), the third largest unit of Teso social organization. The area in which the patrigroup resides is known as *atutubet* (pl. *atutuben*, lit. a portion, fragment). The term has also been extended to cover contiguous homesteads and land of non-kin in some cases. (Note that the glossary lists *atutubet* "cluster" as distinct from *erony* "village.")

The thesis that rights in durable property reinforce the establishment of corporate unilineal descent groups must be qualified to the extent that the nature of the property affects the social response. While corporate descent groups are usually associated with subsistence economies centered in inheritable land rights which stabilize groups of kin in fixed localities, where livestock constitute the basic property, kin are

[114]

often dispersed in each generation.[10] Teso patterns provide an intermediate case since a tendency toward dispersal of kin which is associated with cattle interests is counterbalanced by a trend toward settled dependency as a result of the introduction of cotton as a major cash crop. There are, in effect, two collateral patterns of acquisition and inheritance: one related to cattle and wives gives its corporate body to the descent structure as among most Nilotic pastoralists; the other related to land leads to an increasing use of "residual rights" and affinal ties.

Although it is specifically stated in Gondo that lineages do not have "clan lands" and that land is individually held, there are indications that at least the idea of association with a locality is important when an authoritative voice is required to arbitrate the settlement of newcomers or other local affairs. There are usually three or four clusters within each neighborhood, each containing five or six homesteads. Each cluster has a leader (*apolon lo alutubet*) who is usually the oldest male of the core family. Indeed, each cluster may be looked upon as the moral support group of the patrigroup head since it contains his agnatic kinsmen and dependents either by marriage or patronage ties.

The denial of lineage dominance within specific areas is not surprising since its occurrence reflects contradictions in the social structure. The value of egalitarian coexistence between neighbors, expressed and manifest in the integration of the community, contradicts values attached to clan ownership of land. Such values are expressed only in certain situations—to the anthropologist, for example, but not to those with whom the speaker must coexist for the rest of his life. If values are taken to be views of significance, worthwhileness, and preference held by social actors as a preliminary to action, it is understandable that no respondent would wish to maximize the value of core dominance in a polyethnic community such as Gondo. Yet, sociographically, the unarticulated relationship of certain lineages with specific areas appears more than coincidental.

The cluster is politically important in two respects. First, a core family elder is considered to be the authority within a neighborhood when a boundary is in dispute. Since this is a major cause of conflict in the parish, his authoritative status is constantly being made visible. Secondly, as the head of a cluster, his permission is required before land can be given away: a core elder thus has political sanctions which he can bring to bear on core families and newcomers alike. Moreover, this is one avenue toward prestige closed to political entrepreneurs who are not members of core families.

The dominant kinship ideology is one of patrilinearity and revolves around the nature and rights of the patrigroup (*ekek*). Ekek literally means "doorway" (the Swahili *mlango*, also with this double connotation, was used to clarify this point) and refers to the symbolic common doorway of a hut, emphasizing blood ties shared, or the entrance to a cattle kraal, emphasizing marriage transacted. Ekek is a relative term: in one aspect, a man establishes his own ekek as he marries and begets children; in another, he looks back to the ekek of his grandfather.

Since in Gondo, few Teso patrigroups are without non-Teso ancestors, the public naming ceremony of a child serves as a device not only for the recapitulation of the lineage descent line but also for a reiteration of the nontribal ethos, there being no discrimination between the two. In addition the ceremony serves to keep visible the larger territorial spread of the kin group at the same time as it keeps alive its common tradition. The deeper the ekek, the wider its areal spread. Similarly, when an heir inherits the name of his benefactor along with his property, a sense of continuity is maintained.

In Gondo most patrigroups consist at the most of four generations and usually of three. Genealogies have little depth, and no formal records are kept although this practice is being introduced by a few educated men. The patrigroup goes on record, indirectly and briefly, at one moment in time when contributors to burial feasts (*apunya*) have their names and donations inscribed in a notebook under one of four columns headed agnatic and collateral, male and female, kin. The Teso conscious model is, indeed, akin to that of the anthropologist.

On reaching maturity and prior to marriage, a son builds his homestead near that of his father. Its entrance is reached by branching off the path leading to the parental homestead —an indication of paterfamilial control. Other sons build their homesteads at a distance. These may be on virgin land but are more frequently at the edge of land belonging to a kinsman in a neighboring parish. Gondo youths most frequently seek the propinquity of their father's sister's husband or their mother's brother. Tensions exist between father and son, and cases of patricide (figures were collected for Teso District as a whole) are not uncommon. The chief cause is a son's dependence upon his father for cattle, since the elder may put his own inclination for another wife before the needs of his son. Since a son can inherit the younger wives of his father, his presence within the parental homestead is a constant threat to the old man with several. Moreover, a son may, with the approval of kin and neighbors, charge his father with neglect in the court of the ward headman if he is made to wait too long, thus placing his father in an invidious position with his peers.

Chiefly responsible for the smallness of core patrigroups in Gondo is the rule of inheritance, whereby only one son inherits land outright. In the majority of cases primogeniture prevails, but the actual allocation is always decided by a gathering of elders from throughout the wider community. If the deceased has no son, the eldest son of his elder brother usually inherits. Since his chances of inheriting are greatest, the eldest son settles near his father's homestead while younger sons, on reaching maturity, move away. Where two brothers remain on the same land, one is always found to be childless. Where there are no apparent heirs, continuity of the corporate descent group is maintained, as among the Ilale of Agologolo, by a consanguine being invited into the parish to continue the ekek. Similarly, among the Iunas of Aojabule, where a childless man was selected as heir by default, his elder brother failing to return to Gondo for his father's funeral, a father's brother's son was invited into the parish to continue the line.

In spite of the passing of generations, residential patterns within Gondo are remarkably consistent. As the core group sheds its linear members and adds cognates, the continuity of the residential group is maintained (as one has learnt to expect) through females, in spite of the rule of virilocal residence at marriage. Women are ultimately paramount in the development process although unity is expressed through males. Most frequently it is an invitation to a son-in-law that brings a daughter back to the parish and her father's cluster; often a sister's son comes to join his mother's brother. Since either may well be a member of a different ethnic group, neighborhood heterogeneity is further increased. Subsequently the sister's son may find a wife there, thus continuing the process of assimilation and, in time, enhancing the micro-cosmopolitan nature of social interaction. The maximal phase of a residential group, incorporating adult males from at least three and possibly four distinct lineages, may well contain members of several ethnic groups thus:

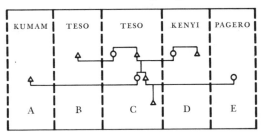

Marriage Relations and the Wider Community

A wider community shared by the three indigenous peoples of Gondo—Teso, Kenyi, and Pagero—is maintained through sons' acquisition of land and daughters' marriage beyond the boundaries of their natal parishes. The genealogy of one core Teso family, Igoria, illustrates both the dispersal phase in the development cycle of the patrigroup and this wider community within which such dispersal takes place (Figure 8). It includes all of the neighboring parishes in Serere and reaches as far as the adjacent parishes of Ngora and Kabera-maido counties. This is the largest area in which can be traced the creation of alliances and the procurement of dependents for strengthening support groups in the parish political arena.[11] The wider community contains the total resources of land and cattle through which support groups may be acquired.

Although the dual role of cattle as status symbols and utilities has been extensively discussed in East African ethnographies, their importance in establishing and maintaining alliance relations and as political facilities has not been traced.

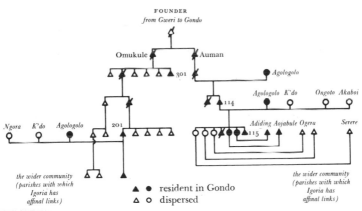

FIGURE 8: DISPERSION OF IGORIA CORE FAMILY

[119]

The basic institution in which people and cattle are brought together, the assemblage and distribution of bridewealth, will first be described in model form; then the interethnic implications of the institution will be discussed in relation to specific bridewealth exchanges among Kenyi, Pagero, and Teso in Gondo. The political significance of status variables will emerge from a comparison of the actual with the ideal. A sample of thirty bridewealth payments drawn from one Teso patrigroup, its affines, and neighbors over a period of twenty-five years provides the basis for the model. Three items are involved: cattle (between six and nine head), goats (between two and six head), and cash (between 30 and 300 shillings).

In all, 72 individual contributors were involved in the thirty bridewealth transactions. Only one man paid the entire bridewealth himself, although in eleven cases one man was responsible for the major contribution. In seven cases, the bridewealth was a direct transfer of what had just been received for an older sister. A special relationship is established between the siblings when this happens. Bridewealth received for a sister was the partial source of a man's bridewealth payment in eight cases. On one occasion a man married a new wife with the bridewealth he had just received for his daughter. Of the local lineage agnates who contributed, Fa did so sixteen times; FaBr eight; OBr three; FaFaBrSo three times; and on one occasion an Osi assisted with a cash payment of 150 shillings.[12] A mosi contributed cash toward one bridewealth payment. Thrice a mo contributed: in one case goats, in the other two cases money. On two occasions an older wife helped her husband acquire a young wife by providing goats and cash. The only affine who ever contributed to a man's bridewealth payment was his moBr, and this occurred seven times.

The area of bridewealth distribution was wider than that

of contribution both in its sociological and in its geographical referents. The recipients of bridewealth gifts lived in Oluben, Ngora, Kateta, Gweri, Atira, Agule, Ongoto, and Kadungulu parishes, a network of kin covering some eight hundred square miles and typical of the wider community of a Gondo patrigroup. Sociologically, the breakdown was as follows: on sixteen occasions the bulk of the bridewealth was given to a younger brother for his marriage. In eight cases it was given to the father and on one occasion to FaBr. On four occasions it was used immediately for a divorce payment. Apart from these bulk distributions within the patrigroup, cattle or goats were given to FaFa once; Fa thrice; FaBr twelve times; Fasi eight times; FaBrSo thrice; and Br twelve times. On one occasion a gift was made to Brwi. Goats were given to Osi thrice and to OsiHu four times. On two occasions mo was given goats and on five occasions mosi received goats. There was also one case of goats being given to momo. In these thirty cases, then, gifts were made to 101 individuals who fell within nine consanguineal categories. There were only three affinal recipients, moBr predominating. About half the prestations were made to persons of an older generation than the marriage partners. No gifts of cattle were ever made to women.

Respondents said that no regular rules governed distribution although an effort was made to see that, over the years, no kinsmen were neglected or forgotten. This does not, of course, mean that no sociological regularities were observed, but it does suggest, once again, that developmental analysis is required.

The pure model of a transfer of facilities which emerges from this analysis of bridewealth cattle may be placed alongside patterns of land acquisition and norms of reciprocity existing between categories of kinsmen and summarized diagrammatically. If one bears in mind the special relationship that exists between the sister whose bridewealth enabled a

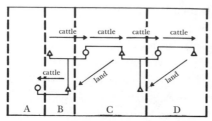

brother to marry and the importance of the moBr/siSo link with its institutional corollary, the nephew clan, the implications for the openness of the society are apparent. Where the lineage members in the paradigm are of different ethnic groups, the transfer of land and cattle between them means that access to the two political facilities is not restricted.

All marriage contracts in Gondo (except those of a few Muslims who are thereby excluded from the parish political arena), both within and across ethnic groups, involve the transfer of cattle according to the Teso model. There are of course idiosyncratic features in some transactions. Kenyi prefer the cash to be an odd sum and value cigarettes and salt among the bridewealth, but a certain number of cattle must be handed over in order that the marriage be socially recognized. The number of cattle paid is determined by the ethnicity of the bride. On this, all groups agree.

The principles underlying trans-ethnic transactions may be abstracted from a sample of 26 bridewealth payments drawn from eight Ilale residents of Agologolo (10 cases) and from the sub-county register of Gondo marriages for 1960 to 1967 (16 cases). (See Table 9.) The registry provides a necessary check since, within the community, the declared bridewealth is inflated or deflated according to the image that respondents wish to project. These 26 cases have been cross-checked and are accurate records of marriage transactions. The general pattern emerging from them conforms with that observed in a larger random sample.

[122]

TABLE 9: SAMPLE OF GONDO BRIDEWEALTH CONTRACTS

Case Number	Marriage Partners		Bridewealth (head of cattle)	Additional Information
	Male	Female		

A. Bridewealth Paid by Teso Youths (Agologolo)

Case Number	Male	Female	Bridewealth	Additional Information
1	T	= T	10	
2	T	= T	10	
3	T	= T	10	
4	T	= T	14	
5	T	= T	12	
6	T	= T	12	
7	T	= T	15	
8	T	= T	13	

B. Bridewealth Paid in Mixed Marriages and Non-Teso Marriages (Gondo)

Case Number	Male	Female	Bridewealth	Additional Information
9	S	= L	5	
10	K	= P	11	
11	K	= K	7	
12	K	= K	5	
13	P	= P	8	
14	T	= K	5	
15	T	= K	7	
16	T	= P	6	
17	T	= P	4	

C. Bridewealth Paid by Big Men (Gondo)

Case Number	Male	Female	Bridewealth	Additional Information
18	T	= T	15	Aringa (T 219)
19	Kum	= T	15	Opolot (Kum 682)
20	T	= T	16	Okello (T 201)
21	T	= T	17	Anyapo (T 109)
22	Kum	= T	15	Opolot (Kum 682)
23	T	= T	16	Odico (T 606)
24	T	= T	16	Ogola (T 203)
25	T	= T	19	Odera (T 114)
26	T	= K	7	Otieno (T 302) = d/o Nakumusana (K 418)

The standard bridewealth agreed between contracting groups of like ethnicity is 10–12 h/c (head of cattle) for a Teso marrying a Teso; 8–9 h/c for a Pagero marrying a Pagero, and 5–7 h/c for a Kenyi marrying a Kenyi. Since the ethnicity of the bride sets the payment, a Teso will give 5–7 h/c for a Kenyi wife and 8–9 h/c for a Pagero. A semi-hypergamous system thus exists whereby Teso contracting marriages with other ethnic groups receive more than they pay for women. Because of the differential, they also tend to receive women from other ethnic groups more than they give their own, and so an upward flow of women from Kenyi and Pagero to Teso is accompanied by a corresponding flow of cattle downward from the Teso to the other two groups.

The non-Teso groups participating in the system must accept this set of ground rules. A Kenyi marrying a Pagero will probably be asked to pay more than 8–9 h/c. He is asked, in effect, to pay both for the woman and the price of marrying up. In case 10 (Table 9) for example, a payment of 11 h/c was agreed upon as fair exchange. A Pagero will pay more for marrying a Teso (the standard price plus mobility costs), and so on.

To what extent are the Kenyi, being fishermen rather than cattle owners, at a disadvantage in Gondo's competition for prestige in which polygamy ranks so high? It is not useful to speak about the average number of cattle per head in each ethnic group since every man may both own cattle and call upon the cattle of kinsmen in the wider community, just as they can call upon him. One can generalize, however, and say that more Teso than Kenyi have cattle at their immediate disposal and that the Pagero are intermediate in this respect. Yet two of the largest cattleowners in the parish are Nakumusana (K 418), the Kenyi ex-chief, and a Pagero, Benefasio Mukasa (P 632) of the Yamia clan who has a Teso wife. This is an oversimplified picture, however, in that it assumes bridewealth is established solely on the basis of ethnic status, as the model purports. In fact, other statuses come into play.

A man of high prestige in the community, regardless of his ethnicity, will pay more for a wife than the common man although he receives only the standard bride-price of his daughters. A man who acquires prestige, regardless again of his ethnicity, will need more cattle in order to contract a marriage than a common man. At the same time, it is his daughters, if he is a Kenyi or Pagero, who will be sought after by Teso, and therefore he is in a position to acquire cattle that is not shared by less prestigious men. Since a system is in operation, such a feedback is to be expected. Moreover, we may note that it is a socially bounded system that we see in operation. The unwillingness of Teso to sell their cattle has constantly worried their administrators. Yet, if cattle are viewed as a political facility, as they have been here, a man's willingness to sell only when the beasts will be transported out of the community (to Kampala markets, for example) clearly relates to the maintenance of the status quo in the parish political arena and in the wider community on which he draws for his support.

PART TWO

WE HAVE SEEN how processes at work in Gondo involve an individual's relinquishing his home-based or familial ties in order to establish new patterns of social interaction by activating other statuses. The ordering of personnel in the polyethnic community requires, with a few exceptions, the setting aside of the nature of cultural origins. While these processes are clearly at work for contemporary immigrants, their operation among long-established Gondo residents can be ascertained only by looking into their past. We can look into the most explicit basis of differentiation between one individual and another: the way in which entry to the community is gained. The mode of entry is related to an unfolding process of landholding, and the two combined permit a division of the community into eight categories of resident and obviate any imposition of ethnic categories upon it (Table 10).

TABLE 10: CATEGORIES OF RESIDENT POPULATION

Code	Category	Total Number	Percentage
C	Members of core families	97	34.5
Cd	Dependents of core families (primary links)	30	10.8
PC	Members of peripheral cores	18	6.5
O	Office incumbents	58	21.0
Od	Office incumbents' heirs	29	10.5
M	Outsiders (marginal)	12	4.3
	Others (in flux)	26	9.4
	Not known	8	2.5
	TOTAL	278	99.5

Core Families, Office Incumbents, and Outsiders

Core families are made up of those who were born in the parish, whose family hold a block or blocks of land there, and whose forefathers lived there for at least three generations. There are twelve such core families in Gondo. They belong to three ethnic groups only; six of them are Teso, three Pagero, and three Kenyi. With 97 adult male homestead owners, they make up 61.8 per cent of the total Teso, Pagero, and Kenyi population, and 34.5 per cent of the population as a whole. Surrounding these core families are individuals not born in the parish who have either married into core families or, as agnatic kinsmen, been invited in from elsewhere, usually in order that they may "continue the line." These I call core dependents. They make up a further 10.8 per cent of the total population and include members of eleven ethnic categories.

A few Gondo parishioners, belonging to nine Teso homesteads in Aojabule and three Kenyi homesteads in Opucet, are members of core landholding families just across the borders. These I call peripheral core families since, living as they do close to the boundaries of neighboring parishes, most of their social ties and many of their field activities are beyond this analysis. They too have their dependents.

The second category of residents are those who enter Gondo to fill occupational niches, setting up as specialists of some kind. These I call office incumbents, the process of their integration being one of office substitution. In 1966, 30.5 per cent of the population fell into this category. Government-appointed officials posted to the parish provide the ideal type of office incumbency, but in Gondo, specialization also relates to trade, skilled crafts, and wage employment. In every case, individuals are brought into the community either by office holders already resident in the parish or by way of an institutional complex or its local representatives. The immigrant finds a niche established for him which he, and certain of his dependents, may wish to maintain. In all such cases, the place of the incumbent within the community is specific and limited. The third broad type of Gondo resident exists because, in order to categorize at all, the process of interaction has to be momentarily halted. Thus the third type consists of outsiders, mainly Asian and Hima (9.4 per cent of the total population) who were outside the system of community relations in operation in 1966.

Each of these three types of resident is characterized by distinctive relationships to the land of the parish. Members of core families and their dependents acquire inalienable rights to family land held within specific wards. Office incumbents inherit or acquire small portions of land dispersed throughout all wards except Aojabule. Outsiders have no land, finding their homes built for them on the land of others.

Core families, office incumbents, and outsiders are also distinguished by the degree to which they are incorporated into the community. The occupational segregation aimed at when Gondo was an administered township has given way to a process whereby an individual is able to move out of his initial ecological niche (in which he resided by virtue of ethnicity, regardless of whether he was related to a core family or to an office incumbent) to establish a new place in the community on the basis of alternative statuses. Through these, he establishes new patterns of social interaction on terms other than those of ethnicity. In other words, the individual moves out of his family nexus or away from his sponsor, whose existence was necessary for his initial entry into the community, to assert ties based on other criteria. He plays down his ethnic status in the changing situation since it is the least flexible, and chooses instead to activate some of the alternative statuses contained in his status set. This choice is frequently accompanied by changes of residence from one ward to another, changes in occupation, choice of friends, and even a shift in religion and language.

In the next three chapters we look at each of these three categories of resident in turn: core groups and their dependents in Chapter 6; office incumbency and substitution in Chapter 7; and outsiders in Chapter 8.

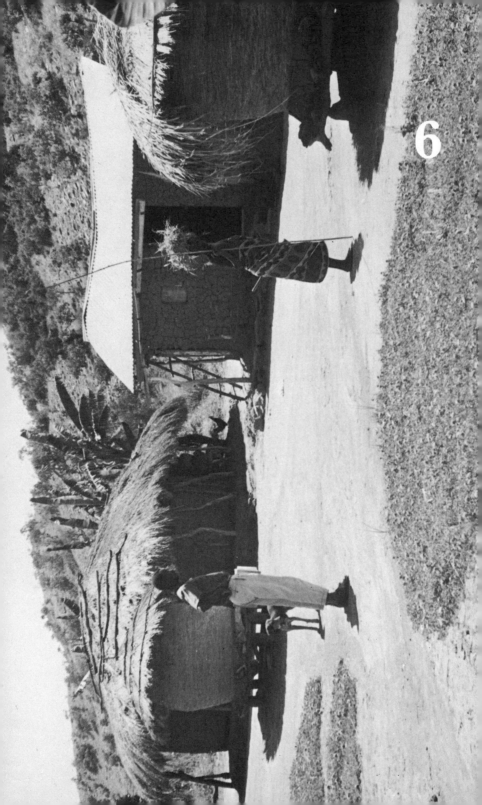

Core Families

WE HAVE SEEN in Chapter 5 that the Teso model of social organization provides a blueprint for individual mobility. The Teso, Kenyi, and Pagero core families, the groups most closely integrated in accordance with this design, are distributed and linked by kinship and marriage throughout the parish as the core family settlement and interaction of Agologolo shows. These, along with relations of the core families in the rest of the parish, suggest that once again a process can be seen at work that cuts across the tripartite division of the population into core families, office incumbents, and outsiders, the end result of which is a distinction between long-established families (including groups other than Teso, Kenyi, and Pagero) and immigrant landholders within the parish.

A core status is in no sense a dominant status. To make an analogy with economics, the status set of a core family member in Gondo is no more inelastic than any other. Although a man may be born into a core family and thus have this ascribed status among those in his status set, whether he chooses to articulate it or not, whether he gives voice to it or chooses to place emphasis on it, is an individual matter. Some members of the Ilale, for example, put occupational ties and friendships before core family in choosing where they live and with whom they associate. Some, such as the Pagero core families, perpetually undercommunicate their ethnic status.

Of the homestead heads of Gondo parish 46 per cent were born there, and, of these, 34.5 per cent were born into core

← *A core family homestead at the foot of the hill*

TABLE 11: CORE FAMILIES AND THEIR DEPENDENTS

Ethnic Group	Name of Patrigroup	Oldest Living Member	Number of Adult Males	Number of Residential Clusters	Number of Core Dependents
Teso	Igoria	Odera (T 114)	4	2	—
	Iunas	Eliedu (T 116)	3	1	1
	Ilale	Ekweru (T 210)	11	2	1
	Imodoi	Odongo (T 220)	14	3	2
	Irarak	Elamu (T 601)	11	3	5
	Icaak	Ocen (T 512)	6	1	4
			49	12	13
Kenyi	Bandije	Nakumusana (K 418)	16	2	1
	Bajwana	Wandira (K 311)	6	1	3
	Bambeya	Kato (K 406)	6	1	—
			28	4	4
Pagero	Yamia	Kasajja (P 324)	10	2	—
	Yachwa	Egimu (P 224)	4	1	1
	Yaiyeru	Magongo (P 421)	6	2	2
			20	5	3
TOTALS			97	21	22

families. Core families are all of Teso, Kenyi, and Pagero origin. There are, however, thirty Teso and two Kenyi (no Pagero) who do not belong by descent or filiation to a core family within the parish. Twelve core families are distributed throughout the parish, each with its lineal descendants (Table 11). Each was founded in the parish at least three generations ago and is associated with a specific tract of land and a recognized elder. The working of the principle of affiliation and dependency is best described by looking at each of the core family groups in turn.

Teso Core Families

All the Teso core families of Gondo give a similar account of the original acquisition of land by their kinsmen. A group of brothers or patrilateral kin came to Gondo three or four generations ago to open new land, either because their patrigroup was harassed by another in the area from which they came or because the land disposed of by their fathers was inadequate for their needs. The older men of the community agree that the earliest Teso settler was Omukule Okello of the Igoria clan who came with his brother Ouna from Gweri, near Soroti, around 1875. He is said to have been recognized as a chief by the Nyoro long before the advent of the Ganda. Omukule built his first homestead in Agologolo where T 220 now lives but moved shortly afterward, leaving some of his dependents there while he himself established a new homestead in Opucet, close to a lakeshore enclave of Nyoro settlers. Such agreement on the history of Teso settlement and the priority of Omukule may be due to the fact that groups of Teso arriving in Gondo later sought affiliation with the Igoria and legitimized their presence, as it were, through affinal and amical bonds with this nodal ancestor of the founding patrigroup. As we have seen, there is little pressure on land in this part of Serere that might lead to manipulations of tradition in support of conflicting land claims.

Among Okello's earliest dependents was Ongosol of the Iunas clan, a former friend in Gweri (possibly an age-mate) whose daughter Omukule married. Following this wife came her brother Oriada, who is looked upon as the founder of the Iunas *ekek* in Gondo. Most Iunas have their homes in the neighboring parish of Ogera, but three Iunas homesteads remain in Aojabule bordering Igoria lands. The heads of these two patrigroups are affinal kinsmen and close friends. At the end of the last century the Igoria lands were not clearly defined since there were no bound-setting neighbors but extended over what were later to be parts of Agologolo, Aojabule, and Kabola in Ogera parish, an area still sometimes called Igoriae.

Sometime between 1893 and 1900, Owinyi of the Imodoi clan moved to join his sister in Agologolo where she had been married to one of Omukule's clan brothers. Owinyi was subsequently joined by three brothers, the youngest of whom was Odongo (T 220), then aged about eight. The other brothers settled in Adiding where their descendants are still to be found and where the sons of Odongo also claim rights in land. The family held the office of "master of the hunt" (*apolon ka eriga*). About 1908 Agetu of the Ilale clan (the father of T 216) moved from Opucet to Agologolo to join his sister, Amonyi, who had married the son of Auman, younger brother of Omukule. The Irarak core family also settled in Opucet, members of the clan having spread there from Ogera and established relations with the Igoria through the marriage of the father's father of old Okulo (T 214) to a daughter of Omukule. Finally, the sixth and last Teso core family in Gondo, Icaak, arrived comparatively recently. Its local founder, Emodingo, came from Ongoto around 1912 after affinal ties had been enjoined with Igoria.

From this sketchy account it is clear that, by the use of affinal links (and here only the most direct have been indicated), a pattern of core family interrelationships was inaugurated in Gondo (Figure 9). In every case but one, a young man moved in to join his sister in the household of a Big Man. This relationship was sustained by further marriages in succeeding generations. Moreover, the affinal links established in one generation were extended to the next through mother's brother/sister's son links in the institutionalized form of the nephew clan relationship. Thus, in the first generation, Imodoi became the nephew clan of Igoria and Igoria of Iunas.

CORE FAMILIES

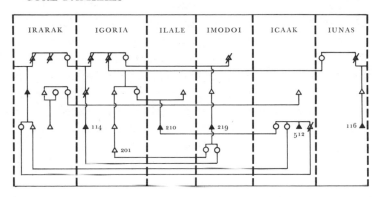

FIGURE 9: SOME KEY AFFINAL RELATIONSHIPS BETWEEN TESO CORE FAMILIES

In the next generation, Igoria became the nephew clan of Ilale, and so on. This relationship is characterized by all the features now firmly established in anthropology.[1] Most of all, the Teso say, a man can deny his sister's son nothing; if he asks for land he should give it to him; if he asks for cattle for marriage he should help provide them even at the expense of his own sons.

The most important feature of this relationship for the structural integration of core families in Gondo is its provision of a mechanism by which ties through complementary filiation gain primacy over agnatic descent. Inheritance of property within the lineage is short-circuited by obligations to respond to demands for land that can be made across lineages. The Teso conscious model of social structure recognizes only the first and, indeed, cattle and women are still acquired in accordance with it. A nephew clansman's rights to claim land from his mother's brother counters the development of closed corporate groups and functions to maintain the open social system which is crucial to the incorporation of newcomers into the community. Cousin marriage is proscribed (terminologically all cousins are equated with siblings), and

[137]

this is said to be because a man is related to the clans of his cousins through his mother and father. A ramification of affinal ties with as many clans as possible is thought desirable, although a shortage of cattle may lead a young man to marry the classificatory or real sister of the man to whom he has given his own sister, so that no actual cattle need be exchanged. The slow multiplication of affinal ties between core lineages and others over the generations (some ties lapse with the deaths of individuals so that the number remains logistically manageable being proportionate to the body of inheritance available) means that demands can be assimilated and limited at any one time.

One such proliferation of reciprocal personal links between core families lapsed with the death, in May 1966, of Suleiman Ocaalo, head of the Icaak in Gondo. This man had contracted many polygamous marriages throughout his long life through which he gained strongly activated affinal ties in five of the six Teso core families, the exception being Iunas. Ocaalo was also related to Pagero families and, through them, with Kenyi and Kumam. He was coordinator (*emorimor*) of Gondo and was succeeded by his younger brother, Ocen (T 512). Ocen was, however, in office for little more than a year. At the time of his election, he was monogamous, his wife coming from Ongoto parish, and by 1966 much of the local power of the Icaak had diminished. As we have seen, Ocen became increasingly poorer as he gave more and more time to his office, so that by January 1967 he was unable to pay his taxes and the parish chief relieved him of his duties. His successor was Yowana Ekweru (T 210) of the Ilale clan and, of all the elders, Ekweru has most firmly established reciprocal obligations with other Teso core families. He also had strong personal alliances with Kenyi and Pagero as well, a characteristic shared by Ocaalo but not by Ocen and, apparently, a prerequisite for the successful coordination of the parish. Although the coordinator is not chosen by his colleagues specifically for his ramifying kin connections, it is nevertheless recognized that "the *emorimor* must always be someone who can get on with everyone in the parish. He must be welcome at all homes." Affinal ties guarantee this.

Kenyi Core Families

There are structural reasons why community leaders cannot be Kenyi. If a rare Kenyi does achieve prominence, it is through status achieved in the outside world and not within the Gondo context of core family relations.

The Kenyi tradition of entry to the community is more individualistic than that of the Teso, just as their way of life is more individualistic. Before the coming of the European administration, the Kenyi lived on small floating papyrus islands in groups of five to twenty. An extended family might occupy two or three adjacent islands. The new administration appointed Kenyi chiefs since the collection of taxes from these people constituted a specially difficult problem and, in Serere County, the first Kenyi chief, Mwambazi, had as his lieutenant Mulojja son of Musana (K 304), whose first task it was to bring the Kenyi to dry land. Mulojja tells of his journeys around the islands with this government order and of how the fishermen with their families and possessions were loaded into canoes, their houses and crops burned behind them. They were given specific rights to settle "anywhere around the lakeshore; the Teso could not stop them because it was an order of the government."

On coming to land, Kenyi families settled in groups adjacent to their previous island neighbors. In return for the land rights they had not sought, they were obliged to cultivate at least one acre under penalty of imprisonment. (Many, as we have seen, chose instead to move to less effectively administered regions on the northern shores of Lake Kyoga so that, today, the wider community of Kenyi kinsmen extends westward as far as Dokolo and Kioga counties in Lango.) Settlement patterns in Gondo reflect this early ordinance. Most homesteads are situated along the shores of Kabola and Adiding for, as Musana Sabiti (K 312), the ward headman of Kabola, puts it, "Have you ever seen a crocodile which is chased from the lake and runs to the land? Where else would the Kenyi settle but close to the water?"

Three Kenyi core families share the two neighborhoods. There are the Bajwana descendants of "Boi"; the Bandije clan to which Mulojja (K 304) and Nakumusana (K 418) belong, along with their many affines and dependents; and, lastly, the descendants of Maji of the Bambeya clan. These three families and their dependents include 76.2 per cent of the Kenyi population of Gondo parish. Like the Teso, the Kenyi core families have multiplex affinal ties, and only the most direct links can be shown diagrammatically in the chart accompanying the map of Kabola and Adiding (Figure 10).

The large Bandije clan occupies a nodal position like that of Igoria among the Teso. Both Bambeya and Bajwana are allied with Bandije by marriage, and the sisters and daughters of Bandije are married into Pagero and Teso core families in Agologolo and Adiding. Their sons, on the other hand, tend to bring in wives from the wider community. The allocation of a large grant of land to Nakumusana when he was a chief was probably the one most decisive factor accounting for both the permanent nature and the extent of Kenyi settlement in Gondo, as well as its spatial distribution within the parish. This permanency is indicated by their demographic structure. Although Kabola is thought of as the main Kenyi neighborhood, Adiding is, in fact, little less their terrain and these two contiguous wards are, largely as a result of three generations of intermarriage, one unit of land settlement. This unit

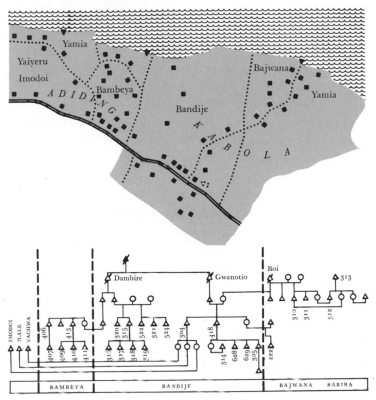

FIGURE 10: KENYI SETTLEMENT IN ADIDING AND
KABOLA WITH A SKELETON GENEALOGY

forms an arc fanning out from the lakeshore to the homestead
of Nakumusana on the roadside at Mile Mbili (the two-mile
point), once the township boundary.

Kenyi core families in Gondo are much larger than those of
the Teso and Pagero, but their clustered residential groups
are smaller and more scattered. The size of the residential
group depends largely upon labor requirements, and as fishermen most Kenyi cultivate less, relying on cash or credit to
obtain much of their food. There is no competition for

dependents as there is among the Teso since fishing crews require only three or four men. As a result, no Kenyi adult, whether he be head of a core family or not, has at his disposal a large support group of dependents, apart from Mulojja and Nakumusana who acquired prestige and patronage powers through their erstwhile chiefly offices. These two are, indeed, looked upon as leading citizens by the community at large. The ward head, Sabiti Musana, similarly has prestige by virtue of his office. He is seen to be an influential go-between in the parish and is popular with Kenyi and Teso alike partly because he is not afraid to stand up to the parish chief. His structural position within the Kenyi social system—as a neutral affine of one of the smaller clans—probably helped his election.

For most of the younger generation of Kenyi, however, and especially the sons of Nakumusana, it is necessary to seek other routes to community prestige. Both Barnabas, son of Nakumusana, and Sharif of the Bandije began as fishermen with dugout canoes, invested their profits in larger boats, and hired porters to fish for them while they themselves opened shops in the township. Their commercial enterprise has set a precedent for other Kenyi. Two other sons of Nakumusana opened shops in the nearby villages of Kamod and Kadungulu, while his youngest son rented a *duka* in Gondo, next door to Barnabas, for the 1966–1967 cotton season.

Although Kenyi settlement is still most dense along the shore, a gradual encroachment toward the road is taking place which reflects both the social mobility of Kenyi in trade and the increasing ecological pressure on them as fishermen. Both coincide with a district-wide trend whereby trade, which was formerly in the hands of Asians and then of Ganda, is being taken over by the scattered, mobile Kenyi. With their widespread kin networks, built up for fishing needs and maintained through elaborate funeral rituals, Kenyi families are able to maintain shops throughout a very wide territory. Within Gondo, however, Kenyi are the most clannish of all ethnic groups, operating as one social unit regardless of whether they live in Kabola, Adiding, or to the west of the township. Their ethnic and residential cohesion is gradually being worn away, however, by this incremental occupational diversity as well as by religion. The pulls of Islam and Catholicism are beginning to counterbalance ethnic and neighborhood solidarity and, in so doing, provide new bases for alliance with sectors of the Pagero and Teso population in the parish.

Pagero Core Families

The Pagero core families are shown here largely in their role of hinge group between Kenyi and Teso. They serve thus in three capacities: first, as fishermen; secondly, as co-religionists; and thirdly, as affines. As fishermen, the Pagero have considerable geographical mobility within the parish, and their residence patterns, along with their consanguineal and intra-Pagero affinal ties, serve to link all but one of the wards (distant Aojabule) in social interaction. Secondly, Christians and secular Pagero operate in an interstitial way to relate Kenyi and Teso in the parish-wide semi-hypergamous marriage system. Lastly, the Pagero are divided as a group between the three major religious denominations in Gondo. Ten are Christian, three are Muslim, and the remaining ten are animists or secular in their belief. Since members of the same Pagero family embrace both Islam and Christianity, they serve to minimize religious differences which are expressed, in Gondo, not in theological dispute but in the payment of bridewealth cattle and participation in work parties rewarded with beer. Islamic marriages are, of course, contracted with the payment of dowry, and alcohol is forbidden to believers. Each of the three Pagero core families in Gondo—Yamia, Yachwa, and Yaiyeru—is bisected by these three dimensions of social living: religion, neighborhood, and marriage alliances. The distinctive social relationships of members of each group are reflected in where they live, whom they marry, and with whom they most frequently meet, both in work and in sociability.

Since this ethnic group is known in the parish both as "Ipagero" and as "Bachopi," a generational cleavage whereby the older generation stress a Chopi tradition of origin while the younger men prefer their Ateso name "Ipagero" seemed likely.[2] This proved not to be the case, however. The division reflects contemporary social relations in the parish and an undercommunication of ethnic status by the Pagero who skirt identification to maintain religious, occupational, or dependency status rather than Ipagero/Bachopi ethnicity.

All but two Pagero individuals belong to core families. Yamia, the largest clan, has two distinct sub-groups which are, contrary to their ideology, affinally related. The two alien Pagero in the parish are affinal dependents of Teso and Kenyi core families and come from neighboring parishes. Like the Kenyi, the Pagero first settled by the lakeshore in Adiding and Kabola as fishermen. Today they are to be found in all wards except Aojabule, their distribution reflecting movement within the parish following upon marriages with non-Pagero. Yaiyeru may be looked upon as the nodal Pagero core family. Its members claim as its founding father in Gondo, Jamlobo, whose son married a daughter of Kijanjaro, a subchief recognized by the British with whom all Pagero lineages try to establish some link. Jamlobo lived in Adiding at the homestead occupied today by his descendants (P 419–422). These families make manifest their rights to land by erecting

[144]

concrete or granite tombstones over the graves of their fore-fathers, a procedure rare in Gondo although found increasingly in Teso as a whole. Although the Yaiyeru family cemetery is well established in Adiding, their land there is small and one son (P 228) has already moved to join his mother's brother (P 224) in Agologolo.

The older generation of Yaiyeru was exclusively Muslim, but the three younger men are nominally Catholic. As in all Pagero families so divided, the affinal links of the younger generation tend to take on a different pattern from those of the elders. Since these links are many and multiplex, extending back over three generations, only a numerical account of them can be given here (Table 12) and a cursory generali-

TABLE 12: MARRIAGE PATTERNS OF PAGERO
CORE FAMILIES BY GENERATION, SEX, AND CLAN

Pagero Generation	Marriages of Sons with:				Marriages of Daughters with:			
	Pagero	Teso	Kenyi	Others	Pagero	Teso	Kenyi	Others
Yaiyeru 1	–	–	1	–	1	–	–	2
2	1	1	–	2	1	1	1	1
3	5	–	–	–	–	–	–	–
	6	1	1	2	2	1	1	3
Yachwa 1	1	1	–	–	2	–	–	–
2	1	1	1	1	1	–	1	–
3	–	2	–	–	–	–	–	–
4	–	1	–	–	–	1	–	1
	2	5	1	1	3	1	1	1
Yamia 1	1	–	2	2	1	–	1	1
2	1	–	2	1	1	–	–	2
3	1	–	–	–	–	2	–	1
	3	0	4	3	2	2	1	4
TOTAL	11	6	6	6	7	4	3	7

zation made. Pagero share with Kenyi their pattern of parochial and wider community marriage alliances related to sex.
As with the Kenyi, Pagero women marry Teso men within
the parish, but marriages of both sexes with other ethnic
groups are contracted throughout a wider community. (The
marriages of five Yachwa sons to Teso women are exceptional
and will be discussed later.) Most marriages to groups other
than Teso and Kenyi are contracted with local Nyoro families
or Kumam in Kaberamaido. The numerical preponderance
of Yamia marriages with these groups in former times may
account for the fragmentation of this family in Gondo today.
The simplified picture that emerges, taken in conjunction
with additional biographical data not presented, is one of
upwardly mobile Yachwa marriage with Teso; Yamia marriage with Nyoro and Kenyi; and their connection to each
other through shared ties with Yaiyeru.

It is the Yaiyeru, therefore, who best illustrate the hinge
aspect of the Pagero in the societal structure of Gondo. The
Yaiyeru living in Adiding have three spheres of interaction.
The first contains fellow Muslims of all ethnic groups who live
around the mosque and border the road through Adiding;
the second embraces their Kenyi affines who are also fellow
fishermen; the third sphere of interaction is with Teso Imodoi
affines who are their neighbors in Adiding and from whom
they first acquired land. The Agologolo Yaiyeru, on the other
hand, interact largely with Teso and Pagero-Yachwa neighbors. Unlike their Adiding kinsmen, they are primarily cultivators and own cattle; they take part in work groups and
drink beer. Some of the social concomitants of the two Yaiyeru
sets of residence choice are shown in Figure 11. Although low
ethnic status may be outweighed by other status considerations
derived from outside the community, it is possible to see, in
this dualism among the Pagero, a form of ethnic redefinition
aimed at further social mobility. Not only can Pagero choose
to be Lukenyi-speaking Bachopi or Ateso-speaking Ipagero,

CORE FAMILIES

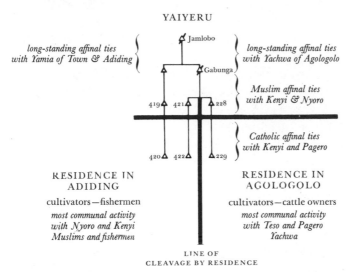

YAIYERU

long-standing affinal ties
with Yamia of Town & Adiding

long-standing affinal ties
with Yachwa of Agologolo

Muslim affinal ties
with Kenyi & Nyoro

Catholic affinal ties
with Kenyi and Pagero

RESIDENCE IN
ADIDING

cultivators — fishermen
*most communal activity
with Nyoro and Kenyi
Muslims and fishermen*

RESIDENCE IN
AGOLOGOLO

cultivators — cattle owners
*most communal activity
with Teso and Pagero
Yachwa*

LINE OF
CLEAVAGE BY RESIDENCE

FIGURE 11: CLEAVAGE IN ONE PAGERO CORE FAMILY

they can also express their choice of allegiance by moving to
new neighborhoods. In this way they challenge social acceptance of their expressed status. In doing so, however, they
forfeit opportunities for community leadership in their own
right, since they become the dependents of Teso and Kenyi
core families. A general picture of the choices actually made,
as they appeared in Gondo in 1966, may be diagramed thus:

Adiding   Agologolo

YAMIA   YAIYERU   YACHWA

KENYI   PAGERO   TESO

Core Family Settlement in Agologolo Ward

The process of interaction between core families of Teso,
Pagero, and Kenyi is most clearly visible in the settlement
pattern of Agologolo where the Teso-Igoria clan was once
dominant. Nineteen Teso, seven Pagero, and one Kenyi home-

[147]

stead are scattered, anything but randomly, over this flat, fertile stretch of land between the eastern marshes and Gondo hill.

The pattern of land fragmentation in Agologolo traces on the present terrain the changes that have occurred during the past eighty years. A skeleton genealogy of the homestead owners of the neighborhood may be compared with a chart showing the distribution of their homesteads to illustrate the relationships which have grown up there (Figure 12). Each homestead, set in its own gardens, belongs to one of the land tracts which has come about, as we have seen, from ties established with Igoria over three generations. Over time each of these tracts has been fragmented into clusters of gardens and plots by gifts of land to dependents and affines. Today there are four such clusters (*atutuben*) each with their own heads, and the Agologolo genealogy may be interpreted as a graphic representation of four clusters of dependents forming four potential support groups around Ekweru (T 210) of the Ilale clan; Egimu s/o Mujwala, a Pagero (P 224); Aringa (T 219) of the Imodoi clan, the son of old Odongo; and Okello (T 201) of the Igoria.[3]

The only direct descendant of Omukule of the Igoria in Agologolo today is Okello (T 201). Although not an important leader in the neighborhood, Okello had a fleeting chance of achieving prestige when he was made village chief of Atirir for a short while just before this office was abolished in 1963. Two Igoria elders live close to the boundary of Agologolo: Odera (T 114) in Aojabule; and Ocheppa (T 301), an adopted son of Omukule Okello—but a man of low rank because he was bought at a time of famine and merely acted as a messenger for the chief—across the boundary in Kabola. The Agologolo elder with authority over land is Odera (T 114); there are no other members of this patrigroup in Gondo.

Ties of Igoria and Imodoi lineages established in the second

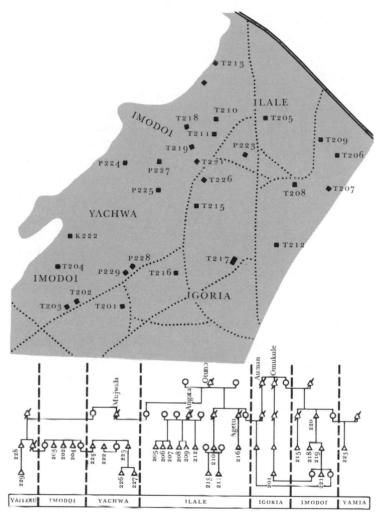

FIGURE 12: SETTLEMENT IN AGOLOGOLO WARD
WITH A SKELETON GENEALOGY

generation have been reinforced in this by Okello's marriage to a granddaughter of old Odongo. Odongo is still alive, but the homestead is recognized as being that of Aringa (T 219), his son, since Odongo spends most of his time inside his hut and takes no part in public affairs. Near this homestead are those of Ocelot (T 215), a single man who migrated to Kaberamaido early in 1967, and Zirimenya Ocoto (P 223), a Pagero who early on in my fieldwork claimed to be a sister's son of Odongo. Ocoto is a member of the Kaweri branch of Gondo's core Yamia family and migrated from Kaweri in 1941 to become a dependent of his kinsmen, Oparo s/o Mujwala, in Adiding. In 1944, a few months after Oparo was invited to join his Teso affine in Agologolo, Ocoto followed him. That Ocoto chose to claim a classificatory mother's brother link with Imodoi in Agologolo rather than reveal his actual link with a real Pagero mother's brother in Adiding reflects the overall ranking system of the three core ethnic groups. He would have been able to "demand" land from either.

The greatest fragmentation of the original clan lands occurs in northern Agologolo where the descendants of Otuno of the Ilale clan and Mujwala, his affinal dependent, live. Five homesteads belong to sons of Angata (T 205–9, 212) and one to Okasu (T 216) son of Agetu, all of whom received land from Otuno through their mother's portion before his death. Later, in 1926, Okasu called Ekweru (T 210), his father's brother's son, from Ogelak to join him since he himself, in spite of three marriages, was childless. Ekweru's two sons (T 211 and T 213) were born in Agologolo, and Ekweru himself is ward head (*apolon ka ateker*). Ekweru's residence in Agologolo coincided with his becoming a clerk in the sub-county headquarters which were then located in Gondo Township.

The Pagero-Yachwa lineage came into Agologolo by activating a link through women; and today the entire core family is to be found only in Agologolo, whither they moved from Adiding when Mujwala inherited Namia, his brother's widow and the daughter of Angata of the Ilale lineage. Mujwala, a fisherman born on Kaweri Island, was "the friend of a Teso in Adiding" who gave him land. This Teso subsequently returned to Adiding but his brother, Eswapu, remained. One of Eswapu's daughters was given in marriage to a member of the neighboring Pagero-Yaiyeru family, and it was through this connection that the two Yaiyeru now living in Agologolo (P 228 and P 229) received a share of the land of the three sons of Eswapu (T 202–4). The other half of the Yaiyeru remained, as we have seen, in Adiding and, in time, married the other half of the Imodoi branch represented there by Emenu (T 402), brother of Eswapu. Such marriages between members of different ethnic groups in which contracts are arranged over the generations, before as well as after shifts of residence, occur a great deal in Gondo. Proximity leads to marriage and marriage leads to increased proximity.

The Yachwa core family is much more closely integrated with the Teso than with any other Pagero in Gondo. Indeed, upon occasions when I wanted to discuss specifically historical problems with a group of Teso elders, it was invariably suggested that Egimu son of Mujwala (P 224) should be one of them. (No such elders' convocations ever did take place, in spite of my attempts to stimulate them. Later, I came to realize that this was partly because ambiguity was the essence of social organization in Agologolo, as elsewhere in Gondo. The only person to reproach me for going around seeing individuals in their homesteads, when, in his opinion, I should have called a public meeting, was Okasu, who probably wanted a chance to speak out his grievances and claim his position as head of the Ilale patrigroup in place of the younger Ekweru, a man whom he himself sponsored into the community.)

Accepting a hypothesis of ethnic hypergamy in Gondo,

Wabwire (K 222) may be considered to have risen in position through marriage into the Yacha family and his acquisition of land in Agologolo. These ties are reinforced by the marriage of his brother in Ogera to the daughter of Mulojja (K 304), the former Kenyi chief, with whom the Teso families of Agologolo all have multiplex ties of alliance.

The Rest of the Parish

Agologolo provides in microcosm aspects of the structural integration of the core families characteristic of the parish as a whole. Differences between wards lie more in their external relations than in their internal structuring. The establishment and articulation of affinal links across ethnic lines, the integrative significance of land rights, and the residence rights entailed in sponsorship relations are all apparent, if less simple, in other wards, too. The Teso kinship model of social integration is the basis for settlement and incorporation for the entire population, with the notable exception of the parish chief. This exception is notable in that it represents the other dynamic in the situation—the acquisition of land in the parish through the action of external forces—in this case, the local administration; in other earlier cases, the ginning companies and the church.

The township and Opucet may be said to have "lost out" as discrete neighborhoods in the face of strong ginnery intervention, just as factors outside of the system affected the process of land settlement and distribution. In earlier times much of the land in these two wards was held by office holders, with all that implies—a matter to be discussed in the following chapter. In general terms, the manner of land alienation affects both the nature and the extent of its fragmentation and the degree of choice any individual has with respect to his neighbors. Only 30 per cent of the Teso homesteads in the township have been inherited; the remaining Teso landholders there are immigrants, most of whom have been in Gondo a shorter time than immigrants of most other ethnic groups.

In Kabola and Adiding, on the other hand, where patterns of population growth and fragmentation of land are identical with those of Aojabule and Agologolo, and where an identical development process in neighborhood settlement has emerged, the replication of the same type of relationship indicates the end of the process. In the township and Opucet no such clear process can be discerned although new patterns in the acquisition of land have been emerging over forty years. Contradictions existing in these two wards make it necessary to focus upon the temporal dimension rather than look for a stabilized, stylized pattern in the spatial design mapped out on the ground. In so doing, yet another of the cross-cutting cleavages that render ethnicity one of the less important variables governing social relations in Gondo becomes apparent: an ideological division between the old families of the parish and the newer arrivals. The process of settlement, dispersion, and fragmentation common to the Teso of the parish, and shared by the Pagero and Kenyi, is, in the township, also shared by well-established Acholi and Lango families. Newly established immigrant homestead owners, on the other hand, regardless of ethnicity, are part of no such process. Thus some Acholi and Lango homesteads (A 669, A 671, and L 672, for example) are seen as belonging to the "older families" of Gondo while incoming Teso are regarded by the long-established residents as upstarts.

Although there is an awareness among the members of the core families that they form a special class in Gondo, this seems to be voiced only in response to inquiries into the past when a distinction is made between "the most important men in Gondo today" and "those who know most about the parish." A further distinction is made between "those who know most about Gondo" and "those who know most about the ginnery." The former category centers around administrative history, the latter around commercial enterprise. This long-standing juxtaposition is not expressed in social action. The recognition of such a dichotomy is but a snapshot in time.[4]

Today, members of core families, their affines, and dependents form over 60 per cent of the population of Gondo parish. This proportion will increase as newcomers claim permanent rights by cementing affinal links with the founding families. In a sense, the large percentage of individuals already sharing multiplex relations is an indicator of the degree to which Gondo may be considered an integrated community. However, at any one time, the parish will contain a certain number of residents not incorporated by these mechanisms of kinship and marriage since members of core families die or leave and newcomers arrive year by year. There must therefore be, at any one time, a working relationship between the two elements—the core families and unrelated individuals or groups —and there is, in fact, this relationship, as we shall demonstrate subsequently.

Immigrants

NOT EVERYONE IN GONDO TODAY is fortunate enough to have been born there or to have been invited into the parish as an affine or a dependent. Yet it is said that nobody comes to Gondo unless he knows someone already living there—not unless one speaks of thieves or prostitutes, that is. There is an ascribed status of community member and a prescribed way of entering the community. If there is a place for the newcomer in Gondo, he stays; if not, he moves on. One can examine the character of these "places" in the community as offices in the table of organization of the parish, observing how their character changes over time.

Although the beginning of the web of connections between core families in Gondo cannot be accurately dated, it is sufficiently well established to form a distinctive pattern compared with that of other members of the community, primarily because the processes involved are those of kinship and affinity. In order to describe the settlement and social interactional patterns of a further 30.7 per cent of Gondo's population, I suggest two concepts, office incumbency and incumbency substitution. Again, it must be observed that, as in the case of core family membership, an individual may choose to relinquish this status and articulate others. Some men remain all their lives in Gondo as incumbents (of the present total, 11.1 per cent were born in the parish); others choose to change their place within the community by advancing, perhaps, from office incumbent to core family kinsman.

Office incumbency comes into being, first, because specialists

← An Acholi settler plaiting sisal

[157]

are a necessary part of peasant society and, secondly, because land within the community is a limited asset. An office incumbent enters the community in one of three ways: as an official appointed to the parish from outside; as a specialist craftsman or trader; or in offices that have come into being with Gondo's "great transformation" as the parish was brought into the market economy. In each case, the office incumbent initially operates within a narrow ecological niche; his place in the community is a limited one; his landholding is relatively small and contained. An office is characterized by the succession of the personnel filling it; it endures as incumbents come and go.

There are currently 56 office incumbents in the parish, 29 of whom have adult male kinsmen living with them who may be looked upon as their successors. Three of these men are government-appointed officials: the parish chief, the fisheries officer, and an inspector for the Lint Marketing Board. All three are Teso.

The peasant prototype of specialist incumbency is represented by such traditional craftsmen as potters, canoe builders, tin smiths, butchers, nut sellers, cattle traders, and shopkeepers. These number some twenty individuals, most of them deriving from Bantu "homelands." Most were born in the parish since this is the oldest type of office incumbency in Gondo. A few came into the community at the end of the nineteenth century as *abakungulu*—mercenaries of Kakunguru who were pensioned off and given plots of land in Gondo— and stayed on as skilled craftsmen.

As the economy of the parish changed, especially after the developments of 1912, other offices arose in connection with the port and the ginneries. In time, as we have seen, homes and land were found for the employees of the ginneries and of the port and steamer service, along with those who served them in secondary occupations—bicycle repairers, schoolteachers, domestic servants, and the like. Later these homesteads and small holdings of land were passed on to successors even when the institution that had brought them into being had passed away. Bus drivers and employees of the Public Works Department who came to know Gondo in their official capacities, recognizing opportunities for economic advancement, stayed on after their retirement. Many became wealthy and influential in the community and, today, provide one part of the leadership element that the community requires.

Incumbency is restrictive for each type of office holder—officials; traditional, peasant prototype, specialist incumbents; and industrial immigrants alike—yet case studies demonstrate a characteristic passage from one status to another by office incumbents.

The Officials

Prebendary officials present the purest form of office incumbency. One of the most striking changes since 1912, when the township was established, has been the decline in the number of resident officials representing "broker" institutions; today there are only three: the parish chief, the fisheries officer, and the Lint Marketing Board inspector. These men are distinctive only in that their houses are provided for them by their institutions and that they receive monthly salaries from outside the parish; otherwise, from their style of living, there is no way of telling them from other Gondo residents.

The parish chief (T 217), a native of Ongoto parish, is polygamous. He has not as yet taken a wife from Gondo although he has one from each of the previous three parishes to which he has been posted. It is perhaps significant that he is negotiating for a wife from Ogera, for, as we saw earlier, that is where the seat of power lies in Bugondo sub-county.

Gondo parish itself is a political backwater. George Henry Ebelu (T 625), the Lint Marketing Board representative at the ginnery, comes from Akaboi in Atira parish and has lived in Gondo for fifteen years. He has made several affinal alliances which have extensive ramifications, his wives being the daughters of Daudi Opolot (Kum 682), his neighbor; the sister of Asani s/o Anderea Oyat (A 670), another neighbor; and the sister of Ocen (T 512) of the core Icaak family of Opucet. Although at the moment Ebelu retains land in his natal parish, he will probably settle permanently in Gondo. On the other hand, Joseph Emulu (T 616), the fisheries officer, is subject to frequent changes in postings. He lives like a bachelor in the small stone house provided by the Fisheries Department, traveling every weekend to Serere, where his wife lives and his children are at school.

None of these officials is considered an important man in Gondo. They are not "men of Gondo" since all owe their positions to official relationships with the outside world. They present the ideal example of official transiency in the parish since their offices are organizational niches filled by an unending stream of incumbents, all strangers as far as the villagers are concerned. The office of parish chief has been in existence for over sixty years; the first Lint Marketing Board inspector was appointed to the ginnery in 1933; the first fisheries officer in 1954.

Specialist Incumbents

The modern European and commercial community provided in peasant Africa, as did caste in India, an organization of middlemen, permanent in residence and function, part of the market system of international commerce. The entire trend toward modernization is characterized by an increase in specialization, and in peasant society, where the familial division of labor is an intricately fashioned sociological relationship between land and man, specialists are likely to be incomers or strangers.

In many societies specialists remain strangers even while their worth is recognized, simply because their ties are efferent rather than community-centered. Where they do not acquire land, they are not integrated into the web of society, as was the case in Gondo during the period when social interaction was patterned by the alien model of municipal organization. The stranger specialist, artisan, craftsman, middleman, and trader appear in common guise in the sociological literature.

Throughout the history of economics the stranger everywhere appears as the trader, or the trader as stranger. . . . The stranger is by nature no "owner of the soil" . . . soil not only in the physical but also in the figurative sense of a life-substance which is fixed, if not in a point in space, at least at an ideal point of the social environment. Although in more intimate relations he may develop all kinds of charm and significance, as long as he is considered a stranger in the eyes of the other, he is not an owner of the soil.[1]

The non-landowning stranger is "in the community but not of it. Economically he is a member but morally he is not and it is this which lies at the heart of the peasant's ambivalent and often violent, attitude toward him. The peasant needs, but dislikes, him."[2] The stranger is not accepted because he is not known as a whole person. He is an individual out of context, out of his kin group. It is imperative for the fulfill ment of his role as a trader that he maintain a widespread extralocal network of relations, an act which may be incompatible with local involvement in the community in which he resides. Yet in Gondo it is clear that, with the passage of time, and given the opportunity to acquire land, the trader and specialist may become, by virtue of incumbency substitution, an integral part of the structured community.

As a result of Gondo's early existence on the trading frontier between the northern and southern shores of Lake Kyoga,

TABLE 13: CAREER HISTORIES OF OFFICE INCUMBENTS

Code Number	Incumbent's Means of Entry	Occupation	Years of Residence	Age Category	Probable Heir
G 424	as a cattle trader	butcher	23	7	wiBr living in Gondo 10 years
P 421	Gondo-born	offal butcher	47	4	Soga wiBr.
N 531	Gondo-born So of a cattle trader	diviner	40	4	?
N 652	from Bugerere to inherit from Fa	potter	32	5	So, now living in Kamod, will return to Gondo
N 417	inherited from Fa now in Busoga	nut seller	38	3	?
N 532	inherited from moBr now in Bunyoro	cattle trader	10	2	?
N 658	inherited from siHu	carpenter	12	4	Br (S 659) with him 10 years
N 639	joined siHu, cook to European	hotelkeeper	37	5	siSo (N 641) his cook for 2 years
J 691	joined Br	fishmonger	16	4	So (J 693) with him 5 years
S 661 S 662 S 663	brought in by Fisheries Department	boatbuilders	4	{ 2 3 2	Gondo Teso (T 107) aged 29, their assistant carpenter?
N 648	inherited from Fa, born in Gondo	bicycle repairer	48	4	K 407? (affine)

N 649	inherited from Fa now in Bugerere	tailor	30	6	So (N 650)
N 650	Gondo-born	bicycle repairer	27	2	Probable heir of N 649
T 606	brought by Asian	tailor	21	5	wiSo by first marriage (T 605) now itinerant cloth seller
T 401	brought by Asian	tailor	25	5	So recently quarreled and left
A 671	joined moEr. Took over from Asian	tailor	4	3	Gondo-born L 672 being trained by A 671
Kum 680	as ginnery worker; trained as tailor by As 699	tailor	11	3	Br (Kum 681)
S 425	inherited from Fa now in Bukoba	itinerant trader	6	3	?

Bantu-speaking traders and craftsmen predominated in western Serere. This was their ecological niche; yet, since the articulation of ethnicity is no more involved in the operation of specialist incumbency than in any other aspect of Gondo life, today many individuals of other cultural backgrounds are also to be found filling these offices. A breakdown of the primary occupations of adult males (Table 5) shows that, of the 40 trade and craft occupations in the parish, only 65 per cent are today in the hands of Bantu speakers. Nor do members of Bantu ethnic groups operate exclusively as traders and craftsmen: of the 13 Soga in the parish, only 7 are specialists of this kind; only 2 out of 4 Ganda and only 10 out of 37 Nyoro. The remainder are cultivators and fishermen like the majority of the community.

The degree of ethnic correlation that exists relates not to tribal or cultural background but rather to ways in which some groups have benefited more than others from the economic developments of the last sixty years. Thus, most of the "traditional" craftsmen and traders—potters, butchers, diviners, cooks, woodworkers, tin smiths—are, indeed, from the former Bantu kingdoms and, furthermore, most of them are Muslim. The more "modern" craftsmen—bicycle repairers and tailors among them—are, with one exception, all Nilotic, and all have been apprenticed at some time to Asian shopkeepers and traders scattered throughout the rural areas. Finally, in recent years, there have come about opportunities to invest the profits from fishing in commerce, and eight of Gondo's eleven shopkeepers are, today, of Kenyi and Luo extraction.

The Dynamics of Incumbency and Substitution

The career histories of twenty traders and craftsmen will suggest the processes involved in office incumbency and incumbency substitution (Table 13). A tendency for older men to invite heirs to reside with them prior to their own departures for their homelands is clear. These young men are mostly in their twenties and thirties. Where there is no previous incumbent, an external agency—the Fisheries Department or Asian merchants, in the cases shown—is seen to be involved. All the immigrants follow in the footsteps of specialist predecessors, reactivating familial links and not creating new ones. There are six phases in the dynamics of office incumbency, a mechanism which allows for both the continuance of familial ties with the homeland and the continuity of structural integration in Gondo. These phases correspond with status sequences for individual immigrants as follows:

(1) émigré
Utilizes home-based ties to make a descent upon Gondo.

(2) affine or client
Establishes affinal ties with Gondo residents, or is sponsored by a neighbor.

(3) settler
Acquires land and becomes established in an occupational niche. Children are sent to the homeland for schooling and live with kin for most of the year. Marriages are contracted in the homeland.

(4) valetudinarian
Reaching the age of about 60, decides to return to his own country "to die" and invites in a successor from his home village or kin group.

(5) incomer
The potential incumbent. He arrives in Gondo, possibly with wife and children, and lives with the outgoing specialist.

(6) incumbent
The newcomer takes over the specialist office in Gondo as the valetudinarian leaves the parish.

The length of settlement of individual specialist craftsmen and traders in Gondo and the structure of their homestead groups can only be understood through this concept of incumbency substitution whereby "post fillers" occupy ecological niches established by earlier kinsfolk or fellow villagers from their homelands.

[165]

Nyoro of Gondo: Core or Substitution?

"Nyoro" (in generic or categorical terms, at least) were resident in Gondo long before British administration was established. Within the community, their affinal ties are with Pagero and Kenyi more than with their Bantu confrères. They have been settled in the parish longer and their affinal links mesh them more tightly into community life, since they are, on the whole, more closely related to core families than to any other groups in the community. A consideration of whether the Nyoro should be categorized as a core group or in terms of incumbency substitution highlights the distinctive content of each concept.

Nyoro genealogies can be traced within the parish over three generations, but, unlike the Teso, Pagero, and Kenyi, no core lineages have developed. Nyoro movement away from Serere County has been increasing since 1915.

As early as 1913 Gondo's parish chief had complained about having Nyoro under his jurisdiction, and an administrative program to move Nyoro from all parts of the county to place them under their own chiefs at Kagwara led to a decrease in their landholdings in the parish. One Nyoro family in Opucet, cattle traders whose economic interests lay more in Teso than in Bunyoro, did not relinquish its hold on land but most others left. The largest exodus within living memory occurred between 1919 and 1925, and is well documented since the draining off of a taxpaying sector of the population caused Teso administrators some concern. The most recent emigration took place in 1963.

Fragmentation of ethnic status among the Nyoro themselves, which may also account for the failure of core patrigroups to develop, is due to their diverse origins. This may appear surprising since in the census the Nyoro appear as the fourth largest ethnic category in Gondo; but, sociologically speaking, the most important fact about *the* Nyoro of Gondo is that they do not make up a unified social group of any kind. Nyoro expansion eastward along the southern shores of Lake Kyoga between the fifteenth and nineteenth centuries led to the growth of separate small satellite states in such places as Bugerere, Buruli, Bulamogi, and Bugweri as well as in Serere, and Nyoro immigrants to Gondo now come from all these places. As a result, the units of Gondo society which fall into the category of "Nyoro" are so small and so numerous that none form viable social grouping on their own. Some family groups among the Nyoro, especially two Bazira lineages which are linked with Kenyi settlers in Adiding, Kabola, and Opucet, look like core families, but Nyoro may more profitably be considered in their synchronic aspect as clients and dependents of Kenyi and Pagero or as office incumbents. Difficulties of categorization only cause trouble to the anthropologist obliged to work with one frame of reference; Gondo residents are skillful in operating within several.

In Gondo a lack of distinction between the ethnic categories of Soga, Ganda, Kenyi, and Nyoro relates to the close similarities in their languages, the overlapping of occupational and religious statuses, and their tendency to operate as specialist incumbents. A Nyoro fisherman is likely to be called a Kenyi by many parishioners, as is a Soga shopkeeper, since most fishermen and most shopkeepers are Kenyi. A Soga who is a Luganda-speaker from Bulamogi, who belongs nominally to no universal religion, and who assists a Ganda butcher is himself described by many as a Ganda butcher and a Muslim, since this combination of statuses is common. An inquiry into social distance revealed that, except for a small percentage of leading citizens who were consistently identified correctly by all in the parish, "Bantu" were constantly confused.

Let us examine for a moment, then, the justification for considering the Nyoro to have no core family groups in Gondo. Bugerere families of the former sub-chief Kijanjaro have six residents remaining in the village; a Batabi/Bachwezi lineage has five; a Bagala lineage four; and two Baziro lineages of Hoima six and four residents each, in landholding units. Their size appears comparable with that of core family groups. Yet, the analytical category of core status must be withheld because, unlike the Teso, Kenyi, and Pagero, no elders of any of these families are buried in Gondo. Their pattern in this respect is that of retiring office incumbents and, in the light of Nyoro behavior, the Pagero practice of not only burying their elders in Gondo but also erecting above their graves large slabs of concrete takes on added significance. The Pagero are solidly staking a claim to land ownership and core resident status regardless of their traditions of a Buchopi-Bunyoro motherland. By contrast, there is among the Nyoro a constant stream of coming and going between Gondo and their "homeland" which exceeds anything to be found among Serere-bound core families. They do not share the same wider community, as do the Pagero. The children of Ganda, Soga, and Nyoro alike are usually sent to their homelands for education since instruction in Teso schools is in Ateso and English. Only Muslim children receive their education in the parish, where Lukenyi and Arabic are taught at the Qu'ran school attached to the mosque. The continuity of the Nyoro contingent in Gondo depends upon external replenishment as a continual mechanism whereas for core families this is a rare device used only when demographic necessity forces its operation. In the structural integration of Gondo, Nyoro vertical continuity brought about by incumbency ties interlocks with horizontal cohesion brought about by marriage with core families of Teso, Kenyi, and Pagero.[3]

Industrial Immigrants

In the past a contrast might have been made between the craftsmen whose working life was contained within the parish and the immigrant ginnery laborers who were more likely to be part of a wider national scene. Today, with the institutionalization of ginning operations within the parish, the performance by Africans of skilled tasks, and their acquisition of land within the parish, the concepts of office incumbency and incumbency substitution apply equally to both. This is not to say that all contemporary ginnery workers are office incumbents or that all are fully integrated into the community. Yet, ginnery labor is today a form of office comparable with the ecological niches created by steamer and rail services or the Post Office in the past. The ginnery similarly provides for office incumbents limited but enduring niches within the parish.

Of the present ginnery labor force 28.2 per cent reside permanently in Gondo (Table 14). The remainder come largely from Ogera and Ogelak (19 per cent), from which they travel daily, or from Soroti, Atira, Kyere, and Kaberamaido parishes (30 per cent) which are also not too distant. Of the total force of 137 seasonal migrants, only 12 come from distant Teso counties (Ngora, Kumi, Amuria, and Usuku); 4 from northern districts; and 2 from the south and west.

Acholi

Regular salaried work is at a premium in contemporary Africa, and a clear characteristic of ginnery employment in Gondo is the procurement and maintenance of niches for relatives and friends. Perhaps most successful at this have been Acholi employees, and their case histories serve to illustrate office incumbency and incumbency substitution among industrial immigrants. As we have seen, it was not the policy of the Protectorate Government to develop the northern savannalands of Uganda but instead to encourage migration southward in search of employment. Thus, during the 1920s re-

TABLE 14: COMPOSITION OF THE AFRICAN GINNERY FORCE

Ethnic Category	Number		
	On roll	Of Gondo men	Of seasonal migrants
Teso	95	20	75
Kumam	3	2	1
Karamojong	5	1	4
Pagero	3	1	2
Kenyi	12	1	11
Nyoro	13	9	4
Soga	8	1	7
Hima	2	0	2
Ganda	10	2	8
Acholi	12	8	4
Lango	9	5	4
Luo	4	1	3
Swahili	1	1	0
Lugbara	3	1	2
Alur	1	1	0
Dama	1	0	1
Kiga	0	0	0
Gisu	2	0	2
Not known	7	0	7
TOTAL	191	54	137
PERCENTAGE	100	28.2	71.8

cruiters went around Acholi District seeking laborers willing to undertake the tasks that the local people of Soroti refused to perform. No one comes just "out of the blue" to Gondo, and the earliest Acholi immigrants were recruited in Kitgum in September 1926 to carry out night soil removal in the township.

Of the eleven adult male Acholi in Gondo, three live in the township and eight in Opucet. A lorry driver who has worked for the ginnery under its various managements for thirty-one years (A 669) and the son of a former ginnery headman (A 670) live opposite the ginnery gates, and an Acholi tailor (A 671, a sister's son of A 669) at the *dukas*. The eight Opucet residents reflect the Acholi presence in 1936 when ginnery workers were, for 4 shillings, given grants of land there. Today for most of them this landholding establishes a base of operations for an assault on the ginnery employment procedure rather than a foundation for encapsulation in the community. As is the case with office incumbents generally, no attempt is made to expand the landholding.

The course of Acholi settlement and the home-based kin ties which immigrants articulate are shown diagrammatically. Incumbency substitution is clearly indicated by their demographic pattern. Few young children are reared in the parish and no old men die there. In four cases wives were brought from Acholi; in all other cases but one (A 670) local liaisons are maintained, for Gondo is renowned for its available women. "The reason I like living in Gondo better than in Acholi," said old Otoo (A 542), "is that the women in Gondo are got for free, but in Acholi it is only when you pay some cattle that you can get one." Such liaisons are in accord with Gondo Teso values. A girl who lives with a man before marriage is, in Ateso, an *apapero*, "a friend." Should she live with many men in this way she will be deemed *amalayat*, a "prostitute." Most of the Acholi liaisons have lasted over fifteen years, including that of Otoo. All three of the present generation of elders established themselves in Gondo by stay-

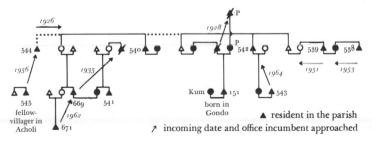

ing with local women. Later immigrants then asserted kin ties through them.

An exception to Acholi incumbency substitution and an illustration of passage from this status is the family of Anderea Oyat, a former ginnery headman, represented now by the homestead of his son, Asani (A 670). This young man was born in Gondo, where his father is buried, is married to the daughter of a Kumam neighbor (Kum 682), himself an affine of a core Teso lineage. One of his sisters has married a local Pagero (P 228) and the other has married a Lango in Lira.

Most Acholi maintain strong ties with their homeland which, by ferry and bicycle travel through Kaberamaido, is not too distant. In the cotton season, those in Gondo become hosts for youths from their home villages who are seeking seasonal employment. So regular is the turnout of Acholi residents when the time comes round for ginnery employment that they are able to count on specific jobs being allocated to them year by year. The management is able to rely on them for a 28-day month, the only group of individuals for whom this is true. Opilo (A 669) and Owino (A 544) have been lorry driver and night watchman respectively for over 30 years, and others have similar more highly paid jobs as oil boys, bale makers, press boys, and office boys. Otoo's daughter's husband (A 543), his heir apparent, is, as a newcomer, the only Acholi to be a mere porter earning only 80 shillings a month. Asani (A 670) is the only Acholi to follow the more usual Gondo pattern of taking employment only on the days that suit him: he is, as we have seen, the only Acholi to be Gondo-born, a cultivator, and less an office incumbent.

Variation on the Theme of Office Substitution

Ginnery employment in its more specialized forms encourages the use of a circuit of incumbency rather than a dyadic flow between "homeland" and parish. Thus groups of brothers will each work for short periods at one ginnery and then vacate their positions to younger brothers, they themselves moving on to take over the positions of older siblings, uncles, or friends. This practice illustrates both the high value placed on permanent wage employment and the restricted nature of landholding for an office incumbent. A group of Ganda brothers (of whom G 668 is one) operate rotating incumbency substitution within a circuit of ginneries in Masaka-Jinja-Soroti-Gondo-Usuku. Similarly, the brothers of Asani (A 670) "follow" a Gondo-Arapai-Mbale-Lira ginnery circuit, since there is land and a homestead for only one adult male and his family attached to the Gondo niche.

Office incumbency as a form of ecological adjustment to the requirements of trade and the modern commercial ginnery is but one ascriptive mode of entry into Gondo. In the past another way was through the sponsorship of Asians or Europeans who were connected with these institutions. Many men brought into Gondo as cooks, household servants, tailors, or porters did not return to their natal villages when their masters left the parish but instead used their contacts, their brokerage positions, and their wages to establish niches for themselves in the community, rapidly acquiring more permanent statuses. Both Gawera, the hotelkeeper (N 639), and Opolot (Kum 682) came into the parish as cooks for European households, similarly, as we have seen, Odico (T 606) and Ejau (T 401) were brought in as tailors by Asians. These four men are among the most prominent spiralists in the community. In a similar manner the first Luo fishermen were brought to Gondo's shores in the 1930s by a European company hoping to exploit the Lake Kyoga waters. Later Luo immigration was encouraged by the administration, which hoped that their deep-water fishing techniques would be emulated by the indigenous Kenyi.[4] Later, as with all incumbents, these men were joined by heirs from their homelands.

These intermediary types of office incumbents—neither peasant-type specialists nor appointed officials—come into the community as the society opens up. For this reason they appear to be the most dynamic; their particular status upon entry (under the patronage of external institutions) seems to carry less risk when it comes to manipulating the entrepreneurial aspects of their positions. However, before enterprise can be initiated, the niche in the society must first be made secure, and four brief case studies serve to illuminate the process by which this is done:

T 607 STANISLAUS ERENGU

Now aged 41, Erengu was born in Usuku. He came to Gondo from Ngora in 1961 to work as a jobbing carpenter at the ginnery. His career is of interest as it shows the fate of a man no one will fully sponsor. Erengu left his office incumbency (the ginnery lines having provided him with a roof over his head initially) and lived for a while in a hut on the land of a Kenyi in Adiding. He was not sponsored and moved for a short while again to the house being built for the parish chief, upon which he had been engaged to work. When this was destroyed by arson he moved, again for a short while, into the house of Stephen Opilo, who was then in prison. On Opilo's release, Erengu was given permission to build a hut on Akora's land (T 611), but he has not been given permission to cultivate. At the moment he borrows a garden seasonally from Elamu (T 601), the ward head of the township. It is unlikely that he will stay much longer in Gondo.

T 521 MULISIO OPAGI

Opagi is aged 25 and was born in Kadungulu, a parish to the south of Gondo. He first came to work in the ginnery in 1964, living in the ginnery lines. At work he met Raymond Obwonyo (A 543) who offered to let him use some of his land. Opagi has built his house and has been cultivating for two seasons, awaiting the approval of Obwonyo's neighbors. He sometimes works as a herder for Opolot (Kum 682). He says that he works at the ginnery only for tax. Although his family has land in Kadungulu, it is insufficient for its needs and there is a possiblity that Opagi will settle in Gondo. He is not married but has an *apapero* (mistress).

T 502 CHRISTOPHER OMODING

Omoding, aged 27, was born in Kapiri, Ngora. He came to Gondo in 1961, to work in the ginnery where his mother's brother had worked before him. He acquired land in 1964, being sponsored by Apila, an elderly Lango (L 549) who has no heir and is likely to return to Lango shortly. He became friendly with Apila because both worked as pressboys together at the ginnery. Omoding says that he likes Gondo "because all the people are brothers; they don't quarrel all the time as they do in Kapiri. However, the educational facilities are better in Ngora." Omoding plans to settle permanently and has built a large, tin roofed house. He currently lives with an *apapero* (mistress). It is possible that he will marry a daughter of Ocen (T 512), *emorimor* until January 1967.

T 601 ELAMU

Now aged about 52, Elamu was born in Kaberamaido parish. His father came to Gondo to work on the steamer service bringing with him Elamu, his six-year-old son. Apart from four years in the army between 1944 and 1947 (with the KAR in Ceylon), Elamu has lived all his life in Gondo, inheriting house and land from his office incumbent father. Elamu married the Pagero daughter of Magongo (P 421), thus establishing marital ties with a core family. When his wife left him, he married a Teso from Ogelak. He has no children, but his present wife's brother is a member of his household. Elamu became Adiding ward headman in 1963.

These four selected cases illustrate the process by which an immigrant becomes a member of the community political arena. The important steps on the way, it will be seen, are, first, the acceptable manner of entry; secondly, the acquisition of a home; thirdly, the permission to own land on a permanent basis; and fourthly, the acquisition of a wife. Marital status is a prerequisite of adulthood and political status in the community and may also be a crucial factor in determining where the office incumbent goes from there. For some, this is the end of a status sequence; for others, it is the consolidation of a base at the beginning of a political career.

8

Outsiders

IN DISTINGUISHING THREE CATEGORIES of resident in Gondo in 1966-1967, I noted the existence of a small number of persons whom I termed "outsiders," individuals marginal to the political system of the parish as it exists today.

Marginal positions tend to protect ethnicity, and for the first time we can see ethnic status as the dominant status stressed in community interaction between certain individuals.[1] At the time of fieldwork in Gondo, two ethnic groups were clearly outside the community political arena: Asians and Hima. Temporal factors accounted for their marginality, for, in the past, the Asian segment of the society had had an important political role. There is no place for them, however, in the present microcosmopolitan society largely because of what is perceived to be their readiness to exploit the community to further their own operations in a wider sphere. If Asians linger on from the days of Edwardian melodrama, Hima are possibly role players in dramas yet to be written. The influx of Hima into Serere County has been so massive and so rapid that it is not surprising a structural lag exists. Since structural integration is a matter of degree, it is inevitable that, at any one time, some elements should be outside of the system. The structural contradiction of their presence in the parish is a function of change. Social reality does not form a coherent whole, and the inconsistencies that provide the anthropologist with an understanding of processes of social change are also essential to the definition of the system.[2] Without outsiders there is no in-group. The perma-

← A Hima herdsman

nent residence of the Asian and Hima outsiders within the community is an essential part of the self-recognition of its members.

The term "outsider" is taken from Maine's description of villages in southern India where he uses it to describe those who form no part of the organic aggregate to which the rest of the villagers belong. Such individuals are not villagers, but rather appendages solidly connected with it, having definite duties.[3] Unlike the true members of the community, however, their relations are not multiplex: they are permitted to activate only their ethnic statuses. Thus, in an inquiry put to a representative sample of Gondo parish which included the question, "Whom would you *not* marry?" only Asians and Hima were singled out for opprobrium, the former because their women do not work in the fields; the latter because "they smell"—an allusion to a former Hima custom of smearing the body with cattle dung and their current habit of smoking very strong tobacco. Together these two ethnic groups form only a small proportion of the total number of homestead owners in Gondo and only 4.3 per cent of the population as a whole. Parish-wide contact with them varies in intensity: all the Asians live in the township and, even on their evening strolls, rarely pass beyond its boundaries. The Hima, on the other hand, are scattered throughout the parish in every neighborhood except Aojabule (Table 15).

Apart from the Asians, the Hima are the only people who might be immediately recognized by their appearance. The tall, angular men are distinguished both by their features and by their slouch hats and idiosyncratic pipes. The clothing of their womenfolk is more colorful than that of any other Africans in Gondo. By virtue of their occupation, the Hima are scattered through the parish; nowhere is a group of Hima males ever seen. They are few in number and live in poor, grass huts on the land of the man whose herd they are mind-

TABLE 15: DISTRIBUTION OF HIMA AND ASIANS

Ward	Hima				Asians			
	Adult		Infant		Adult		Infant	
	Male	Female	Male	Female	Male	Female	Male	Female
Aojabule	0	0	0	0	0	0	0	0
Agologolo	0	0	0	0	0	0	0	0
Kabola	1	1	1	0	0	0	0	0
Adiding	1	1	1	1	0	0	0	0
Opucet	3	1	1	0	0	0	0	0
Township	3	1	0	0	4	2	2	1
TOTAL	8	4	3	1	4	2	2	1

ing. Many of them are bound only by one- to three-year contracts; everyone knows that Hima are transient.

Hostility against Hima is rationalized as being due to their
stealing calves or taking too much milk for sale so that calves
die. On the other hand, it is grudgingly agreed that Hima
have a way with cattle. The herds they mind are well behaved; and the Hima himself, walking behind the cattle, talking to them, whistling his directions, playing on his flute,
is seen to be a man with pride of occupation, a specialist.
Yet there is no permanency in his office holding: a man can
herd his own cattle; the cattle may die. Elsewhere in Teso,
Hima are the constant object of attacks at night, not because
of ethnic antagonism in itself but because, living in isolated
homesteads and known to have cash on the premises from
their daily sales of milk, they are most vulnerable. And it
is well known that no neighbor will respond to the cries of
a Hima.

It is tempting to look for the causes of this hostility in the
relationship of Teso with their cattle. Although they themselves (in Gondo, at least) showed none of the loving care

that true pastoralists are supposed to feel for their herds, they have a cattle ethos which manifests itself in childhood games and a complex ritual symbolism linking cattle with lineage structure. The presence of Hima in their midst gives visibility to the contradictions in the Teso value system. It shows, for one thing, that some men in the community have achieved more than others.

The Hima herdsmen in the village, like the cattle, represent loose ends. Their lives are not knotted into the whole. They represent ties with other places rather than community integration, even as do the cattle they herd. They represent within the community a visible reminder that the outside world can impinge, and that it is alien, and thus, by definition, hostile. Hima look different; they dress differently; they speak a language no one else shares. They are seen as exploiting the community, giving nothing in return.

Yet even here, the case is somewhat different in Gondo from the rest of Teso. Elsewhere in the district, many of the Hima are members of the proselytizing, evangelical Balokole movement, and this doubles the antipathy felt toward them by the people among whom they live.[4] In Gondo, however, on Christmas Day, Nakumusana's Hima attended the Native Anglican Church along with his family. He, like the ethnographer, arrived an hour too early—an indication that he too was a stranger unused to the ways of the parish—but he joined the community.

Moreover, and more importantly, one Hima family appears to be permanently settled in Gondo. Most of its members are dispersed throughout Serere County, from Mpingire in the east to Kagwara in the west, individual males herding the cattle of Teso, but their nodal core lies in Gondo township where the old man, the father, lives with two of his sons, a daughter, and several grandchildren. They do not work the land, but they have built a rambling warren of semipermanent mud and wattle huts at the foot of the hills. The older son has been accepted as a member of the gambling groups that play outside Eria's hotel—a popular member since he usually has cash and he usually loses.

It is too early to tell whether time will justify the choice made by this Hima family to settle in Gondo, but it seems possible that their decision to do so reflects the diminishing administrative intervention in the affairs of the parish referred to earlier. Throughout the district, the administrative belief that the employment of Hima herders hindered Teso cattle breeding and the development of a cattle market bequeathed to the Hima a scapegoat role in relations between cattleowners and the veterinary officer. This has been consistently expressed in complaints taken up by the District Council in its more chauvinistic moods.[5] In Gondo, the parish chief aired his grievances freely:

The Banyankole don't build houses. They just build huts which look like anthills which are made of grass only. That is one of the problems I am facing. If you tell a Munyankole to build a house, he doesn't know how. They only drink milk and buy cassava. They don't eat *atap* (millet gruel). Their children are fatter than the children of the Iteso and they send them to school. Many are permanent here in Gondo and are very, very rich, richer than the Iteso.

Attempts to discriminate statutorily against Hima have failed in Teso, but as throughout East Africa, there has been a long history of political discrimination against alien Asians. By 1966 it was clear that Asians had no place in the Gondo community. They are few in number. Two Hindus are employed by the ginnery and live there all the year round, one as a supervisor, the other as a mechanic. Their families are in Mbale and, though children join their fathers occasionally for vacations, most of the year the two men live alone at the ginnery. There is, however, a sharp contrast between them:

the mechanic lives in a stone house, mosquito-proofed and with electricity; consorts only with fellow Asians; and speaks only Gujerati and bad Swahili. The supervisor, on the other hand, lives in a tin shack which is always open to visitors, pays very little tax (an indication of his poverty), and speaks fluent Ateso. This man, Valji, came to Gondo from Gujerat in 1914, when he was eight years of age, to join his father who had a shop in the bazaar. Later he himself kept shops in Kadungulu, Kyere, and Ngora before returning to live in Gondo in 1955 when he obtained a job as a ginnery clerk. He is looked upon as a useful go-between by many of the parishioners in their dealings with the ginnery. They rely on Valji to see that they are not cheated. In response to a questionnaire (part of an inquiry into the workings of the cotton cooperative society in Ogera) many respondents gave Valji's presence as their reason for preferring to sell their cotton to the ginnery rather than to the African-run cooperative.[6] Yet Gondo comes to Valji; his world does not extend beyond the ginnery gates. It was most apparent from his answers to a Big Man inquiry that he had no sensitivity to statuses in the parish at large. Valji is the poor man's friend.

The remaining Asians in Gondo are a newly arrived Hindu shopkeeper who is unlikely to stay long as his prices are being undercut constantly by Mulisio, the Soga trader; and a seventy-year-old Sikh shopkeeper with a Somali wife. During the 1966–1967 cotton season the Hindu worked in the ginnery as a cotton inspector. The Sikh's shop is poorly stocked, and he appears to stay in business only because he rents his stoop to Odico (T 606) who works as a tailor during the cotton season. Singh had been in Uganda most of his life but in Gondo only five years.

The day of the Asian shopkeeper in Gondo is clearly over. The last of the successful traders left in 1963 when a wave of night-marauding *kondos* (a Luganda name for armed rob-bers and extortionists) swept Serere County. By 1966 most of them had set up in business in Serere or Soroti where street lighting and the presence of police give protection. During the 1966–1967 cotton season one of these men returned briefly to Gondo, but it was a poor season, the cotton price was low and business bad, so he went back to Serere at the end of the few cash-circulating months, cutting his losses. He did not return for the 1967–1968 season.

In Teso District long-standing administrative regulations discourage the alien trader from becoming a permanent settler in rural communities and small townships, but, even without this, the way of life of the Asian is so alien and inward-looking that he could never be integrated into an African community like Gondo. The Asian is a man of the outside world: in his person he is deeply encapsulated in an intricate web of family relationships that in no way impinges on that of the African. The place of the Asian in the economic sphere was fixed within the larger framework of the plural society. As an economic broker he introduced the African to the skills of the modern world and gave him access to tools and machinery that, in those days, would otherwise have taken a lifetime to acquire. The careers of many Gondo men who have made their way in the world owe much to their initial apprenticeships to Indian shopkeepers, tailors, and middlemen.

African shopkeepers and tailors have taken the places of Asians in the community life of Gondo and, since ethnicity does come into play in gaining customers and bestowing patronage, Asians are fast losing out. Only the ginnery remains in alien hands, and because the Gondo ginner is responsible for the selection of cottonseed strains for distribution throughout the Eastern Region of Uganda, a task for which high management skills and experience are demanded, it seems likely that this will remain so for some time to come.

Elsewhere throughout the country, ginneries are being taken over by African cooperative unions. In a sense then the ginnery, like the parish itself, is an anachronism outside of the mainstream of political activity—a situation in which it is somewhat firmly kept by the external pressures of the wider world.

PART THREE

9

The Politics of Agriculture

To ACHIEVE PRESTIGE and prominence in Gondo, a man must invest his status as a member of a core family or as an office incumbent in the agricultural activities of the community. To be a leader, he must gain a larger share of the resources of the community than the average villager, and he must invest these resources in building up a following in whose eyes he will be prestigious. Forces in the society may be seen to operate against such aggrandizement of the individual, not least among them the combined activities of other individuals who see themselves as challenged by the rising entrepreneur.

I want to describe the nature of the spiralism in a peasant economy and suggest that the spiralism of the individual may best be analyzed with respect to his agricultural transactions. We have been concerned mostly with social interaction; the introduction now of the concept of transaction brings us to a consideration of competition and conflict in the parish.[1] The political value placed on people, a scarce commodity in the agricultural community, leads to competition over the organization of work parties and plough teams in Gondo. Measures of success are cotton production and the sale of millet beer, the cash transactions that revolve around beer proving in the hands of a political entrepreneur a means of building up prestige and power in the parish.

Since the monetary economy is not pervasive (and could not be except for four months of the year when an outside supply of cash flows into the parish as payment for ginnery

← *Around the beer pot in Agologolo (above)*

← *A plough team (below)*

[187]

labor), cultivation needs unify the community. The status attached to land using rather than to mere land holding is a prerequisite for prominence. In Gondo's agrarian economy a high value is placed on egalitarianism and good neighborliness. Cash can buy porters, but it cannot buy prestige; for that it has to be reinvested in resources that are valued by the community at large. The most prestigious men in Gondo are not necessarily the wealthiest, although to acquire wealth is one way of acquiring the resources that are valued. Techniques of spiralism are thus established and restricted by community values which set bounds upon the behavior of a political entrepreneur. Gondo's community spiralists work through a sequence of status sets to rise above their fellows, usually a tedious and lifelong process in this rural community.

The process by which core family members and office incumbents spiral to prominence begins for both on the solid earth of the parish. To begin his ascent, a political entrepreneur has to own and work land in Gondo. Cultivation is a unifying force in the community, cutting across ethnicity and all other statuses. Only the Hima and the Asians do not cultivate. Crops are homogeneous as is technology, which, being simple, requires the cooperation of groups. These are, for the most part, mustered within neighborhoods; where they are not, this is politically significant. The heart of the transactional process in Gondo lies in the homogeneous agricultural routine of the parish, and the careers of Big Men depend upon their successful manipulation of the agricultural system. All, having entered the community by devious paths, then invest their status, so to speak, in the same competitive arena.

The political struggle in Gondo may thus be seen as revolving primarily around agricultural transactions. At the outset of a transaction political actors aligned themselves in groups, segments of human activity upon which the analyst focuses for the purposes of one specific inquiry. The membership of groups is determined by the nature of the transaction, which is seen analytically as a dialectal process. "The trans-action regards both sides of the group struggle as a single process. Each side gets its meaning from that struggle. One does not exist without the other. The meaning of one side *is* its relation to the other side."[2] A distinction between social interaction and transaction emphasizes an acceptance by the actors involved in transactional relations not of a common set of shared values but merely a mutual recognition of a value specific to a situation. Notions of competition for scarce values and the restriction of access to the strategic resources of the society do not challenge the usefulness of the distinction but represent at the macro level the outcome of a series of field situations characterized by transactional competition, "sequences of interactions which are systematically governed by reciprocity."[3] The ideology of transaction exists to a marked degree in the rural peasant communities, and political actors operate on the assumption that, first, they have a secure support group within which reciprocal relations are en-trenched (in Gondo this is the cluster or *atutubet*) and, sec-ondly, that beyond this group, all must compete for coopera-tion. Conflict also arises from discrepant values and less than fully compatible commitment to the rural transactional ethos.

To some extent, the moral interaction of core families, the moral interaction of the office incumbent with his heir, the home-based network in which he is encapsulated, and the ethnic solidarity of Asians represent, in Gondo, relationships of incorporation in opposition to transactional relationships. It is necessary to define the field of social action involved in each case since there is a clear movement in such groups away from descent and incorporation toward alliance and the establishment of transactional relationships.

The principle of reciprocity underlies the existence of the office incumbent in the community since the office holder acquires a smallholding in the parish and permanency of tenure in exchange for his specialist services. It also underlies the whole system of sponsorship. Indeed, our taxonomy of Gondo residents may be viewed as a recognition of their varying involvement in the transactional system from which, for example, migrant workers living in labor lines are excluded, as are transient herders and all those who do not possess land. The officials of the externally controlled institutions are excluded as are the Asians in independent commercial enterprises, since these actors operate within a wider political arena unbounded by Gondo's set of values. Transactions involve competition for what is valued within Gondo situations, and this competition is between permanent landholding individuals regardless of whether they are core family members or office incumbents.

The Value is People

The tempo of the agricultural routine mobilizes people, regardless of ethnicity and neighborhood, in a round of common activities. In its day-to-day aspect much of the manual labor is carried out by women, but the need for timely and sizable labor organization for weeding and harvesting demands the activity and cooperation of men regardless of their primary occupations. This need for timely agricultural action cannot be overemphasized.[4] Time is a crucial consideration in planning agricultural activities. Food crop planting has to be carried out when cotton demands are heaviest; weeding and cotton picking have to race the rains. The demands of the cotton crop—clearing new land, weeding, and picking—all call for a concerted effort if the needs of subsistence are not to be foregone. While the routine of the women with regard to food crops is leisurely and ordered, the growing of cotton entails harassment and anxiety. The small modern homestead is neither a viable labor unit nor a self-sufficient production unit in Gondo. Many agricultural tasks are beyond the capabilities of the nuclear family working alone if best advantage is to be taken of seasonal variation. Erratic rains are chiefly responsible for the pressing need for timely planting and sowing, picking, and weeding of cotton. If any one operation lags, the rest suffer.

The amount of land owned is less important in determining production than the amount of labor that a man can call upon. In the deployment of agricultural labor, women and adolescent children are wholly appendages of the head of the household, and agricultural transactions largely involve competition between men for the cooperation of their neighbors. The main expression of, and vehicle for, such competition revolves around the composition of work parties. These are used mainly for weeding, harvesting, and clearing operations. In Gondo they are institutionalized as eitai (from the verb *aita,* to work for beer), and this is their distinguishing characteristic. Work parties rewarded with millet beer coexist alongside wage labor on a daily and monthly basis.[5] Cooperation is also required for ploughing, a transaction which involves reciprocal labor relations or the hiring of a plough and oxen, perhaps along with the ploughing team, for cash.

Neighborhood Work Parties

Work parties are used for weeding and harvesting millet (June–August), heaping sweet potatoes (June–July), and weeding cotton (June–November). For these tasks a group of between nine and twenty people is usually mustered by invitation. Sometimes a written message is sent but more frequently the word is passed on—*Loso eitai ore Ocen aicap epamba* ("Arrangements are being made to work at the home of Ocen weeding cotton")—and the day or days named. It is said that the number of workers invited depends upon the amount of millet beer available for their payment, but, in fact, each man is found to have a set of persons he always invites and who may be said to make up his eitai group. If he has enough beer for this group for two days' drinking, the work will last two days even though it could be finished in one by a larger group. Only under stress conditions when every man wants to muster a large work party on the same day is the system tested.

An ironic correlation exists between rainfall, the prolixity of weeds, and yields of finger millet planted with the rains, whereby beer for work parties always seems to become available the year after it is required. Frequently it happens that the more need there is for eitai, because of the rapid growth of weeds with the heavy rains, the less millet there is for brewing eitai beer, although the promise of the following year is excellent—provided some other means of obtaining labor can be found to stop the weeds from choking the growing millet. The home that produces and is able to store a great deal of millet, not being obliged to sell it for cash as the hungry months proceed, can make most use of eitai organization, while poorer homes are rarely able to exploit it at all.

Such management of resources requires entrepreneurial attitudes, initiative in administering resources, and the pursuit of an expansive economic policy. Above all, it requires the organization and coordination of many interpersonal relationships in order to succeed in entrepreneurial endeavors. In Gondo beer is considered to be payment for work, and men cannot organize work parties at their homes if they lack either women to brew the beer or millet for its foundations.[6]

Most work parties consist of both men and their wives; sometimes the group consists only of men and sometimes only of women. When men and women work together, they drink separately afterward, the men indoors and the women outside under a tree; but there is no fixed rule that calls for their segregation. When the drinking group that follows eitai is mixed, a wife always sits at the side of her husband since the etiquette of commensality is not relaxed. An explanation is given that a man may not sit next to his wife's consanguines; to put the emphasis in structural terms the other way around, a wife, by positioning herself at a distance from her brothers and fathers, indicates her movement away from her natal lineage and into that of her husband. Politically, she has become a member of her husband's support group.

Since work parties are in operation for six months of the year, from June to November, their effect in keeping visible the prestige of those in command of the labor resources, as well as their integrative function, is evident. Work usually begins soon after daybreak and continues until midday when participants return to the home of the organizer and deposit with his wife their hoes, knives, or baskets, ready for the next day's work. They then go briefly to their own homes to wash and change before returning to the eitai homestead for beer. Usually they will sit around the beer pot until dusk or even later, so that five hours' work is followed by six or seven hours passed in talk, game, and drink.

At the peak of the harvest season or when weeding is exceptionally heavy, an individual may be engaged in work parties five days out of seven, moving from the gardens of one member of the group to another. A man who cannot take part when he is asked to do so sends a substitute, usually a kinsman, sometimes a wife. Such an arrangement is essential for those who have herding duties or for men like Ekweru (T 210) who became the coordinator (*emorimor*) in January 1967. The services of an eitai group are never lost as long as beer can be provided for its payment.

Although on any one occasion a work party is mustered by an individual, reciprocal obligations underlie its composition and a pattern of interaction may be discerned. A man works, just as he plays, primarily among equals. Only in this

[193]

way can the potlatching of reciprocity be avoided. A record
of work parties formed in Agologolo in 1966 and 1967 illustrates this. In Agologolo there are two categories of cultivator
as far as eitai is concerned: those who cooperate and those
who do not. Twenty-five cultivators are involved, Ocaet, the
parish chief, being excluded since he employs porters to
assist his wives and plays no part in the systemic transactions.
He is not a contender for the prestige stakes of the community.

An economic profile of the Agologolo residents is given in
Table 16. Four men are too poor to take part in eitai: Ekamu
(T 204), Okasu (T 216), Okello (P 226), and Ocoto (P 223).
The first two live alone, Ekamu being described as simple-
minded and Okasu because his three wives have left him
since he is "sick in the mind sometimes." Ekamu occasionally joins his brothers' work parties. Okasu explained their
predicament:

I can't take part in the *eitai* proper (i.e. the reciprocal transactions) ; all I can do is join an *eitai* group for one day if anyone asks
me to do so. I can't belong to an *eitai* group because I am alone
now with no wife to prepare beer to drink after the work.

Ekamu, along with Okello, sometimes works as a wage laborer for the parish chief or men such as Odico (T 606) in
the township. Zirimenya Ocoto, the Pagero sister's son of
Aringa (T 219), is too poor to do eitai although he has a
wife. He has too little land for his family needs (three gardens
and two plots only), and his poverty was officially recognized
in 1967 when his tax was reduced from 60 to 50 shillings,
one of the few cases of tax reduction in the village. Every
other man in the ward (except old Odongo who is too old
and feeble to leave his homestead) is a reciprocating member
of an eitai transaction.

In Agologolo three basic groupings form the minimal units
of transaction (Figure 13). Most men are able to muster only

TABLE 16: WEALTH PROFILE OF AGOLOGOLO HOMESTEAD HEADS

Number	Name	Amount of Land in Gardens and Plots a	Number of				Cotton Income in Shillings		Tax Payment in Shillings	
			Ploughs	Oxen	Cattle	Wives	1965/6	1966/7	1965/6	1966/7
T 217	Ocaet	10/6 +	1	10	8	4(3)	1489	268	60	100
P 224	Egimu	8/3	1	2	4	1	657	NKb	60	60
T 219	Aringa	10/5 +	1	2	8	1	485	199	60	60
T 210	Ekweru	6/4	—	—	—	2	400	280	60	80
P 228	Wagule	5/2 +	1	4	13	2	295	240	60	60
T 203	Ogola	4/3	1	4	10	1(2)	286	NK	60	50
P 227	Enyengu	3/2	—	—	—	1	280	140	60	60
T 215	Okot	6/2	—	—	—	1	275	85	50	60
P 226	Okello	4/2	—	—	—	1	271	148	60	60
T 212	Eladu	4/2	—	—	4	1	250	198	60	60
K 222	Wabwire	5/2	1	2	—	1	250	180	60	60
P 225	Oparo	4/1	—	—	—	1	248	220	60	60
P 229	Lasile	3/2 +	1	—	—	2	245	120	50	60
T 201	Okello	9/4	1	4	17	1	245	169	50	50
T 202	Esangu	3/4	—	—	—	1	245	140	50	50
T 221	Oriada	4/2	—	—	—	—	198	140	50	60
T 209	Ouna	4/2	—	—	—	—	189	98	PETc	PET
T 216	Okasu	5/2	—	—	—	1	NK	90	60	60
T 218	Ocomu	5/2	—	—	—	1	150	120	50	60
T 211	Opit	4/2	—	—	—	—	150	98	50	60
T 208	Ocele	4/2	—	—	—	—	150	85	50	60
T 206	Opulo	4/-+	—	—	—	—	150	50	50	50
P 223	Ocoto	9/2	—	—	—	1	148	94	60	50
T 205	Angata	2/2	—	—	—	—	140	140	40	50
T 207	Enyang	2/2	—	—	—	1	125	100	60	60
T 204	Ekamu	4/2	—	—	—	—	95	63	50	50
T 213	Oluko	4/2	—	—	—	1	—	—	50	60

a. For the measurement of land in gardens and plots, see Chapter 4, fn. 2.   b. Not known.
c. A pensioner and/or one who is exempted from paying tax on account of age, disability, etc.

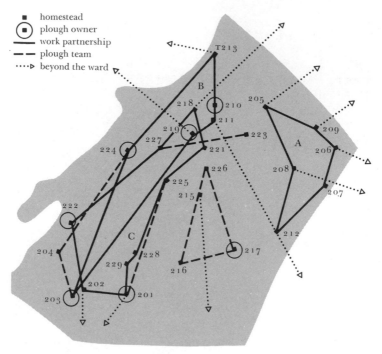

FIGURE 13: WORK PARTIES AND PLOUGH TEAMS
IN AGOLOGOLO

one of these; only four men are able to aggregate more than
one. This means that these four men control twice as much
labor as the average cultivator. The composition of the minimal groups is as follows:

GROUP A: *men 6, women 6*
This group consists of the six sons of Angata of the Ilale clan.
Four of them also work land in Kabola but only the heir, Opulo
s/o Angata, has more land there than in Agologolo. This land
crosses the boundary and Opulo also belongs to a Kabola work
party.

GROUP B: *men 6, women 10*
This group consists of Ekweru (T 210), head of the Ilale, and

[196]

his two sons (T 211, T 213). Elija Aringa (T 219), of the Imodoi lineage, belongs but not his brother or son, both of whom are politically independent of the head of the family. Aringa and his son (T 221) fought over bridewealth cattle and Aringa's brother, Ocomu (T 218), quarrels constantly with Ekweru over boundaries. For Aringa to be in the same work party as Ekweru, his own brother has to be excluded from it. It pays him to do just this.

With the inclusion of Egimu s/o Mujwala (P 224) and Martin Ogola (T 203), his wife's brother, the composition of this group cuts across ethnicity, contiguity, and herding relations. The help of a large work party is more valuable to the individual than any of these. This group musters a large number of women since the four elders' seven wives, one adult daughter, and two adult sons with their wives regularly take part.

GROUP C: *men 9, women 11*

This group contains members of all the core ethnic groups of the parish. The fulcra of the group are Benefasio Okello (T 201) and Musa Wagule (P 228), each of whom has two wives and many cattle. Wagule and his son (P 229) have land in Adiding among their Pagero kinsmen in addition to the acres in Agologolo. Okello's land lies across the Aojabule boundary and he takes part in *eitai* there as well. He shares ploughing activities with a partner in Aojabule as well as with Ogola (T 203).

Structurally Group B appears to be the interlocking eitai unit, largely because Egimu and Ogola are brothers-in-law. (Again we note the function of women in relating groups in the community.) From the point of view of individual trans-actions in the competition for the labor force of the neighbor-hood, Group B contains the only four men who are able to count on dependents from the other two groups, thus:

Big Man	Groups
Ekweru (T 210)	A and B
Aringa (T 219)	A and B
Ogola (T 203)	B and C (plus poor Ekamu)
Egimu (P 224)	A and B (plus two members of C plus Okello, the single man)

These four men are among the wealthiest and most influential in the ward. Their comparative wealth may be assessed from their cotton production, itself an indication of ability to form work parties (Table 15). There is political significance in the fact that all four, unlike the rest of Agologolo, market their cotton at the cooperative store rather than at the ginnery.

A mechanism at work in agricultural transactions in Gondo which encourages the greater interaction of cohorts (men of the same life experience) and coevals relates to the amount of land and the number of cattle, wives, and adult daughters a man has. Ogola's somewhat marginal economic position in eitai group B in 1966 is due to his once having had two additional wives whom he has not yet replaced. Temporal factors are reflected in the static model.

Ploughing Teams

Not all men in Gondo own ploughs. There are thirty-nine in all, or (since one man has two ploughs) one plough for every 6.1 land users. Their distribution is not uniform throughout the parish since 35 per cent of Aojabule cultivators have their own ploughs compared with only 8.1 per cent in Opucet.

All plough owners are actual or potential Big Men in the community. Those names italicized in Table 17 belong to individuals we have already seen to be potential Big Men in the society by virtue of either their genealogical positions in core families or their large holding of land, or both. Large landowners may be expected to have ploughs, and this is, indeed, the case. The only exceptions are two landowners in Kabola more interested in fishing than in their marginally productive land: Okasu, the Agologolo man whose wives have left him; and one young landholder in Aojabule (T 105) who works as a carpenter for Gondo boatbuilders. Owning

TABLE 17: DISTRIBUTION OF PLOUGHS AND
PLOUGH OWNERS

Ward	Number of Residents	Ploughs	Plough Owners	Code Number	Resident Status
Aojabule	20	8	Eliedu	T 116	C
			Odera	T 114	C
			Abilo	T 111	PC
			Anyapo	T 109	Cd
			Ekwaru	T 104	PC
			Ekwaru	T 104	PC
			Okiror	T 108	C
			Okwi	T 103	PC
Agologolo	26	7	Ocaet	T 217	—
			Egimu	P 224	C
			Aringa	T 219	C
			Wagule	P 228	C
			Ogola	T 203	C
			Wabwire	K 222	Cd
			Okello	T 201	C
Kabola	35	6	Otieno	T 302	PCd
			Ogamba	N 332	Cd
			Sharif	K 315	C
			Ajula	K 305	C
			Wandira	K 311	C
			Mwereza	K 314	Cd
Adiding	28	2	Nakumusana	K 418	C
			Emenu	T 402	C
Township	103	11	Mukasa	P 632	C
			Ogot	J 692	O
			Mukaya	N 651	O
			Gawera	N 639	O
			Bin Salim	S 658	O
			Opolot	Kum 682	O
			Elamu	T 601	C
			Oreda	T 610	O
			Akora	T 611	C
			Odico	T 606	O
			Mugala	P 634	O
Opucet	62	5	Okurut	T 506	C
			Elasu	T 517	C
			Asilo	P 527	C
			Kamusera	N 528	O
			Kinunge	N 532	O

a plough gives control of a commanding resource in the community; and the several men of high status by other criteria are among the ploughowners, as well as spiralists who, although they have not yet attained Big Man status, appear strategically well placed to do so.

Ploughing teams generally consist of three or four persons including the owner of the plough or oxen. Each member is entitled to three days' ploughing of his own land in return for helping the owner. Under normal conditions, one large garden takes two mornings to plough, working from seven until ten. The maximum number of hours that oxen may be spanned is restricted by district statute. The plough is used to prepare two gardens for each member of the team in turn and then may be hired out either complete with team or simply as owner with oxen and plough. Some ploughing teams have worked together for more than ten years. To hire a plough, oxen, and porters costs a man between 30 and 45 shillings depending upon the acreage to be ploughed. Out of the money, the owner pays the two porters 3 shillings each upon the completion of the task.

Oxen may be borrowed from those who have more than four and, in return, ploughing is done for the owner of the oxen. Whether two or four oxen are required to pull the plough depends largely upon the condition of the soil. At the time of borrowing, the hirer may plough three of his own gardens and one for the owner of the oxen. It is a common sight between March and May to see ploughs being carried on the backs of bicycles from one homestead to another.

Just as there are more plough owners than oxen owners in the parish, so there are more individuals without either. Although the cost of neither plough (40–60 shillings) nor oxen (400 shillings) is exorbitant, nevertheless the concentration of ploughs and oxen in the hands of a few individuals is apparent. Since ploughs are in use for only four-and-a-half months of the year at most and oxen are not used for any other forms of draught, it is more economic to share the capital investment even at the cost of loss of profit due to late planting. This being the case, the actual investment in a plough indicates entrepreneurial initiative that is out of the general run.

Since time is a crucial factor in the preparation of land for planting, agricultural needs drive an individual beyond the bounds of his own neighborhood for ploughing partners.[7] In most cases links with mother's brothers, sometimes with sisters' husbands, are called into play in the formation of regular ploughing teams. Among Agologolo's twenty-six homesteads, for example, there are fourteen ploughing groups. Of these, only four are wholly contained within the ward. Others are formed in cooperation with partners in Adiding and Kabola and in the neighboring parishes of Ogelak and Ogera. Where ploughs are not shared in this way, they can be hired for cash. Five plough owners hire out their ploughs on a regular basis: two Aojabule owners (T 116 and T 104) annually to a Nyoro and a Kumam (Kum 679) in the township, and three townships owners (N 651, Kum 682 and T 611) to residents in a different part of their own ward. Akora (T 611) is the only plough owner to operate on a large-scale basis, hiring his plough out seasonally to five regular customers. With the exception of Elamu (T 601), none of the Big Men of the community exploit their ploughs for cash. All share on a neighborly basis, alliances outweighing cash transactions.

Ownership of a plough gives the entrepreneur a further resource for the building up of reciprocal obligations and for making alliances. By sharing with his neighbors he incurs dependents: since there are twice as many potential plough groups as ploughs and since the amount of land held is fairly uniform, there is a favor bestowed on those a man agrees to recognize as partners. Yet the essence of timing imbues cooperation with conflict, and so the socially dangerous resource is shared with those with whom relations are already ambivalent or stressful, with affines and mothers' brothers, so that relations are not imperiled. Similarly those who loan their ploughs for cash do so to cultivators who are neither close neighbors nor potential supporters.

In Gondo, the delayed planting which results from this peripatetic use of ploughs could be avoided by engaging a tractor from the group farm at Labor, twenty-five miles away. This has been done only on one occasion. Although a garden can be ploughed by tractor in half an hour, there are disadvantages to the scheme which highlight both the system-binding effect of close relationships between working the land and reliance on neighbors and the forces that operate against the spiralism of an entrepreneur. A tractor costs only 45 shillings an acre, which is little more than plough hire, but the date of its hire has to be fixed well in advance, a prepayment being made. The tractor team is not sent such a distance unless there are several acres to be ploughed, and it is almost impossible, according to the Gondo men who have tried, to find one cultivator with sufficient acreage ready for planting at any one time, or sufficient cash to pay for this amount, or enough individuals willing to put their fields together to be ploughed by tractor.

The political structure of each ward partly accounts for this. Within his cluster (*atutubet*) each man is surrounded by dependents and is apart from coevals. Yet only coevals can share on an equitable basis the hire of a tractor. It is stipulated by the authorities that only adjacent strips of land may be ploughed in fulfillment of a contract. On the one occasion when the tractor was brought to Gondo, Otieno (T 302) persuaded Ekweru (T 210) to share its hire, their land being contiguous across the Kabola-Agologolo boundary and providing a sufficiently large acreage for the contract to be accepted. Odico (T 606) and Ogot (J 692) in the township and Anyapo (T 109) in Aojabule have all tried to persuade neighbors to cooperate in this way but have been unsuccessful.

Millet Beer and Cash Transactions

The command of labor resources both brings and reflects prestige. Since labor may be obtained by cash and beer transactions alike, it is in these spheres that the entrepreneur must handle his resources skillfully. Two distinct patterns of agricultural labor are found in Agologolo: on the one hand, cultivation for cash by the poor and unmarried men; and on the other, reciprocal, rotating work parties paid in beer. These same patterns are found throughout the parish although everywhere, except among Muslims abstemious of alcohol, the eitai is considered the ideal. Wealthy men in the township engage in eitai (although they may rather frequently send substitutes) and, at the same time, employ porters.

As might be expected, there is more employment for cash in the township than elsewhere in the parish, but the activities of the Agologolo cultivators suggest that this should not be thought of as a "modern" form of labor organization supplanting a "traditional" form. A work party is but one of several ways to organize agricultural labor, just as it is only one form of labor open to a resident in the community. Five Agologolo cultivators—Ogola, Egimu, Aringa, Musa Wagule and Ocomu—regularly employ cash labor for cotton picking, for instance. Others hire groups of four or five people (men and women) as the occasion demands. A hundred shillings is paid for the picking of a 45- by 120-yard cotton garden. If one man is hired for the task, he receives 120 to 140 shillings and is then responsible for subcontracting the job. To the owner it is worth the extra shillings to have the cotton picked more quickly.

[203]

The amount of labor paid in any one year depends upon weather conditions. All things being equal, a man and his wife with two children can generally keep pace with the cotton as it ripens. The demand for porters increases whenever cotton buds rapidly or heavy rains threaten to destroy the crop; and, once again, it is at inclement times that competition between Big Men comes out into the open. Cotton picking time coincides with both the harvesting of food crops and the penniless months, since cash is acquired almost wholly by selling the cotton crop and the last of this may well have been expended on house thatching, building, or school fees. Yet cotton picking is rarely paid for with beer. On the whole, the average household determines the amount of cotton to be planted by the labor it has available, and only exceptional wealth or exceptional climatic circumstances call forth cash labor.

The above-average householder (the agricultural entrepreneur and potential Big Man) looks at this time to other resources and opportunities. He finds one such opportunity in the sale of millet beer, one of the most profitable sources of cash in the agricultural community. Two types of beer are distinguished in Gondo and both, in different ways, become facilities in the political arena. Beer given to peers within a cluster, to work parties, and to ritual gatherings is known as *ajon* or "free" beer. Its gift sanctions the maintenance of reciprocal relations. *Esonde,* on the other hand, is "sold" beer which is available during the cotton season when everyone has cash enough for its purchase. A 5-shilling licence is supposedly required for the manufacture of esonde.

Some of the social and economic transactions involving beer and cash may be shown diagramatically. The value of millet beer as a political facility follows from the elements of the agricultural system. The availability of ajon for work parties is one of the factors making for higher status within a geron-

MARCH	APRIL	MAY	JUNE	JULY	AUG	SEPT	OCT	NOV	DEC	JAN	FEB
→	← WEEDING →			HARVESTING				←	COTTON SEASON		
				MILLET					*house building*		
	eitai groups								*and thatching*		
	rewarded			*hiring*					*school*		
	with beer			*porters*					*fees*		
									money in circulation		
	"EARNED"				"FREE"				"SOLD"		
→	← EITAI BEER →				← AJON BEER →	←			ESONDE BEER		

tocratic society in which some ascribed statuses are already valued. And, in this competitive arena in which the political value is people, esonde beer also operates, like ajon, to pave the way of the spiraling entrepreneur.

A bowl of millet beer sells for one shilling and is drunk from a gourd or calabash. Alternatively, and more usually, a customer pays one shilling to drink in company, sitting around a beerpot at the homestead of the brewer. Millet for esonde beer is rarely provided from domestic granaries but is nearly always bought. Those who need cash between August and November, when the cotton season begins, sell small quantities of millet to Gondo shopkeepers as their cash needs arise. Millet that is in excess of homestead needs (estimated by the number of households or wives with children) is about 25 per cent of the total harvested in a good year, and this is sold as a surplus as soon as the granaries become full between June and August. From three gardens, two sacks of scavenged millet (*emono*) can be gleaned, and this is straightway threshed and taken to be sold for 20 cents (one-fifth of a shilling) a plate.

Prestige and Visibility in the Agricultural Arena

Not everyone in the parish has sufficient cash before November to purchase millet for esonde brewing. For those who have, it is a profitable business and clearly not unrelated to the Big Man paradigm, involving amount of land, number of cattle, number of womenfolk, and the maximal aggregation of work parties. Besides needing ready cash to purchase millet from the shopkeepers, a man also requires many women in his household, for beer making is a time-consuming operation and the manufacture of esonde coincides with the cotton picking period when domestic group labor is at a premium.

To make three pots of beer requires 25 shillings worth of millet, and the actual time spent on its manufacture will be in the neighborhood of sixteen hours. This is the time actually spent at the homestead; time spent collecting firewood and fetching water varies according to the location of the home-stead. After the millet is ground and mixed with water and the fermenting yeast added, the mash must be left for seven days. It is then boiled again, and spread out for drying; water is again added and, after fermenting, it must be again left for three days, after which it is ready for sale. And all the while, the women engaged in its brewing are also called upon to pick and sort cotton, slice and dry sweet potatoes, fetch wood and water, cook, look after children, and perform other daily duties. The importance to an ambitious man of selecting a hardworking wife is apparent. The wife, too, acquires satis-faction and prestige from the progress of her husband.

Quantitative data on the sale of millet beer were collected in January 1967, halfway through the cotton season. In the whole of Gondo only eight men regularly had large quantities of beer (3–5 pots) for sale at their homes during this time. They were Odico (T 606), Ebelu (T 625), Opolot (Kum 682) and Amecu (Kar 687) in the township; Ocaet (T 217) in Agologolo; Ejau (T 401) in Adiding; Otieno (T 302) in Kabola; and Asilo (P 527) in Opucet. A further nine men in the township, five in Aojabule, five in Agologolo, four in Adiding and four in Opucet—twenty-seven in all—had between one and three pots of beer for sale twice or thrice a week for a few weeks of the season. The location of a man's household within the parish did not limit his opportunity to profit from esonde. Although Aojabule was too remote to attract cash customers, Ekwaru's daughter brought esonde to sell at the township home of Amecu, their former Karamojong herdsman. Similarly women from Opucet brought esonde to sell at Opolot's "licensed" homestead opposite the ginnery gate. George Henry Ebelu's brother's daughters came weekly from Akaboi, twelve miles away, traveling by evening bus with sacks of dry millet beer (akiria) to which water was added at Ebelu's house where it was sold.

Millet beer is not the only form of alcoholic nourishment in the parish. Nubian gin or waragi is also made and is more profitable although the profit is less elastic, since waragi customers take away a bottle whereas esonde buyers have their brew replenished with hot water as the evening draws on so that the beer grows weaker for increasingly unfastidious customers. An estimated profit of about 16 shillings is made on every twelve bottles of waragi; the profit from millet beer must fluctuate well over the hundred per cent mark. Banana and cassava brews are also in circulation, and bottled "European" beer is available at Eria's hotel. None of these forms of beer enters into the prestige and prestation system as does millet beer.

The nucleation of millet beer in both its forms around certain individuals in the village is reflected, of course, in the behaviorial patterns of consumers. The overall structure of drinking sets in Gondo and the interaction and transaction involved cannot be described here, but a delineation of the three types of drinking groups is relevant to an understanding of the power and prestige structures of the community. There are, first, small cluster (atutubet) drinking groups around their ajon; secondly, work parties rewarded with ajon; and thirdly, groups of individuals who sit together around esonde. A cluster, as we have seen, is composed of the moral support group of the individual. A work party is a group of dependents won by an individual through his success in the competition for agricultural cooperation. The last category of beer drinkers, comprised of groups of peripatetic individuals casually and occasionally brought together at the homesteads of brewers by their mutual possession of cash, serves to maintain the visible prestige of specific men. (Those who send their beer to be sold at the homestead of another gain cash but not prestige.)

Gradually, then, the composite circle of prestigious individuals has been narrowed down. Everyone belongs in a cluster; most men belong to cooperative work parties; a few may muster more than one—but only a very few indeed can maximize beer as a social lubricant for all twelve months of the year.

Crisis, Violence, and Arbitration

CONFLICT OCCURS OVER LAND, cattle, and women in Gondo; institutions exist to counter its expression and others to bring about its resolution. Both are, on occasion, ineffectual. It is in the daily operations of the elite as its members move about the parish tempering violence and mediating disputes that the consolidated nature of the gerontocracy and their command over the various mechanisms for enforcing social control within the range of their vested interests are most apparent. Beyond their jurisdiction much domestic violence occurs without mediation, patterned, for the most part, by seasonal economic activities. No conflict appears to be mounted along ethnic lines.

Much of the conflict in Gondo parish is reconciled through mechanisms of social control operating informally among small groups of kin and neighbors as they move in contact with each other in their daily activities. These mechanisms operate at all levels and range from "mother-in-law" avoidance and taboos on childbirth and affinal visiting to "customary" payments for the breach of peace at rites and ceremonies. Social control is maintained, too, through a recognition that sickness and death are due to antisocial behavior; informal discussions of their causes as well as healing and divination rites provide numerous occasions for reiterating social norms. The recently institutionalized registration of marriage procedure, with its recording of bridewealth, also operates to counter conflict. Those few marriages registered

← *Seller of sorcery medicine in the local market*

[211]

at the sub-county office are, as far as Gondo is concerned, contracts ripe with latent dispute: marriages of the elite and their offspring in which bridewealth is high and attenuated or intraethnic marriages. Occasions for open expression of hostility and rivalry arise when dance competitions (*atenus*) are held between villages. In the past these have seen physical violence, and carrying dance sticks is now banned as a result; nevertheless quarrels occur. It is on such occasions that Elamu (T 601), Gondo's best *atenus* dancer, appears as a Big Man. Within the community, hostility is often expressed through ribald songs composed to express disapproval of an individual's behavior. These songs ridicule those who have breached the norm: the fisheries officer who "stole" the catch of the poor man who fished without a licence; the sub-county chief who tried to "rob" a poor parishioner of his rooster on the way to market. Men who flaunt their power or abuse their office (as defined by the community) are subject to such constraints.

A distinction between competition and conflict suggests that power in relations between like groups—agricultural entrepreneurs, for example—be discerned as power in competitive relations—competition, in this case, for land and labor as political facilities. When the power relations are between unlike groups, we address ourselves to conflict.[1] Relations between like groups in Gondo involve cohortative politicking in the horizontal dimensions of the informal structure since egalitarian values are expressed; unlike relations evolve out of the confrontation of husband and wife, father and son, parish chief and parishioner, landowner and sponsored immigrant, employer and porter, ginnery management and labor, permanent landowner and transient herdsman. Conflict in these relationships has three possible outcomes: recourse to institutions for mediation and arbitration; retreat from the political situation; and open violence.

It is in their powers of arbitration that the Gondo elite is most evident. Quarrels at the domestic level, and all fights between women, are settled by male homestead heads; most of those occurring between neighbors are settled informally by ward headmen. A few may reach the hierarchy of courts or moots which are held in the community as the occasion arises. Within the community, power to determine intent in disputes is divided between three officials: the ward headmen, the coordinator (*emorimor*), and the parish chief. In general, when fighting is not serious, when quarrels concern cattle damaging crops or are between man and wife over money or small debts, the ward headman is called to the home of the complainant to decide the matter. Sometimes kin or neighbors join the discussion but rarely does the event draw persons from outside the cluster (*atutuben*). The ward headman's decision alone is usually accepted, and there are fairly standard rates of compensation. Should cotton be involved, however, or should the debt include cattle, or any financial matter over 100 shillings, the litigants are more likely to go straight to the emorimor for settlement. More serious fighting that might call for fines between 20 and 30 shillings also goes to the emorimor, as does extensive cattle damage and quarrels between persons of different wards. The parish chief handles all cases of serious assault, theft, and large debts. He is among the first to be summoned for murder, arson, or hamstringing and immediately escorts those involved to sub-county headquarters, from whence the Uganda Police post at Serere is informed. In 1966, 14 Gondo cases went for hearings at the sub-county level, most of them having reached there by appeal from one or more of the lower courts. Seven involved debt; four land; two divorce; and one compensation for injuries. In 1965, 18 cases were heard at the sub-county level, five involving debt; five divorce; three cattle damage; three tax offenses; one adultery; and one assault.

Quarrels, Fights, and Litigation

In discussing quarrels and fights, legal cases, and crime generally in Gondo, distinctions are made between three kinds of conflict: quarreling with words (in Ateso, *ecelet*); fighting with fists or sticks (*ejie*); and an accusation leading to a court case (*aiwosa*). An attempt was made, late in 1967, to obtain a clarification of the type of quarreling that does not reach the courts by carrying out a specific inquiry designed to supplement field observation. All respondents in the representative sample were asked to recall quarrels in their neighborhoods during the past few months. Of these, 50 per cent were over land, over cattle damaging crops, or over women, and a further 25 per cent were domestic disputes between husband and wife or quarrels over petty debts. The remainder concerned thefts (of hoes, cotton, or fishing nets), quarrels between fathers and sons over bridewealth cattle, altercations with the parish chief, blows being exchanged at beer parties, squabbles over ploughs, or work relations at the ginnery (Figure 14). Of these quarrels, few of which reached the courts, 53 per cent occurred in the Township, 43 per cent in Agologolo and Opucet, and only 4 per cent in Kabola, Adiding, and Aojabule, the more densely populated wards of the parish clearly proving the most conflict-ridden. The nature of each of these types of conflict will be examined in turn.

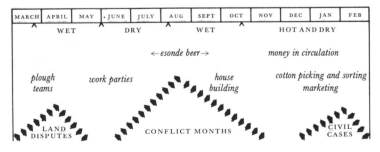

FIGURE 14: CALENDAR OF LITIGATION AND VIOLENCE

The most serious land disputes occurred seasonally in northern Agologolo where Ekweru (T 210) was in constant altercation with the sons of Angata over the amount of land he let them use, and with his neighbor Ocomu (T 218) who annually attempted to plough over boundaries in order to extend his own property. It is this persistent quarreling that sets Ekweru and Ocomu apart in different work parties (*eitai*) and, along with a related quarrel between Aringa (T 219) and his son Oriada (T 221) over cattle, aligns the entire ward into three political camps. Although shifts in eitai membership are rare, when they occur they reflect conflict, as the cases of Oriada, Ocomu, and Ocoto make clear.

The accounts these men give of why they have changed eitai groups are presented in their own words so that both the sequence of events and the rationale used may be seen:

OCOMU: I work in Okello's party now but since childhood I worked in Ekweru's but there I quarreled with Ekweru and Aringa over land for they had more land than I did and they used to plough over the boundaries of my land. I decided not to work with them any more and a few days later I was invited to drink *eitai* beer with Okello. I drank with his work party twice and on the third time I was invited to work for *eitai* beer which led me to join his party. This was in 1951. Now Okello has married my brother's daughter, there have been no quarrels and we get on well as work party members.

ORIADA: I share Okello's work party since I quarreled with my father and left Ekweru's group where my father never wanted to share beer with me. I was invited to work for *eitai* beer by Okello five years ago but I am now thinking of going back to Ekweru's group since my quarrel with my father is over. I recently quarreled with Okello because he stole my fishing nets (he was fined one ox and 50 shillings for this) and so I must leave his group for fear that further fighting will break out between us.

OCOTO: When I first came to Agologolo I drank with Ocomu and Ekweru's group but when they quarreled, Ocomu was invited to join Okello. I was not asked to stay on by Ekweru and so, because Aringa belongs to that group, I was for many years alone.

The rivalry of the Agologolo neighbors and kinsmen is apparent in their day-to-day squabbling, but when the question is one of support for Ekweru in competition with others for the office of ward headman, all except Ocomu subordinate their neighborhood differences and line up behind him.

Since Otieno (T 302) settled in Kabola, being given a portion of PWD land by the parish council at the urging of his sponsor, Odico (T 606), in 1951, quarrels have broken out periodically between Otieno and his two Kenyi neighbors, Sharif Musa (K 315 with his array of adult sons) and Wandira (K 321). All three men are spiralists through ginnery employment, commerce, and fishing respectively; both Otieno and Sharif have many wives (Wandira is currently a widower); all paid 80 shillings tax in 1966. Their dispute is made possible by the council grant of land not having built into it the safeguards of sponsorship outlined in Chapter 4, so that common boundaries are shared (as with Ekweru and Ocomu) by individuals in competition. This competition becomes conflict, in this case, by virtue of Otieno's position on the parish council whose support renders the opposing factions unequal. A land dispute in Opucet has reached neither the proportions of the Agologolo quarrel nor that of Kabola and is not likely to since no officials are involved. Otoo (A 542) has permitted dependents to settle on land he was originally given by Emalu (T 504) without consulting him. While only his son-in-law (clearly his incumbent heir) was involved, no trouble arose, but when the son-in-law lent a share of his land to an industrial immigrant (Mulisio, T 521, whose career was described in Chapter 7) Emalu began to complain. Neither the quarrel between Ekweru and Ocomu, the two Agologolo elders, nor that between Otoo and Emalu has been taken to court, both remaining *ecelet*. That between the Kabola residents was recently mediated by the parish court in Otieno's favor, whereupon Sharif appealed to the sub-county court.

Quarrels over cattle and goats damaging crops are most prevalent in the Township and, in every case, are settled on the spot by the ward headman, the herdsmen agreeing to pay compensation to the owner of the garden. Fights over women most notoriously involve young bachelors and wives in polygamous households, but adultery is by no means rare and many domestic disputes are probably of this nature. Quarrels with the parish chief involve two major issues: the payment of tax and the building of latrines. After a period of haranguing, the chief usually makes summary arrests. Debts are almost entirely a township matter between specialist incumbents and their customers, frequently from outside the parish. Although credit is not offered by the African shopkeepers, the Hindu merchant is beginning to do so in an attempt to revive his failing business, and sellers of milk and esonde beer often accept payment at the end of a month; most quarrels over debts revolve around failure to pay. Porters have difficulty, too, in collecting their wages for casual weeding, housebuilding, and water carrying.

There is a seasonal rhythm to conflict in Gondo. Dry seasons are more tense than the rains; there is money from cotton around at this time and so more social intercourse at the dukas and at beer parties; cultivators have more time on their hands. The dry season from January to March is a time of litigation (*aiwosa*): first, cases of seduction, adultery, tax evasion, and theft reach the courts; and later, elders and councillors are called upon to settle land disputes which arise with the rains at the onset of the ploughing season. From June to October, on the other hand, is the open season for fighting (*ejie*), some of which reaches the courts and much of which reaches the dispensary, as Table 18 indicates. During 1966, 113 women and 50 men were treated for beatings or local injuries (including injuries from falls, stab wounds, lacerated wounds, and abrasions with no way of distinguishing which

TABLE 18: GONDO INJURIES TREATED AT
APAPAI DISPENSARY

| Month | Beatings and Minor Injuries | |
1966	Men	Women
January	0	0
February	1	1
March	1	0
April	1	6
May	5	3
June	0	21
July	8	15
August	6	24
September	7	14
October	7	13
November	3	6
December	11	10
	50	113

were violently incurred); the seasonal distribution of injuries is apparent from the table.

Violence in Teso has long been of concern to the administration, and bylaws limiting the sale of beer, the carrying of dance sticks, and the presence of a chief or headman at any large gathering are all directed to its control. Research has been made into the alcohol content of millet beer, the relationship between manslaughter cases and drink, and even the physiology of the Teso male since ruptured spleens loom large in the mortality reports.[2] Although no violent deaths occurred in Gondo during fieldwork, murders were committed in Kamod, Ogera, and Kadungulu during this time. Records of manslaughter and murder charges show Gondo to be consistently the parish with the lowest number in the sub-county, and the five cases which have occurred there in the last twenty years are all recalled in detail. At the same time, every death in Gondo, except those of children, is attributed to malevolence of one kind or another. Poison is usually seen to be the instrument, and a doctor (*emuron*) is brought in to discover the reason for the death and to arrange ceremonies whereby matters may be restored to normal. An outline of one case in which a Gondo diviner (N 652) was called to adjudicate an Omongolem death illustrates characteristic features and, in conjunction with other cases, permits generalizations to be reached. Crisis situations which arise in the life cycle of any individual are moments of potential conflict for the community. All inexplicable illness is attributed to human agency, generally that of deceased kinsmen, or to recent quarrels which have driven one protagonist to ask the help of a sorcerer. In such situations of subjective social reality, those seen to be involved are generally kinsmen, very rarely neighbors, never strangers.

The case of the hungry ancestors

Enyuku bought a medicine from Byamuka (N 652), a medicine to kill (*ekia*). It consisted of a bottle of liquid, a small pot and a piece of wood. When Byamuka sold them to Enyuku he warned him that they must be used in a certain way or their strength would turn against the user. Enyuku needed them to kill his young wife's lovers, for she was very nice to young men around.

It is a rule that before using *akia*, you must kill your eldest son or daughter, whichever the *emuron* tells you, then the *ekia* will work. Enyuku consulted his elder wife about doing this but she refused to let him. Enyuku then used it to kill his eldest wife's brother's daughter without her knowledge. He did so and she died after being ill with pain, growing thin and coughing. Enyuku then returned to the *emuron* and said "I have done what you told me, *akia* was used on my wife's brother's daughter." But the *emuron* said that it had been misused and that the medicine would now be on him. At ten a.m. after a week, the thing caught him and he fell sick. He was taken to Serere hospital, given a bed and after a week he died.

After the mourning ceremony was over, two weeks later Oriada, Enyuku's younger brother and Enyuku's oldest wife went back to the *emuron* and asked him to divine. Using cowrie shells, he threw them down and began to tell what had been happening, what had gone wrong and what must be done. He said that he must go to Enyuku's home and remove the parasites or they would increase and cause more deaths. This he did for one cow and 200 shillings in payment. At night, 6 p.m. he came with a friend, mixed medicines . . . looked around Enyuku's home for medicines and then with a calabash of water and medicine sprinkled Oriada who was now living in Enyuku's house since he had inherited his wives.

. . . Oriada thought the *emuron* had done everything and there would be no more troubles. But in 1963, their fifteen-year-old boy fell sick, so Oriada went alone to see the same *emuron* to see what was wrong. Byamuka said that it was the dead man's spirit (*emusimu*) that was attacking the youth. Enyuku needed a black goat to eat, the *emuron* said, and a large ceremony must be held to let him eat it. They must get an *emuron* to do this. They asked Byamuka himself, got a goat, killed it where the grave was, put blood on the grave and left a piece of meat there. The rest of the goat was eaten by Oriada and his wives; half the goat was taken home by the doctor. At the ceremony all the neighbors were present; they watched and waited and afterwards sat drinking beer. The mother's brother had to be there as it was his sister's son who was being cured (of Enyuku).

The boy got better but in March 1965 the youngest daughter fell sick. As they believed something must still be wrong, they went again to Byamuka who told them that it must be Etolu who wanted to eat a black ox. (The same ceremony [*ainakin*] was again carried out, the ox cooked from the grave nearby and this time the patri-group was gathered within Enyuku's hut while Byamuka used his medicines on them.) The *emuron* reassured them all was well; the girl recovered.

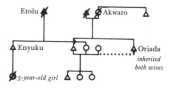

In March 1967, the sixteen-year-old daughter fell ill, her head spun, she fell down, she cried and they knew the *emusimu* was still around. They went to Byamuka who told them that Akwaro, Enyuku's dead mother, wanted a black goat. . . .

Although the actual ceremonies performed by *imurok* in Gondo vary, the institution operates to direct animosities away from objective conflict situations, reinforcing social norms of harmony, conformity, and egality. All the healers/ sorcerers in this part of Serere are Nyoro, Kenyi, or Soga, and all used by Gondo people come from other parishes—Kadungulu, Kaberamaido, Kateta, Pingire, Madochi, and northern Busoga. The practice of sorcery, an ambivalent art, cannot be used as a basis for power within the community and thus no spiralist can use extra-societal powers of this nature to compete within the cohort of Big Men. Illness is in every case attributed to restless, "hungry," deceased kinsmen and is seen to strike the patrigroup. No illness is treated in isolation; each is seen as one more link in a chain of maladjustments. The initial cause is diagnosed by the emuron as a social ill, frequently a woman's wrongdoing as in the case above. Most imurok seem to have a run of about seven or eight years in the office, during which time they receive supplies of cash, meat, and cattle. The calling in of a new emuron begins a new chain of diagnosis, with the seeking out of a current social malfeasance. Diviners are also called in to "find things that are lost." Anyapo (T 109) of Aojabule is believed to have this power, but he usually places it at the disposal of men outside of the parish and has no medicinal skills for good or evil.

While there is great recourse to these informal, substratum judicial techniques within neighborhoods and kin groups, most crises beyond these narrow limits are taken readily to the court of the emorimor and, less readily, to the parish chief. A striking contrast exists between the immediacy of action by the emorimor and the quick consensual settlements he arbitrates, and the slow process by which the parish chief, notified of a grievance, prepares to take action and sends messages in writing by way of headmen to summon witnesses to a moot held at a public place on a date usually set a week or two later. One party is then brought unwillingly to court, and the concerted voice of neighbors and witnesses, Big Men loud among them, is called forth to testify to the "crime." In the settlement by the emorimor of day-by-day disturbances, concern is expressed more for making things quiet again as speedily as possible than for attributing blame and arranging compensation. The strength of precedence, reconciliation, and forgiveness are emphasized.

Court of the Emorimor

An analysis of the cases settled by the emorimor between January and March 1967 gives an idea of their nature and magnitude. There were ten cases in all, and their character illustrates the role of the emorimor in the maintenance of external relations by Gondo parishioners. Four were cases of debt between Gondo residents and men from Ogera, Ogelak, Atirir, and Ongoto. One marital case involved a young Kenyi in Adiding who had sent his new wife back to her father's home at night upon discovering that she had conceived before their marriage. The father (K 406) brought the case since the girl had been driven out in the middle of the night, but the husband took the occasion to plead for his wife's return and this was the decision reached by the court. Another domestic conflict was settled at this homestead at the same time when the court decided that a young Lango girl staying there should be taken back in spite of her frequent quarreling with the women of the household.

One township land case settled by the emorimor was brought by T 611 who claimed his right to plant millet following upon cotton in a garden he had borrowed from a neighbor. The owner's right to refuse was upheld. One case between a Township beer seller and a customer was dismissed for lack of witnesses. A name-calling incident involved two of the emorimor's neighbors (the wives of T 200 and P 225), and it appears that it was the presence of Odico (T 606) that made Ekweru feel that he was acting as emorimor rather than as ward headman in this instance. The fine was only 5 shillings, the name only "as foolish as a dog," which would not seem to have been a serious enough offense to call out the emorimor, neither party being Muslim. One crop destruction case was settled by the emorimor rather than the ward headman of Adiding because damage was so extensive, compensation of 200 shillings being granted to the owner of a garden of potatoes.

At these courts elders in the vicinity drop by and join the emorimor in mediating the case. Proceedings are marked by six phases. First, a declaration of offense is made by the complainant after which the defendant is given an opportunity to reply. Witnesses for both parties corroborate their statements; there is rarely anything very controvertible, and defense witnesses seldom appear. (From all the records it is clear that men guilty of the more serious crimes run away rather than face charges.) The matter is always one of compensation and not of punishment, and so it is intent not guilt that has to be determined. Following these statements one of the Big Men speaks out, giving his assessment of the case, passing moral judgment, condemning stupidity, and suggesting what he considers just recompense. He is followed by another of the elders who takes care to point out possible alternatives to the first weighing-up, and then each Big Man speaks in turn. At the end the emorimor either suggests the compensation to be paid or, if the defendant refuses to accept this judgment, recommends that the case be taken to the *eitela* court.

Parish Chief's Court

Data on parish court cases for Gondo are much less reliable than those for the emorimor's court since, from the beginning, it was clear that my attendance affected decision-making. Toward the end of fieldwork, the parish chief twice invited me to attend his courts (*adieket alo eitela*) but prior to this, I had dropped in on three sessions, like other passers-by, when I had chanced upon them. Most of my understanding of their operation had been obtained from attendance at such courts in other parishes. The moot in November 1966 dealt with the inheritance of a bicycle in a quarrel between two township Lango and an accusation that Emenu (T 402) of Adiding was poisoning his son Esangu (T 217) of Agologolo. Both cases were apparently referred to the sub-county level, but later I found that they were merely dropped. In December cases involved a fight over a woman (*amalayat*) in the township, a quarrel between Ekweru and his son Opit (T 211), and name-calling between Emenu and Esangu. This case between father and son had been smoldering for three years, and again the intervention of Emeru, whose father sponsored past Imodoi entry into Agologolo, reveals a political entrepreneur gaining supporters from rifts between kinsmen. The third meeting was held in Aojabule and consisted of a marital case in which the girl had left her Ogera husband and a case of assault between two of the wives of Odico. Characteristic of the courts at the parish level was the attendance of three or four headmen or councillors as well as the elders of the neighborhood. All were notified; some attended. Frequently they, or their cohorts, were involved as litigants.

Thus far in our discussion we have been dealing with confrontations in which a distinction between the "ground rules" (cultural rules by which competition and conflict are fought out) and "sets of strategies" (alternatives selected to maximize values within the context of the ground rules) is valid. Many indigenous or customary "fines" act as well-established sanctions and an overt value is placed on avoiding open confrontations. Once they break out, however, the level at which mediation is sought is part of the strategy of the plaintiff. There are also occasions when individuals choose to move out of arenas of conflict (that is, they choose not to play the game at all) as when a man elects to move to another ward in order to avoid extended conflict with his kin or neighbor, or when he leaves the parish entirely. On the other hand, certain running feuds exist in which protagonists face each other in court case after court case, seeking compensation and revenge.

Conflict may also flare up beyond the control of institutionalized norms. During fieldwork one such outburst occurred in Aojabule which climaxed a long history of conflict between two feuding patrigroups. This extended case history suggests some of the sociological factors underlying supra-individual violence in Gondo.

Feud in Aojabule

In April 1966, Okiror s/o Yokonia (T 108), a resident of Aojabule, began to plough his gardens close to the Ogera swamp. These two gardens had belonged to his father before he had migrated to Ogera allocating them to his youngest son. Okiror had ploughed one of the gardens and was about to prepare it for cotton planting when Oyara, an elderly Ogera resident, intervened. Although Okiror had used both gardens four years earlier, then allowing them to rest, Oyara claimed that these were his gardens since they belonged to the Irarak-Ibokita clan dispersed throughout Kadungulu, Ogera, and Aojabule where Ekwaru (T 104) and his son Okello (T 105) are its representatives. Since Okiror claimed that the land belonged to his father Yokonia of the Ikapelo clan, the matter was taken to the Ogera parish chief for arbitration. At the court which was summoned immediately, Oyara and Ekwaru claimed that the land was Ibokita land which had merely been lent to Yokonia, an affine, a long time ago, but judgment was passed by the chief, councillors and elders present that the land rightfully belonged to Ikapelo. At this, fighting broke out between Ekwaru, Oyara, and Okello on the one side and Yokonia and his two sons, Okiror and Eledu, on the other. This was stopped only when a large

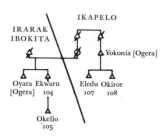

crowd of neighbors was able to pull the combatants apart. Okiror was carried, critically beaten, to Apapai dispensary, while Oyara was detained at sub-county headquarters for three weeks until it was certain that Okiror would live. On August 17th Okiror appeared at the sub-county court to demand compensation. The magistrate granted him 100 shillings and Oyara was fined an additional 150 shillings for assault and disturbing the peace.

Meanwhile, in July 1966, Ekwaru had accused one of the Ikapelo sons, Eledu (T 107), of using part of his land which he was willing to share but in which he did not wish to relinquish rights. Eledu won the case at the sub-county court level and was given the land. An appeal to the County Court by Ekwaru in September 1966 was disallowed.

From this time on, conflict moved beyond the bounds of litigation into open violence. In early October, two of Yokonia's oxen were stolen, it was said by thieves hired by Oyara from Atira parish. A few weeks later, two of Ekwaru's cows were stolen, for which Yokonia was unofficially held responsible. In November 1966, Oyara's cotton was stolen from his house and on December 26th, Eledu's house was burnt down, his mother narrowly escaping death. The arsonist was known to be a man from Kamod, hired presumably by the Ibokita, but no evidence could be found when he was brought before the Gondo parish chief at the end of the year and the case was dismissed.

Matters then passed quietly for several months until the death of Eledu on June 20, 1967 provoked another set of outbursts. Ekwaru and Oyara were held responsible and it was widely believed that they had obtained poison from Anyapo (T 109) who had some slight reputation as a doctor (*emuron*) in Aojabule and Ogera. On July 15, Oyara's house was set on fire at night, two goats were lost in the blaze, and Okiror was believed to have been responsible. Two nights later Okiror was dragged out and beaten by a crowd of men armed with spears, pangas and sticks who set fire to his thatch and ordered him to leave the neighborhood. This he immediately did, setting out for his father's home across the swamp in Ogera. Although no case was brought, it was widely held in Gondo and Ogera that Oyara had hired men from Kamod to terrorize Okiror.

In August 1967 the three houses of Anyapo, situated farther down the valley in Aojabule, were fired by unknown persons during the night. This was said to have been done by Okiror and his two brothers from Soroti and Okidetok. Anyapo was warned to leave Gondo. He had not done so by October 1967 and was involved once more in the Ibokita-Ikapelo feud on the death, on October 16, of Okiror's wife since this was believed to have been brought about by his medicines placed at the disposal of Ekwaru and Oyara.

Three observations may be made. First, the isolated position of the disputed gardens meant that no local pressures were likely to be successful and, since residents of two parishes were involved, the conflict was immediately escalated to parish court proportions. As it happened, the Ogera parish chief with his councillors proved ineffectual in restraining conflict. Only the rulings of the sub-county court were sanctioned and imposed, and resentment was allowed to smolder. Since this resentment could not be fanned into conflict with neighborhood support, in each case of further violence, outsiders were hired from beyond the bounds of the parish. Finally, since there is a tendency for every death to be attributed to sorcery or to the remiss behavior of the deceased or his kin, any conflict is likely to be perpetuated if no positive action is taken to wipe out the feud. Only one such ceremony was observed in Gondo during fieldwork, and the feud between Ikapelo and Ibokita of Aojabule seems likely to be a prolonged one.

[227]

Conclusion

Challenges to the system of values which the gerontocratic institutions of social control uphold—as when sons demand cattle of their fathers or land users try to infringe upon the rights of those who have helped them—may be brought to resolution by the informal arbitration of ward headmen and the emorimor with the assistance of elders, or through the parish court, or by opting out of the system when claims can more profitably be made of kin or neighbors elsewhere. The informality of the judicial processes reflects, in large part, an interest in muting differences, which facilitates the operation of contradictions and the avoidance of confrontation. With rare exceptions, all competition and conflict tend to have only an individualistic dimension, and the parish-wide lack of identification in ethnic proportions is matched by the use of all three types of court by every member of the polyethnic community irrespective of his cultural background.

Both the archival record and contemporary officialdom speak highly of the readiness and promptness of Teso communities in reporting crime. Gondo is not atypical in that, in most cases, one man is ready to share responsibility for another's actions; kinsmen and neighbors call in ward headmen, the emorimor is quickly on the spot, and it is the community itself which offers up the wrongdoer to the parish chief when this is deemed necessary. The converse is also true: kin and neighbors will themselves beat up a felon caught in the night; a headman may "punish" an accused on his way to the sub-county jail. The community sub-stratum which we have seen to be operative in matters of political action generally includes social control and a great deal of judicial behavior and, in these matters too, reaches into a wider community extending beyond the boundaries of the parish. Whether in relations between affines, in explanations of sickness and death, or in recourse to self-help in feuding situations, Gondo parishioners have recourse to a horizontal dimension of societal organization that cuts across the political units of the administrative hierarchy. It is in this dimension that rural radicalism mobilizes to defy authority and rural conservatism proves resistant to change.[3] The Big Men of Gondo seen daily in their peacemaking roles provide a potential leadership for both.

The Elite

GONDO HAS BEEN DESCRIBED as an open society in which transactions between individuals rather than interactions between moral groups provide the basis of community life, and emphasis has been on contradictions and ambiguities, on selective articulation and redefinition, on working agreements and compromise. The point has come at which to suggest that Gondo is something besides an open-ended network of social and economic relations since, in its political dimension, it has been created a unit. To define itself in relation to the external political world and to protect its interests, Gondo recognizes a strategic elite—an elite, that is, not with respect to the purveyance of communal values (for we have seen that these need not exist in the light of the cross-cutting ties between individuals and groups) but in relation to the society beyond its boundaries.

The composition of the elite serves to represent the interests of a polyethnic community, although it is neither socially nor economically representative of the community at large. Yet it is an imitable elite within the value system of a microcosmopolitan culture.

The Social Profile of the Elite

The basic determinants of elite rank in Gondo are sex and social maturity. No woman and no young or single man can acquire elite positions, and the institutionalization of extramarital sexual activity serves to support the overall ranking system of the community whose first principle is gerontocratic

← *Eight of the Big Men*

privilege.[1] We have seen how the status of residents in Gondo is a prerequisite for entry into the political arena and how this is related to an individual's mode of entry into the parish and his accumulation of a structured status sequence within it. To achieve prestige a man gathers supporters around him, and the processes by which he does this have been outlined. Ascribed statuses, whether they involve ethnicity, place of birth, or familial connections, count for less than achieved statuses. Some of the processes of spiralism have been described. The final process by which certain men and not others achieve pre-eminence in the community is best discerned from a consideration of actual cases, from which further generalizations may then be made. The results of an inquiry into Big Man status in Gondo in 1966 provide our starting point.

The existence of a prevalent notion of "Big Manship" became apparent within my first week in Teso, and, when the matter was pursued, respondents had no difficulty in naming those whom they considered, at any specific time, to be the Big Men of the parish. It has been suggested that constructed reference groups such as these are first conceived and then used by the individuals of a localized society to structure their social world and to make comparisons and evaluations of their own behavior and that of others.[2] The construction of identical reference groups indicates community consensus, and since in the polyethnic situation it is especially valuable to have a measure such as this, our sociological concern with the various statuses of individuals (such as ethnic, religious, occupational, land holding, resident) can now be complemented by the subjective view, the actor's model of what makes for pre-eminence in the community.[3]

Over 140 respondents, randomly chosen, were asked at three-month intervals to name the ten persons they considered to be the Big Men of the parish. Variations in their responses over time were significant as was the large area of agreement between them, regardless of their ethnicity, resident status, ward, or age. Follow-up formal interviews were arranged with a 20 per cent representative sample of the population at which respondents were asked to account for their choice and encouraged to discuss the qualities they believed made for Big Men. Changes in evaluation during the course of the eighteen months in the field confirmed that the factors people said influenced their rankings did in fact do so. Their changing assessments also made it clear that Gondo elites are not likely to develop into classes while the openness and fluidity of the local-level social and economic systems remain as they are. Detailed results of the inquiry appear in Appendix B, but Table 19 summarizes the details relevant here. First, I will review the status sets of the ten individuals listed in the light of the analyses of the preceding chapters.

Among the ten Gondo Big Men the average age is fifty-eight, which supports the suggestion that a gerontocratic principle is markedly operative. That political groupings take the form of cohorts is confirmed by the age span of the elite, which ranges (with one exception aged 40) from 51 to 75 years. Five ethnic categories are represented among the elite. Two of these, as might be expected, are core group Teso and Kenyi; that the Pageru have lent their political support to other core groups and that opportunities for elite status have been sacrificed for social and economic ends were made apparent in Chapter 6. In the terms of the present analysis, they have chosen not to convert ethnic status into political currency. The other ethnic categories represented are Acholi, Kumam, and Nyoro; the elite appear to be drawn from the five largest ethnic groupings in the parish.

With respect to the resident status of each member of the elite, only three belong to core families (two Teso and one Kenyi); one is a Teso core family dependent; while the re-

TABLE 19: SOCIAL PROFILE OF THE ELITE

Code Number	Name	Votes Rec'd.	Age	Religion	Residential Status	Official Position	Primary Occupation	Number of Gardens	Wives	Cattle	Tax Status
T 512	Ocen	51	60	P	C	emorimor	cultivator	7.0	1	—	6
Kum 682	Opolot	48	51	P	O	—	cultivator	8.0	3	130	8
T 606	Odico	41	52	P	O	councillor	tailor	11.5	4	6	6–8
T 210	Ekweru	38	66	P	C	headman	cultivator	7.5	2	—	6–8
K 418	Nakumu-sana	33	75	C	C	chief (retired)	cultivator	7.5	2	106	PET
T 601	Elamu	29	52	—	O	headman	cultivator	9.0	1	6	6
N 639	Gawera	21	52	P	O	—	hotel keeper	6.6	2	16	8–10
T 109	Anyapo	17	62	P	Cd	councillor	cultivator	14.5	3	29	8
A 542	Otoo	16	70	—	O	gin headman (retired)	cultivator	7.0	1	—	PET
T 302	Otieno	16	40	P	O	councillor	cultivator	12.0	4	18	6–8

mainder all entered the parish as office incumbents, two being brought in as heirs and four by external agencies, the ginneries, the Public Works Department, or Asian and European employers. Only Ocen (T 512) was born in the parish, although Elamu (T 601) lived there as a child, and both Nakumusana (K 418) and Ekweru (T 210) entered as young men. All but one (N 639) are owners of the land they work.

A dynamic analysis reveals that all ten of the Big Men have made polygamous unions; the tabulation shows only the circumstances of November 1966. Divorce and death in child bearing are not rare in Gondo, and while most men make three or four marriages in a lifetime, Big Men generally make seven or eight. The number of wives that a man has at any one time significantly affects his prestige in the community at large: Otoo, for example, with only one wife, and Nakumusana, now with two remaining out of nine, are facing imminent passage, with age, out of the elite, as is Ocen.[4] Ekweru and Anyapo, however, are each about to acquire another wife. We have seen the importance of wives and affinal dependents in the creation of support groups; in addition, each of the Big Men within his neighborhood aggregates the largest possible number of work parties. The distribution of the Big Men throughout the parish is, itself, significant, for it is as if each ward has a carrying capacity of Big Men. Four live in the township; two in Opucet; one in Kabola; one in Adiding; one in Agologolo and one in Aojabule. Gawera, the Nyoro hotelkeeper, is the only one not to take part in work parties, although his wives join those of kinsmen. He takes his turn in herding although he employs porters for cultivation. Odico, Opolot, and Otieno also employ porters, especially during the cotton season when Odico becomes the busiest tailor in the parish; Opolot's homestead, located as it is on the ginnery doorstep, figures prominently in the esonde market; and Otieno works as a cotton inspector at the ginnery. Opolot is not the only Big Man to make the sale of esonde beer a basic part of his spiralism since, as we saw, Odico and Otieno are also among the leading brewers (each has four wives), and all do, in fact, increase the visibility of their prestige in this way. Although members of core families and office incumbents alike may become heads of their *atutuben* (clusters), something more is required for parish-wide recognition of leadership. Within his neighborhood a man gains recognition by his sponsorship of others, by his aggregation of large work parties, and by his plentiful supply of beer. This is true of all those shown to be Big Men in Gondo, but it is also true of eight or ten others; something further must still be sought to account for the composition of the present elite.

All but three of them have their own ploughs; two of the four largest herds in the parish are owned by Big Men, but the ownership of cattle clearly does not rank high in their present positions. The use made of them in bridewealth contracts is generally more significant. Similarly, only four of them are among the largest landowners in the parish; the use to which they put their lands—its allocation to kinsmen and dependents—is more important for political advancement. By indicating in Table 19 the tax which each of the Big Men was assessed in both 1966 and 1967, something is captured of the dynamics of the situation. The two men in their seventies (K 418 and A 542) are both exempt from tax by virtue of bad health; Ocen and Elamu are both in the average 60-shilling category with respect to their assessed wealth; while the increased prosperity of the spiralists is clearly indicated.

Paths to Leadership

A comparison of the career résumés of these men illuminates the further social characteristics that they share. In their retelling an effort is made to retain the emphasis the Big Men

[236]

themselves placed upon the events in their lives as they narrated them. The reasons for this approach should be made explicit. Barth has suggested that the conventional structural analysis of community as a basic scheme of social statuses organized in persons and corporate groups and interconnected through patterns of recruitment allows one to discuss the pattern of localization of entrepreneurial activity in sets or types of statuses within the social structure, but one can say little about the factors affecting this distribution, or hope to make any prognoses or *post hoc* explanations of changes in the pattern.[5] By focusing on the careers of Big Men in the parish as a process, on the other hand, as a chain of transactions between the entrepreneur and his environment, we see the community as composed of actors who also make choices and pursue strategies, and we can analyze community life—routinized and institutionalized as it is—in terms of the choices that are available and the values that are ascribed. The entrepreneurial Big Man, through his relations with other people, is subject to these factors, but he may also, by his very activity, modify and change them.

1. T 512 ENOSI OCEN

Ocen is a Teso and a resident of Opucet. He is sixty years old and has one wife, and two young children with him. His other children are married. One son lives "on the doorstep." Ocen was born in Opucet but was taken to Agule in Kaberamaido County when his father migrated to join his clan brothers there. He returned with his father in 1920 after a quarrel with their kinsmen. Ocen went to school for a few months at the Catholic school at Kamod but he did not then get a Christian name "because his father did not buy an Ateso prayer book and so baptism was withheld."

Ocen worked on the steamers from 1928 until 1932, marrying his first wife in 1930. From 1932 until 1935 he worked as a ginnery porter. During that time he had two children killed by witchcraft, one by the Nyoro village chief of that time, the other by the sub-county chief as retaliation against Ocen for complaining that he was not given a receipt for his tax. Both men were fined because of his complaint. After this incident he felt that all the men were against him in Opucet so he left to stay with his wife's brothers in Kamod. In 1939 when all his clansmen were dead, Ocen inherited the land in Opucet and returned to live there. From 1951 until 1957 he worked as a ginnery headman but resigned suffering from venereal disease. In 1958 he assisted Emmanuel Otala in his campaign as the Democratic Party candidate in the national elections but they were unsuccessful.

In 1959 Ocen was elected apolon k'ateker (area headman) for Opucet and in 1962 chosen as emorimor (coordinator). In December 1962 he was baptized at Gondo's Church of Uganda school and received his Christian name, Enosi. In 1967 Ocen refused to work as emorimor because Odaet would not pay him. Odaet said that he was fired because he had not paid his tax. He was unable to do this because he had spent two hundred shillings having his sick daughter cured by a doctor from Bukedea County. In October 1967 Ocaet with Ekweru (the new emorimor) came to Ocen's house to arrest him and take him to the sub-county court. At this, Ocen's sick daughter threatened to commit suicide. Odico intervened to guarantee that Ocen would pay his tax as soon as his cotton was sold, as he had a good crop that year.

Ocen speaks Ateso, Lukenyi, Swahili, Kumam, and Acholi. I interviewed him in the little hut where he stays when the animals have to be kept off the crops. It is his habit to sit there at times with his pipe. As emorimor, Ocen was to be seen striding through the village with his walking stick, a dog at his heels, and his felt hat pulled down over his forehead. He strode his fields like an English country farmer, raising his hat courteously in greeting. Often he was seen, squatting on his heels in the yard of a homestead, listening to complaints and settling quarrels among the people.

2. KUM 682 DAUDI OPOLOT

Opolot is a Kumam born in Soroti County fifty-one years ago. He first came to Gondo in 1936, brought by a European for whom he was a cook. The European was transferred to Gondo from the Soroti ginnery and Opolot accompanied him since he had already been working for him for nine years. Shortly after his arrival he was able to buy land from a Ganda woman who was returning to her homeland. He paid twenty shillings for it "which people thought was a lot of money in those days." He has land in Soroti but this is worked by his brothers; his family is large and he plans to stay in Gondo where he has made three marriages, one to a Pagero, the other two to Teso. One adult son remains with him with his wife and children; his other sons and daughters are married and live in other parishes. An old unmarried brother joined him seven years ago and he helps with the herding. Opolot also employs a Hima herdsman. His house is situated on the corner opposite the ginnery gates and he probably sells more *esonde* beer than anyone else in the parish. He has now been a retired gentleman farmer for many years. In 1964 he sold cattle in Kampala but has not taken up this occupation. He is on visiting terms with Otala, and one of his best friends is the sub-county chief of neighboring Kadungulu who has a car and a gun. This man usually stops at Opolot's homestead on his way to Serere and Soroti.

3. T 606 ERISMASI ODICO

Odico is a Teso, aged fifty-two, with three wives for whom he has paid bridewealth. He has established two homesteads in the township. Odico has a permanent liaison with Sara Apio, the widow of an Icaak clansman and a highly respected, progressive woman, who has a daughter and a son "on the doorstep." Odico has had no children, but this is explained as due to his having always married women too old for childbearing. One wife is a Pagero, two are Teso.

He was born in Ogera in 1914 but was taken to Madochi at the age of four when his father migrated, joining his wife's brother. Odico went to school in Asuret, living with a Kenyi school teacher for whom he worked in lieu of school fees. Leaving school, he went to live with his mother's mother on his mother's land at Oburin near Serere. He learnt tailoring from a Ganda in Serere and lived at his home as a "houseboy" in 1929. He then worked as a tailor for two Asians in Serere where he stayed until 1946. In 1933 he married and built a home at Serere where he lived until he was brought to Gondo as the tailor of Tulsidas (now a Soroti cotton buyer). At first Odico stayed in the dukas, then built his own home on land near the PWD camp. Later he joined Sara on the land her son (a schoolmaster at Kamod) had bought for her from a Ganda "prostitute," in the township. He married the daughter of Engutu in 1953, the daughter of a Kadungulu man in 1954, and Ocen's daughter in 1960. In 1958 Odico campaigned for the Uganda Peoples' Congress Party, being the party's agent in Gondo. He was a founder member of the Cooperative in 1953 and has held office as Treasurer, Vice-Chairman or Chairman for all but two years ever since.

4. T 210 YOWANA EKWERU

Ekweru was born in 1900 in Ogelak parish, although he spent most of his childhood in Gondo with kinsmen. He came to live permanently in the parish in 1927 at the invitation of Okasu (T 216) of the Ilale core family. Although Okasu is older, and claims to be the head of Ilale, this claim is not recognized by the parish at large. Okasu is childless and often "sick in the head." Ekweru has the largest core of consanguines around him of anyone in Gondo and is ward head (apolon ka ateker) of Agologolo. In January 1968 he succeeded Ocen as parish head (emorimor). Ekweru worked as a sub-county clerk on arrival in Gondo and later worked in the ginnery until 1932. He was a parish councillor in 1938. As a child he spent some years in Lango where his mother was married to a Kumam. Later he was appointed clerk in the parish of Pingire and he returned to Gondo on retiring in 1943.

5. K 418 KOSTANT NAKUMUSANA

Nakumusana of the Kenyi Bandije core family is now over seventy and lives in Adiding in a house vastly superior to any other in the parish. He has the second largest herd in Gondo; has four sons who are shopkeepers in neighboring parishes or at the dukas; and a homestead full of many dependents. He has made several marriages and his many daughters are married to Teso and Pagero as well as Kenyi in the neighboring parishes and Gondo. Some Kenyi settle with their father-in-law, since he is rich and influential and, in return, he has their services. At present his homestead consists of many transient clients. In November 1966, besides his wife and children were two Karamojong; his Kenyi brother-in-law; the son of his senior brother from Kampala; a Teso porter; and seven Hima (3 men and their families). Most Kenyi traveling in Serere County visit him.

His wealth and influence were founded upon his period of office as a Kenyi sub-chief from 1910 until 1923 when the office was abolished. He then became village chief in Gondo until 1940. Nakumusana was born in Busoga and was about eighteen years of age when the Ganda administration was set up. His brother, Mulojja, was the lieutenant of Mwambazi, appointed chief of the Kenyi of Serere County, and now lives near Nakumusana. The majority of their kinsmen are settled in Serere County, although they still occasionally visit Busoga and Kobwin where they also have kin.

6. T 601 YOKANI ELAMU

Elamu is a Teso born in Kaberamaido near the Lango border. His father worked on the steamers and acquired land in Gondo. Elamu, now fifty-two, came to join his father and inherited land from him in 1920. His brothers and sisters are still in Kaberamaido. He has married twice, first to the daughter of the Pagero core family of Gabunga (Yaiyeru) and second to a Teso in Ogelak parish, but he has no children. His wife's brother recently joined him and would appear to be his heir. Elamu served in the army in India and Ceylon from 1944 until 1947. Four men in Gondo parish have army experience, but apart from Otieno (T 632) and a Ganda (G 668), none seem to have used this training or experience to further their positions within the parish. Elamu is currently ward head of Adiding, but the people are not pleased with him and it is unlikely that he will be chosen again.

7. N 639 ERIA GAWERA

Gawera is a Nyoro, aged fifty-two, who was born in Hoima. He came to Gondo in 1929, following his sister. Gawera cannot speak Ateso in spite of his long residence in the parish. From 1929 until 1948 he was employed as a cook by one of the European owners of the ginnery. In 1934 he started a small shop at Ogelak on his sister's husband's land in which he sold only cigarettes. In 1940 he built the Gondo hotel on its present site. This mud and wattle, tin-roofed building has been expanding ever since. It now has small huts alongside where the bus drivers can sleep overnight and the hotel is now the bus terminus whereas formerly buses stopped at the *dukas*. The radio in Eria's eating house is always playing and a gaming board is set up under the tree outside, both of which attract customers. The eating house is always open, being run as a family affair.

Gawera receives his goods weekly from Asians in Serere. A few years ago he bought cattle with his profits and sent them back to his kinsmen in Bunyoro where most of his children are being educated. The cattle died and he has sent no more. He employs a fellow Nyoro as a part-time herder and shares the herding himself. He is usually the first cattleowner in Gondo to ask the veterinary assistant for injections or sprays.

Gawera has two wives, both Nyoro, and twelve small children living at the hotel. His father's brother's son was with him until recently as his potential "heir," but they quarreled and the lad was sent back to Hoima. Gawera borrows land year by year from his father's brother in Opucet and his wives join the work parties of that neighborhood, although he does not.

8. T 109 LEVI ANYAPO

Anyapo, a sixty-two-year-old Teso, lives in Aojabule. He was born in Atira parish but taken to Kamuda in Soroti County when he was two years old to stay with his mother's family. There he went to school where he was taught by a Ganda teacher, from 1916 until 1927. He was baptized and, in 1927, married for the first time. He then worked for one year as a village school teacher and for nine months at the Agricultural Research Station in Serere. He was selected to go to a course held in Buganda, but his father refused to let him go, so instead he returned to Kamuda. In 1929 he married again; this time to an Ilale woman whom he accompanied to Aojabule where she was joining her sister. This sister was married to Ebeju, one of the Big Men of Ogera parish, just across the boundary from Aojabule.

Anyapo married again in 1931, 1941, and 1948. His last marriage was in 1961 to the daughter of Odera (T 114) of the Igoria core family. He currently has three wives and seven children at home.

When he first arrived in Gondo in 1929 Anyapo lived in Adiding near the ginnery. For a brief while, between 1931 and 1932, he went to Arapai Ginnery near Soroti as a cotton weigher. He taught school again for a short while in 1933 and 1934. In 1935 he became a fish trader between Kamuda and Soroti Town and in 1940 migrated finally to Gondo where he built a permanent home on the land of Ebeju in Aojabule. Until very recently he traded cattle to Kampala for several months of every year.

Anyapo is renowned in Ogera parish as a diviner. He joined the Cooperative Society in 1954 and was Treasurer from that date until 1962 when he resigned. He was elected to the parish council and thence to the sub-county council where he is still the Gondo representative. Anyapo says that he will never return home to Kamuda, although his kinsmen may often come and visit him; Gondo is now his home.

9. A 542 OTOO S/O EJAU

Otoo, a seventy-year-old Acholi, lives in one of the largest homesteads in Opucet. As a young man he traveled southward from

Acholi looking for work, first coming to Gondo ginnery via Kwera in Kaberamaido. There was no available work in Gondo so he stayed in the neighboring parish of Madochi looking after cattle. He acquired seven head of cattle with which he married a Teso Ngoratok wife. He had left his first wife and children with her kinsmen in Kitgum. After two years as a herder, Otoo moved into Gondo where he got work as a night watchman at the ginnery. In the 1940's he was transferred for four years to be a watchman for the ginnery manager in Soroti Town but he was glad to return to Gondo where he had been able to get land in 1936. Shortly after his return his Atesot wife died and he sent for his Acholi wife who joined him in Opucet where they raised seven children. The oldest son, whom he had hoped would inherit his land in Gondo, died in 1964. This son used to visit him regularly, bringing him sesame every Christmas when he worked for a few months at the ginnery. One of Otoo's daughters is married and lives in Madochi; others are married in Acholi. One lives with him in Gondo, and her husband (A 543) was the office incumbent heir throughout most of my fieldwork. When his Acholi wife died, Otoo took up with several local women in turn, finally settling with his present Teso wife (for whom he says he paid one bull) from Pallisa whom he met at the dukas. Otoo returned to Kitgum in January 1967 when I drove him back to his brother's son's home shortly after he had sold his cotton and obtained his exemption from paying tax (on the grounds of old age and sickness). He died in Kitgum in March 1967, and his Gondo home is now occupied by his son-in-law, his daughter, and their young children.

10. T 302 CHARLES FREDERICK OTIENO

Otieno is a Teso, aged forty—the youngest of the Big Men—who lives in Kabola. He has four wives: a Kumam, Pagero, a Soga, and a Kenyi. The first is a daughter of Opolot; the second of a core Pagero family; and the last of Nakumusana. Otieno was born in the neighboring parish of Ogera but as a child was taken by his father to live with clan brothers in Soroti. He went to school there, acquiring a Primary Grade Two education. At the outbreak of war Otieno joined up and was sent to fight in North Africa. He was in the Army until 1945 when he took a Public Works Department course and examination on his return to Uganda. He was sent by the Department to work in Buganda, at Mbale, and finally at Gondo. He "retired" from the Public Works Department in

1956 and obtained land from the Parish Council next to the road camp in Kabola where he built a homestead.

Otieno was elected to the Parish Council shortly after his arrival and has served on it ever since. He is one of the few men ever to have used a tractor on his land. His homestead, situated on the road between Kabola and Agologolo, provides a drinking place for the men of the two neighborhoods and many of the votes he received in the Big Man poll came from his Kenyi neighbors.

Conversion of Social and Economic Facilities into Political Currency

Prestige and authority in Gondo represent the two facets of community life: its internal structure and its external relations.[6] We may discern two paths by which Big Men reach the top. Some rise through the established echelons of the gerontocratic society, and these we may call authorities or conservators according to whether status or function is being described. Others, who may be termed influentials or mediators in respect to status and function, rise by way of external institutions. This dichotomy is, however, only a question of the predominance of one career pattern over the other since there are elements of both in almost every man's life, Gondo having been in the mainstream of a nationally oriented economy since 1912. In the final analysis, the man who rises in the prestige hierarchy is an entrepreneur who makes the best use of all the facilities at his disposal, and the prestige of both types of spiralist depends on what they make of their positions in the community itself.

Within the authority structure of the parish, all but one of these men (Gawera, the hotelkeeper) are heads of neighborhood clusters, focal points in peer group sociability. Three of them are among the five ward heads of the parish. Factors which work against the other two ward heads becoming Big Men in the parish as a whole are the distance of one of the wards, Aojabule, from the heart of the community, and the overshadowing of the ward head of Kabola by the two former Kenyi chiefs, Nakumusana and his brother Mulojja. All four parish councillors are Big Men, two of them mediators and two conservators. Significantly, in the light of the earlier analysis, the two members sent up to the sub-county level are the mediators.

All the Big Men have obtained some of their social and economic facilities outside of the parish. Both Odico and Anyapo have made their play for recognition in the external arena, as has Otieno. Odico was one of the founders of the Cooperative Society which serves the three parishes of Ogera, Ogelak, and Gondo. He has held office as Treasurer, Vice-Chairman, or Chairman in all but two years since its formation. Anyapo was Treasurer from 1954 until 1962. Upon his retirement Otieno was nominated as his successor but lost to an Ogera man who, according to the Secretary-Manager, "couldn't even count," but who was sponsored by powerful men within the wider community.

The careers of the elite are alike in status sequence. All had characteristically mobile infancies, followed by minimal schooling. Only Anyapo and Ekweru advanced by virtue of their literacy and, in the case of Anyapo, his father's conservatism acted as a brake to his progress, so that he was obliged to improve his position through the more conventional entrepreneurial activity of trading. Two of the Big Men, Opolot and Gawera, owe their start in life to employment by Europeans; one, Odico, to his apprenticeship to an Asian. Two others, Otoo and Otieno, have held posts of minor responsibility at the European-owned ginnery; and three others, Nakumusana, Ekweru, and Anyapo, have been salaried officials in government service. Elamu alone has gained his position without, at some time, stepping outside of the mesh of kinship organization into the world of contract, for he appears to have made no use of his father's office incumbency in the steamer service or of his own experience in the army. Yet one reason given for his elite status is that he is the best *atenus* dancer in the parish, a performer in a competitive institution in which talented individuals uphold the prestige of their parishes within the wider community.

Yet, in spite of these external relations prominent in the lives of all the Big Men, all have reinvested their differential status so acquired back into the parish in which they have chosen to live, accepting community values with respect to age, polygamy, and the working of the land—the three cornerstones of the prestige paradigm which forms the base of the pyramid of power in Gondo.

Change and the Prestige System

Some entrepreneurial activities in Gondo do not contribute to status prestige, the hiring out of ploughs or fishing craft being among them. Activities which revolve around day-by-day activities in the ginnery, at fishing, or in religious institutions are not part of the Big Man syndrome. The outcome of ventures in these fields is uncertain so that they cannot, at present, be a part of the spiralists' systemic operations. As we saw, 15.8 per cent of the population are fishermen, and success at fishing is one of the quickest routes to economic advancement and social mobility. But profit made from fishing must be reinvested in cattle, land, wives, and dependents—that is, back into the system—if it is to be converted into political currency. Part of Nakumusana's current prestige is due to his sons' commercial successes, which reflect to his glory since they are his political dependents. But Otieno and Aringa, both of whom rent fishing craft to Kenyi and Pagero neighbors, receive no praise for their enterprise. Just as the plough owner who seeks prestige lends his plough to neighbors rather than renting it to others, so their cash operations bring them profit but not prestige. Such activities are still outside of the prestige system of the community, although, of course, this is not to say that they always will be.

One of the functions of an elite is to innovate,[7] and commercial fishing is a new form of enterprise. Other prestigious possibilities related to other value systems have been introduced in the past. The values of Christianity, for example, bring some prestige to men who contract "ring" marriages. Two of the three men in the parish who have done this are Nakumusana, a Catholic, and Aringa, a Protestant. On the whole, however, where Christian values such as monogamy and premarital chastity conflict with community values, the Christian values have lost out. In some cases there may be compromise, but there is no enhancement of an individual's position through such compromise. Strict adherence to Islamic principles certainly limits opportunities for spiralism in the community at large, and it may be seen that none of the Big Men is Muslim although 12 per cent of the parish is nominally Islamic.

Systems change and individuals pass out of a system. The very old (such as Odongo, for example) lose eminence as they take less and less part in social activities. Leaders in public life are mature and active. They are typically described as active men, men who have strong voices politically, men who are fond of asking questions, reasonable men, and, above all, popular men. There is a plateau of prestige which men may attain and from which they may fall. (Parish chiefs, by contrast, are thought of as cunning, out to trick people, choleric, and unpopular.)

Property, Visibility, and Deference

We have seen how certain property rights become the distinguishing attributes of specific status relations and do, indeed, mark the various steps of a man's progress in the social climb. As Gluckman has observed, some transfer of property is necessary not only to mark changes but also to validate them, to legitimize success in the status encounter.[8] Yet a Big Man is not necessarily a wealthy man since prestige may be gained from distributing wealth. The relationship between wealth and authority among the elite is as follows:

	Wealth	Authority
Core family	0	3
Immigrants	5	2

A Gondo-born man who has acquired authority does not need to acquire wealth to become a Big Man; an immigrant to the village becomes a Big Man by virtue of his wealth, among other things, but rarely becomes an authority.

There are several clear visual indicators of elite status within the community. Paths to their homesteads are unusually wide and well cleared, and there is always plenty of beer at their homes. Deference is clearly accorded to the elite;[9] a Big Man is always given a chair, a younger man vacating one for him if necessary. This is not formalized in any way but is consistently observed. It is the pecking order of the village manifested at its highest level: a son gives a chair to his father; a poor man to a wealthier; a host to his guest if the guest is of equal or superior status. Disputes are avoided upon occasion by the uncomfortable sharing of a narrow seat. Should a Big Man drop in at a homestead when a ward headman or the parish chief is hearing a case, he will join the panel of adjudicators facing the witnesses and will speak out at the end of the hearing. He attends all funerals within his neighborhood and often plays a leading part in the proceedings, helping to dig the grave, contributing a conspicuous amount of cash to the burial fund, or being responsible for recording the gifts in a notebook. The reputation of a member of the elite will be known beyond the boundaries of the parish, and his homestead will receive more outside visitors than most.

The Elite as a Corporate Body

Recording of "who does what with whom in what sequence and under what conditions" was an important part of the inquiry,[10] but a full account of the activities of Big Men within the community and across its boundaries cannot be given here. We can, however, describe one situation in which the elite may be seen in operation. On January 9, 1967, a meeting was held to assess the tax of Gondo parishioners in accordance with the regulations of the Teso District administration. This was the only occasion during my fieldwork when, supposedly, the entire parish was assembled; a second meeting was, in fact, held two weeks later to assess absentees. The meeting was held on neutral ground under a large tree opposite the *dukas*, tables and chairs being supplied for the sub-county chief, the parish chief of Ogera (who was acting as his second-in-command), the Gondo parish chief, and the askari responsible for the tax register and for handing out statements of tax due. Three benches were placed in a semicircle around the tables, and these were occupied by the older and more prestigious members of the community. Young men sat on the grass; no women or children were present.

The structure of the parish was dramatized in the public ceremony, the positioning of individuals indicating clearly the extent to which neighborhood ties outweighed those of ethnicity. A man stood with his friends, and the cohortative structure of the community became apparent. In its diachronic aspect, positioning also revealed the complementary facets of the elite. According to the regulations under which such meetings are held, a parishioner is supposed to leave the meeting under penalty of a fine once his tax has been assessed. Accordingly, most of the parishioners turn up for half an hour or so during the day since they know the order in which names are listed in the tax register and the order in which they will be called. On this occasion, a photographic record was kept of the entire two-hour proceeding, and an average of between thirty and forty parishioners was on the scene at any one time. It was noticeable, however, that most Big Men took their places before the arrival of the sub-county chief, regardless of their place in the register, and were therefore present throughout most of the proceedings. As each came along, one by one, to the meeting, a space was made for him on one of the benches, alongside his fellows. The mediative spiralist Big Men were not as conspicuously in evidence as the authorities.[11] They came along just before their names were called, and in two cases were actually fetched from nearby, a procedure that was not followed for lesser mortals. As they joined the assembly, they too were given seats and, after being assessed, they left. The reaction of Otieno (T 302) to the fact that his tax was being increased since his wealth was perceptibly greater than the previous year was revealing. Whereas others attempted to plead their case, calling upon the parish chief to attest to their poverty, Otieno laughed and jested about his higher tax and jokingly shook his fist at his assessors.

Part of the definition of an elite is that it display some degree of corporateness, group character, and exclusiveness.[12] We have been concerned with barriers to admission to the elite and the ways in which individuals overcome these in their journeys to pre-eminence. In their day-by-day activities there are few opportunities for the elite to perform as a self-conscious unit within the society since most of their social interaction is within their own neighborhoods and with kin, affines, neighbors, and clients. The tax assessment meeting provided a stage on which their corporate nature was given self-conscious recognition and exhibited. In a subsequent in-

TABLE 20: RANKING OF ELITE MEMBERS BY
EACH OTHER

Code Number	Name	Poll Results		
		20% Sample of Parishioners	Big Men	Peripheral Elite
T 512	Ocen	51	6	4
Kum 682	Opolot	48	9	11
T 606	Odico	41	8	11
T 210	Ekweru	38	8	13
K 418	Nakumusana	33	8	9
T 601	Elamu	29	9	5
N 639	Gawera	21	2	5
T 109	Anyapo	17	4	5
A 542	Otoo	16	4	2
T 302	Otieno	16	4	4

quiry each Big Man in turn was asked privately who he
thought were the leading men of the parish and the criteria on
which he judged them. Agreement was considerable. (Table
20).

A Satellite Elite

The private interviews with Big Men and a re-examination
of the photographic evidence of the tax assessment meeting
revealed the existence of a peripheral or satellite elite around
the clearly visible Big Men, and, in a third inquiry, each of
seven men appearing next in order on the parish poll was
asked whom he considered to be the most influential men in
the community. Each of these fringe influentials had been
named by at least two of the Big Men in the earlier interviews.
A sociogram (Figure 15) brings out the interrelations of the
various sets of choices, showing (1) the mutual choices of the

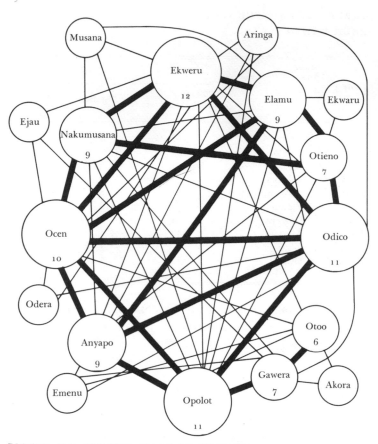

FIGURE 15: CHOICES MADE BY LEADERS
IN GONDO ELITE POLL

elite; (2) the single stranded choices of the elite and their satellites; and (3) references to other individuals in the parish who were not recognized as leaders by either the representative or random sample of parishioners. In the figure, each circle represents a member of the elite involved in one or more mutual choices with other Big Men, the size of the circle indicating the relative number of votes he received.

Elite recognition of their corporate identity is apparent, as is their personal recognition of "men behind the scenes," minor influentials whom they can count upon as part of their support groups. With the exception of Ekwaru, an Aojabule man, most of these influentials are well known within sectors of the community. The influential fringe positions of Sabiti Musana, Ekwaru, Aringa, Ejau, Emenu, Odera, and Akora, for example, represent the neighborhood patterns and sponsorship relations discerned in our analysis of group interaction and agricultural transactions, where the politically oriented activities of all of these men have provided the bulk of our data. Each is a Big Man within his own cluster, neighborhood, and ward but has not achieved pre-eminence in the ranking system of the community at large.

Polyethnicity and the Strategic Elite

The satellite elite represents (with the exception of Musana, the Kenyi ward headman) the Teso gerontocracy. To be a member of the parish elite requires an outward face as well as an inward pose, and none of these men are in a position to represent the polyethnic community as a whole. Elites are standard-setting groups which enact the values current in the society[13] and, in Gondo, these values relate to the polyethnic situation in which neighborliness, filiation, and optation are placed above descent and ethnicity. Each member of the constellar parish elite is able to make his way in all cultural worlds as evidence of his claims to the social capital of the specifically microcosmopolitan heritage; this is not true of the satellite elite, which may be seen rather as part of the orbit in the power struggle between the pre-eminent.

Gondo's polyethnicity is predicated upon dramatic social and economic change, and a structural analysis of the role of Big Men within the community must stand alongside a functional explanation of an elite's high amenity to the forces of development. The elite is the cutting edge of societal change within the parish but it is also one of the mechanisms by which the extent of contact and interaction with the outside society is controlled. The problem of community leadership is to associate within the state without relinquishing parochial integrity. Most change in Gondo, as in much of Africa today, is exogenous change, and the parish elite serves to funnel governmental and administrative demands in a highly selective manner. In anthropological writing individuals such as those who make up the Gondo elite have been termed cultural brokers, gatekeepers, hinges, mediators, and middlemen, but no structural delineation of their type has been made.[14] Nadel, following Eisenstadt, has discussed how elites have the power to facilitate or hinder new developments, attributing this to their personal contact with the community at large, to explicit instruction, and to their communication of the values of the community by enacting them and hence demonstrating them *ad oculos*.[15]

The results of the Gondo inquiry suggest the need to recognize the dualistic nature of an elite, in the corporate body of which is encapsulated community in continuity and change. Hence my description of Gondo's Big Men as a strategic elite, which, by their strategies, serves to select and adopt those elements of the wider societal context which allow for stability in momentum. A characteristic of any elite is its determination to uphold the status quo and this study has shown how eminently placed are Gondo's Big Men to control access to the strategic resources of the community. But a complementary elite characteristic is that its members constitute also those who have been able to avail themselves of the opportunities of change in the outside world and are thereby able to introduce new values, making them, by their practice, acceptable to the community at large. Both the internal structure of the community and its external relations are

[254]

captured in the composition of the elite. As one historian has suggested:[16]

> In the most elementary sense, societies may be said to meet the problem of change by concentrating their efforts alternatively . . . on defending the existing conceptions and relating them to an altered conception. It is not by chance that political struggles have come to be expressed in terms of an incumbent government and opposition, the ins and the outs, conservatives and liberals, parties of order and parties of movement. This fundamental choice between inflexibility and adaptation . . . reflects the accumulation of an infinite number of smaller choices that it is virtually impossible to trace in full detail . . . .

We have weighed the actual freedom of maneuver for each individual to discern whose strategies and choices, in effect, carry megaton values. The structural aspect of our findings suggests that one way in which a community gets round this either/or predicament perceived by the historian is in the complementary composition of a Janus-faced strategic elite. Gondo residents have found a way to eat their cake of stale custom and to have it too.

Conclusion

GONDO WAS SELECTED FOR STUDY precisely because of its ethnic heterogeneity; but in taking individuals as a starting point and observing them in an environmental context, the analysis began by setting aside tribalism and ethnicity, the categories in which many studies of African townships have been framed. This was possible largely because the population of Gondo was small and because its increase in heterogeneity had been gradual, thus permitting an appreciation of the establishment and growth of communal relations between peoples of different cultural backgrounds. It was possible to trace the initial use of ethnic ties as people were brought together by common economic interests. At the end of the nineteenth century, when Gondo lay athwart the moving frontier of Teso expansion westward, shifting agriculturalists and pastoralists came into contact with the Kenyi and Pagero fishermen on the shores of Lake Kyoga and with Nyoro who traded in cattle and iron hoes around the periphery of the lake. For some time economic specialization was maintained mostly along ethnic lines only as the western end of the Serere peninsula became an outlier of the Nyoro kingdom across the lake. The land was fertile and invited conquest and settlement by the Ganda at the end of the nineteenth century. Nyoro petty chiefs were replaced by Ganda, and the local population was administered within an imposed hierarchical structure which recognized different ethnic elements in its composition. This administrative organization was taken over by the British when they began to develop Teso District. This early phase in Gondo's polyethnic contact is characteristic of much of Africa, the Middle East, and many parts of the world where peoples interact within societies that are interdependent by virtue of their exchange economies. This is what Coon has called an ethnic and ecologic mosaic in which the division of labor is by peoples rather than by persons.[1]

The establishment of a port and township at Gondo in 1912 imposed upon people of different ethnic groups already living there side by side an alien structure based upon segregation and limited social interaction, along with the dominant ideology of a plural society. This was an era of the politicization of ethnicity, largely along racial lines but also containing the recognition of privileged ethnic groups. Intercourse was largely that of the marketplace, and political relations were based upon coercion and the sanctions of an outside power.[2]

A contrast may readily be perceived between the multiplex, many-stranded relations of the small-scale society and the single-stranded plural society.[3] Today a measure of the integration of Gondo's internal structure may be found in the number of multiplex relations existing between the various members of the polyethnic community. Historically, with the withdrawal of outside attention, the use of ethnic status gave way to the situational selection of other forms of identification according to the interests and goals of the individuals involved in each social transaction. Interaction now occurs on the basis of sex, age, occupation, religion, politics, and prestige as well as on that of ethnicity. An initial hypothesis that the existence of tribal categories in the census of a small parish did not necessarily indicate that tribal in-group identification would be found there had quickly to be modified and observations made of how and when ethnic status was used, placing it within a range of statuses open to the individual. A process was discerned whereby the basis of transactions shifted from ethnicity to neighborhood and thence to group coevality (extending the concept in the sense that "cohort" may be extended beyond the criterion of age to general life experience). It became apparent that in the historical process factors of sheer size of group and mode of organization besides pure matters of sequence were important in determining intra-ethnic relations. In the contemporary polyethnic scene, while ethnic separation and identity remain apparent on specific occasions and under certain circumstances, the situational use of ethnic status and its strategic redefinition is much more evident. Generally, however, there is an underemphasis on ethnic identity. "Terms like role and status" it has been suggested, "help us to isolate and analyze the parts played by people in social life. This is elementary. What is fundamental, however, is that roles and statuses must be legitimate in the society in which they occur; that is to say, they must have moral and jural sanction."[4] The appeal to ethnic status is not legitimate in Gondo today, unlike the early part of the century when it was the cornerstone of political interaction. In the early days of the administration, ethnic identification was recognized and its growth fostered by chiefships and discriminatory legislation; yet, as early as 1925, economic and ecologic factors were beginning to operate which rendered this action ineffective so that a tribally plural society based upon mechanical solidarity in time gave way to an open, polyethnic, integrated community.

A great deal of the analysis of urban Africa has relied on ethnic categories, distinguishing between tribalism in the town and tribalism in the reserve; between townsmen and tribesmen. There has been little questioning of the circumstances in which this emphasis on tribal identification is, indeed, useful. Although in extended case studies and explorations of urban networks, categories have given way to ego-centric analysis, many outside observers continue to attach a primordial significance to ethnicity as a basic or initial form of identifying individuals. Questions most relevant to Gondo centered upon how it was that so many peoples have become persons in the polyethnic setting.

Similarly, while elsewhere in Africa concern may relevantly

fasten on the interplay between "urban" and "tribal" phenomena (just as ethnic arithmetic may be more relevant in American politics than in British), by virtue of circumstance this proved a false dichotomy in Gondo through a historical failure of the administrative design; and this framework, too, had to be set aside in favor of an ecological, field approach. At the time this could not be done lightly, but a questioning of whether preconceived categories of "tribe" and "urban" might to some extent be ethnocentric, and a belief that a more objective focus might well be on communication and economic development, was confirmed when it was found that the affairs of the parish were indeed conducted along quite other lines than those leading to tribal and urban termini. Ethnic categorization was played down and an overt evaluation was placed on egalitarianism regardless of cultural origins. A conscious striving to identify as post-independent Ugandans, which the times themselves did much to shape, cut indiscriminately across all ethnic categories and all generations. Gondo has been swept along by the currents of modernization, and it may well be that the long-established polyethnic community provides a natural breeding ground for national ideology. Middleton's perception that it is these middle-range townships that provide the main loci for the dissemination of external influence to the rural areas clearly suggests their importance for an understanding of political socialization and the processes of national integration in contemporary Africa.[5]

Since a description and analysis of African society in tribal categories is still common in the anthropological writings on sub-Saharan Africa (Fallers even suggesting that it is his competence in tribal studies that qualifies the anthropologist to study the contemporary African nation-state[6]) and is widespread among other social sciences in Africa, I have labored the point that ethnicity alone does not, cannot, account for everything. Ethnicity is a cultural phenomenon and, as we have seen, definitive historical or temporal bounds may be placed upon the politicization of ethnicity and its articulation by any sectors of the society. This observation calls for a more detailed account of the Teso Administration than was possible here, but it cannot be overemphasized that, since much change in contemporary African communities is exogenous change, studies of administrative organization, ideology, and the changing needs of government and administration are required in order to counterbalance the existing emphasis on peasant receptivity and rural transformations. It may, indeed, be even more important in accounting for the social changes that actually occur at the grassroots level. From the Teso archives it was clear that an understanding of the unfolding nature of the administration, as of the polyethnic community, adds a necessary dimension to any perception of the contemporary rural scene.[7]

Thus, in Teso it was found more useful to inquire into administrative measures to create a public from the shifting sands of acephelously organized pastoralists and peripatetic fishermen than to look into the cultural traits of tribal peoples. It was clear that a Teso awareness, as opposed to ongoing social interactions between culturally related groups, came about only with the establishment of British overrule, and so one may profitably inquire into how this awareness was created. There were many centralizing procedures. During the first twenty years, boundaries were constantly changed until linguistic homogeneity was achieved and the Ngoratok dialect recognized as that of the District, this vernacular being used in schools. Statutory distinctions were made between "natives of the district" and "settlers"; the unification of the land tenure system was attempted; exchange of cattle bridewealth was required of all natives of the district apart from Muslims; cotton growing was made compulsory regardless of primary occupations of different ethnic groups; District by-laws were molded upon Teso tribal customs relating to clan elders, witchcraft accusations, the adoption of children, and so on. The culmination came with an effort to provide Teso with a symbolic figurehead like that of the western kingdoms or, an analogy perhaps more apt, the Kyabazinga of Busoga.[8]

Teso data bear out a suggestion that "tribe" in Africa may validly be thought of as a form of social organization given concrete expression by European administrations rather in the way that Colson found the Makah Indians coming into being on the northwest coast in response to economic opportunities offered by an external agency.[9] Recent accounts of tribal identity in the wider anthropological literature suggest that there is nothing peculiar or sacrosanct about the African tribe.[10] Perhaps it provides one index of a stage in political development, for a different form of societal organization is surely manifest when the inhabitant of an African community can say, as did Odera (T 114),

There are many more people in the parish than there used to be because there are many immigrants who come to work in the ginnery. There are Luo from Kenya; Imiro from Lango; even those from Ngora (Ngoratok) come here for work . . . .

The Ngoratok, it will be remembered, are fellow "tribesmen" of Odera from Ngora county in southern Teso.

In an analysis of changing society in Africa, it is necessary to recognize the peculiar and temporal character of the "tribal" baseline. Much anthropological fieldwork in Africa was carried out in the days of tribes, that is, under colonial regimes. When trade unions are found to transcend tribal organization in the urban areas, it must not be forgotten that this transcended urban tribal organization operated within European parameters.[11] We have attempted to show the significance of this for social relations by comparing the Gondo of 1912 with the Gondo of today. Today tribes are no longer corporate political groups except in rare cases where the ideology of a dominant ethnic group has pervaded the lower strata. Yet it would be overstating the case not to recognize that in some situations it may pay a political entrepreneur even in the post-colonial setting to perpetuate the articulation of tribalism.

Although the unit of analysis in rural Africa today is no longer the tribe, there is as yet a dearth of studies of nontribal forms of societal organization. Anthropologists have contributed their perspectives to problems of land tenure, resettlement schemes, customary law, migration, and other contemporary topics, but there are no structural studies of rural communities: no Roussillons, Suye Muras, or Tepotzlans. Yet developing nontribal communities are not rare, and comparative study would provide valuable African data on a form of social organization with universal provenance. A cross-cultural comparison of societal types is an established goal of social anthropology, and the process whereby the hamlet becomes involved in the larger societal structure has been described as "the one constant and most important constituent of social evolution."[12]

Since, in the past, the tribe was taken as the unit of analysis, it was no accident that most African ethnographies turned out to be studies in "political anthropology" with a characteristic lack of distinction between political and societal processes and forms.[13] Yet, with colonial indirect rule went, hand-in-hand, the introduction of cash crops, the increased mobility of the cultivator, and the mushrooming of nucleated settlement. Even without a Great Tradition, much of African society today is best analyzed as an emergent peasantry.[14]

In Gondo, the local society was envisaged as having moved from colonially structured tribal society to a peasant community based largely on subsistence cultivation and thence to a modern society in which industrialization and urban living rest upon an agricultural base. Taking the community on its own terms, as it existed, and as its people interacted in 1966 and 1967, it was possible then to look back at what had gone into its making and outward at the change it was currently undergoing. Several trends could be discerned, some of which are certainly more universal in character than others, being phenotypical of changing peasant society and incipient urbanization wherever they occur. These trends I have described and tried to measure, not in relation to increased education, distance from larger towns or the seat of government, technological modernization, or agencies of innovation, but with respect to the changing societal structure of the community itself as it is reflected in the altered patterns of social relationships between the individuals living there.

In doing this it was helpful to recognize the fixed nature of a locality in a world of developing economies and changing human relations. Administrators and community settlers were alike transient, but the setting remained constant. A pursuit of ecological relations allowed the handling of analysis over time and a closer appreciation of the changes that actually took place in a way that other models of social change do not. An ecological perspective also led to the establishment of interrelationships between development processes in family growth, in the unfolding of a spatially delineated village structure, and in the gradual coming together over time and in place of a polyethnic community.

This is no place to review the ecological dimensions of the study, but in a continent such as Africa where movements of people have been extensive and the recorded past elusive, this is a useful anthropological approach the value of which has already been demonstrated in studies of pastoral societies.[15] In Africa the settled community may be looked upon as the locale in which peoples become persons as economic and political development brings with it increased room for maneuver for the individual and an expanding range of choice. Much of this is due to the fact that ecologically determined boundaries can more easily be crossed and contact extends beyond contiguous groups. The rural community is no longer an island in a sea of communications and interactions.

In Gondo, the unit of analysis was clearly the parish within a wider community, but, in the short space of fieldwork, the pattern (as opposed to the spread) of relationships in that wider community could not be traced. It was clear, however, that this is an integrative unit of some significance and perhaps one more strategic for the analysis of rural African life than either the nation-state or the tribe. It must be observed that the wider community does not necessarily coincide with the county or the district; in determining sociological units in modern Africa it would be as much an error to focus upon contemporary administrative segments as upon historical cultural entities. The dynamics of their interrelationship, in fact, provides the very stuff of administrative and development politics.[16] As I have drawn it from the Gondo perspective, the wider community is a network of kindred ties which serves to provide a forcing ground for the society's influentials—a catchment area of political facilities. From a structural perspective, such units might be delineated by means of their shared ecological features. Again we observe that interconnectedness of social and ethnic groups based largely upon economic interdependence within shared ecological zones.

This ecological perspective also leads to a constant emphasis upon the dualistic nature of any social unit and the need to recognize its two dimensions of identification and delineation: internal structure and external relations.

Membership in a group, incorporation within it, is dependent upon a category of the excluded, a sense of otherness. . . . That a notion of the other may contribute towards solidarity is probably well established, but the idea is also of importance for the definition of the social unit and for delineation and maintenance of its boundaries. Simple knowledge of the other is not adequate as a means of definition of social boundaries, however, and differentiation and exclusion are best maintained by interaction and not isolation.[17]

Two processes of structural integration and change were distinguished in Gondo. One has its roots in the needs of conservatism and finds its purest expression in primitive society: this is the kinship model of social interaction. The other reflects the widening of social boundaries characteristic of peasant society and involves the use of mechanisms of office incumbency and incumbency substitution. Although these may be viewed in developmental sequence—paradoxically as they coexist—the application of the kinship model contains necessary elements of change, and the most important aspect of the incumbency model is its function in preserving continuity and coherence. The delineation of these two processes focuses upon the choices of individuals faced with alternative paths of action and upon aspects of individual activity. Yet, such individual action is clearly structured; our analysis has been of systemic behavior, since underlying such action is a measure of agreement on the "rules of the game," the working consensus of the community. This revolves around three interrelated aspects of community structure which we will now examine in turn: first, the sharing of a common model of social organization; secondly, the common mode of entry into the community and relationships to land; and thirdly, the recognition of a community elite which has been called, here, a strategic elite.

The common Teso model could only be analyzed for the purposes of this study with respect to the establishment and maintenance of transethnic relations in the microcosmopolitan community. A view of kinship and marriage as development processes affecting political relations between and within ethnic groups provides some insight into alliances in societies practicing bridewealth exchange. Ethnic and class hypergamy arising from the control of cattle, and the even more strategic control in contemporary Teso of legislative bodies that might affect changes in the current system, were not examined. Their existence has repercussions, as has been shown, in the small community, and also has a bearing on national-level politics in an East Africa fast unifying (on paper at least) its statutes relating to marriage practices.[18] The subject of interethnic marriage is, of course, of great import in African urban studies generally, and Gondo would appear to present a case in which compromise has been reached between diverse established patterns and the needs of the immediate situation, without any explicit, new formulations.

Had Teso social organization been previously analyzed, a more cursory comparative presentation of the Gondo-Teso model would have been possible; instead, a chapter of minutiae was required. From our selective analysis, several lines of inquiry emerged which could not be dealt with here. Among them were the following.

1. The coexistence of dual patterns of acquisition and inheritance in a society where new values have been introduced; in this case, the increasing value of land where once cattle provided the major capital asset.

2. The relevance of the house-property complex in a heterogeneous society both for fostering integration and as a vehicle facilitating economic change. The implications of this form of domestic organization might be considered in relation to successful and unsuccessful agricultural innovation in different parts of sub-Saharan Africa.

3. The political implications of dependents (wives, children, and followers) at the grass-roots level in relation to the labor force required for cultivation and the power syndrome that develops.

4. Differences in the mode of integration of outsiders and

the acceptance of a common set of values, a difference that may be reflected in the secessionist problems of modern African states.

5. The utility of using ethnographer's tribal models as the basis for an analysis of political attitudes in nation-states today.

We would expect kinship to be an important element in the social structure of any rural community and, in Gondo, kinship ties are most numerous among those most closely integrated, those who have lived there a long time regardless of ethnic differences. Common, known, shared antecedents are more important than ethnic status. The carry-over from a closed corporate community to a peasant community may be measured by the degree to which a newcomer is embedded within a known kindred. In Gondo we find that (1) kinship ties already exist between many of the immigrants before they settle in Gondo, and (2) that, through incumbent substitution, the antecedents of a new settler are already known to the core of the population. From this initial observation, Maine's perception of movement from kinship to contract in human society may be placed within a bed of other variables. Chief among these are matters of individual choice, manipulation, and status definition. Here, it may be argued, we have shifted from one level of analysis to another. This is indeed the case, for by doing so we are able to provide elements of degree within the generalization. Accepting an overall trend in society from interaction to transaction, we may then ask whether a point is reached at which the community can be said to operate more harmoniously when there is more of one element and less of another. At what point does urban living breed individual stress? Such a question is clearly beyond our jurisdiction, but as the study of industrial organization has shown, "individual behavior changes in kind and degree *after* individual and collective attitudes undergo change, and that these in turn change *after* prior shifts in basic social relationships."[19] The starting point for the inquiry must lie in the spatial dimensions of societal designs for living.

In determining the nature of daily interaction in Gondo, we were led to recognize individual distinctions based upon the mode of entry into the community and the relationship to land established therein. This appreciation of the place of land in the life of Gondo is not an attempt to portray the romantic ethos of the peasant (as a substitute for the cattle complex, perhaps?) captured by Handlin in his account of the peasant origins of immigrants to the United States of America.[20] Connected with land—a zero-sum quantity in most societies—is a built-in sociological mechanism which operates to maintain integration and stability and is therefore valued. This appears to be a mechanism which determines the relative proportion of non-indigenous to indigenous landowning. In Gondo the amount of land at the disposal of "strangers" or incumbents has been constant for at least three generations, and it may well be that the principle of land allocation related here to office incumbency and incumbency substitution has a wider reference.

Land grants indicate recognition that alien specialists are a necessary part of village life. In several English parishes, "certain pieces of land in the common field have from time immemorial been known by the name of a particular trade; and there is often a popular belief that nobody not following the trade, can legally be the owner of the lot associated with it."[21] Similar restrictions on the growth of alien families of Christian smiths who own 1.4 per cent of the land of a Muslim village have been reported for Lebanon, their population remaining static.[22] Any increase was curtailed immediately by emigration. We remember, too, that in Roussillon, a French commune,

. . . an illusion of demographic stability is created primarily by two factors. The first is that the people who move into Roussillon are very much like the people who leave. It is not so much that the young are replaced by the old, but whole families move away and are replaced by families of about the same composition and professions. Even more important in creating the illusion is the existence of a surprisingly small group of people, the core population, which remains in the commune. In most respects they are similar to the immigrants, but it appears that a large proportion are property owners. The political power is largely in their hands. . . . They set the tone of life and maintain it as migrant families come and go. They are the culture bearers.

When one returns to Roussillon after a long absence and sees Madame Icard, "La Léoncie," sitting in the same chair in the town square surrounded by women of her gossip circle, one has the impression that nothing has changed . . . one feels the continuity of life. The fact is, though, that the members of Madame Icard's group have changed, and the owner of the cafe and the men standing at the bar with Aimé are not the same people we left ten years ago. On seeing our old friends, we have a sense of stability. We know, now, that outside the small hard core all is flux.[23]

This passage is quoted at some length, for it clearly suggests a similar situation in which office incumbency and substitution are operating. The flux around a stable core in a peasant township is, as I have tried to demonstrate, a structured flux which contributes to the integration and perdurance of the community. Both Roussillon and Gondo are specific responses to similar historical conditions. Roussillon has had a largely cash economy for a hundred years now and, moreover, as Pitt-Rivers has suggested, the centralization of France following the Revolution has had its impact.[24] A similar pattern of community integration and adjustment to change has come about in Gondo with the introduction of a cash crop, a controlled system of labor migration, and the centralizing effects of the colonial administration. The species of community to which both Roussillon and Gondo belong is not governed less by areal than by temporal factors: both are communities changing in the face of pressures toward modernization.

The flux, the changing elements around the central core, is

structured. Although the non-core individuals may as individuals be transitory, the fact that they are replaced on departure by substitutes, similar to themselves, permits within Gondo the maintenance of transactional ties of mutual obligation and reciprocity which are the essence of community. Thus continuity is maintained in two senses: landholding is not only a vested interest for the family group of the individual incumbent and his successors; it is also an interest of the community at large since the community depends upon the continuing interrelationships of the same categorical elements for the maintenance of the system. The continuity of personnel is important to the integration of community. Situations may differ over time, but individuals meet on the same known and accepted terms because of a set of community-defined statuses they have in common. Gondo remains a single arena in which multiple group affiliations are an important feature of interaction. Multiple ties which, in time, come to take the place of exclusively ecologic or purely economic relationships make for mutual commitments which, expressed in one situation, greatly influence behavior in another. One might question, however, whether certain incoming individuals could not upset the system. Here we may observe that the immigrant's position is analogous with that of Barth's entrepreneur. Since his niche in the community is identical with that of his predecessor and since his assets are within the same limited range (that is, limited to what he has inherited in Gondo and what connections he has brought with him from the world outside), his enterprise within the parish is subject to the same set of restrictions which prevailed prior to his entry. These restrictions "thus describe the effective limits which are imposed on the entrepreneur's choice, once his assets are given and his choice of niche is made."[25] There is a mold into which the stranger incumbent must fit or there is no place for him in the community.

The economic transformation of rural communities currently receives high priority in African development schemes and yet the involuted relationship of landholding and agricultural systems with local integrative and political processes is perhaps insufficiently realized by those who are trying to change them. A community such as Gondo has a set of related mechanisms which preserve its integrity, relate its residents, and structure its change. Programs for development, on the other hand, have, for the most part, been introduced piecemeal by inadequately integrated government agencies. In Gondo this is most apparent in the schemes for marketing cattle and cotton, which fail to recognize the extent of gerontocratic control of peasant land and labor and which fail to assist the spiralist in his long climb through the intricate web of exploitation and Big Man politics. Again, since much community change is exogenous change, an exploration of how it comes about requires that we pay attention to the structure and organization of those administrative organs responsible, at different times in its history, for the communication and inculcation of new alternatives and their accessibility to the people of the community. In this study we have not been able to explore adequately the power of gerontocrats to limit the range of choice open to younger generations or the expressed conservatism of the Teso with respect to cattle, but it certainly seems more useful to view these as rational responses to the rapidity and uncertainty of induced change than as survivals of customary norms or traditional behavior.

Writing of the nineteenth-century European peasantry, Handlin has suggested that "Stability, the deep, cushioning ability to take blows, and yet to keep things as they were, came from the special place of these people on the land. . . . For the peasant was part of a community and the community was held to the land as a whole."[26] This is but one thread in the design of rural persistence; continuity comes also from the structuring of changes in an individual's relationship to the land, and, through the shared land, to others in the community.

It is, of course, in this sphere, that the external administration is often in conflict with the elements that make for coherence and continuity in a community. Peasant perspectives on a cohesive and harmonious way of life may be opposed to external evaluations, based on national economic criteria, of the desirability for change; this is one reason for the composition and structure of the Gondo elite taking the form it does. The elite functions strategically in Gondo, both to maintain the integrity of the community by representing its internal structure, integrating its polyethnic components, and upholding a microcosmopolitan set of values based upon an egalitarian ethos, and to relate the community to the wider world. It is a truism that every society is maintained by pressures toward conformity: the Gondo elite operates to permit a changing society to retain its integrity. Value systems and land relationships both are bound up in change while, at the same time, they perpetuate continuity. The structure and function of the elite reflects this paradox, and its appraisal supplements, by observation of influentials at the grassroots level, existing studies of administrative chiefs and national elites. From the composition of the Gondo elite, we are led to hypothesize that a balance is maintained, through the fluidity of this form of power-and-influence structure, between the consolidating and integrative requirements of the community and the acceptance of change from the outside. The leadership stratum of the polyethnic community integrates and maintains the cohesion of the community in the face of the world. Most important of all, it is a group composed of two elements, "traditionists" and "modernists," in which the man of authority is one who can speak with the voice of either of two worlds: the conservative, stable, inward-looking world of the community or the outward-looking other face of that community which maintains its identity.

The study of elites is a way of closing in upon the elusive and ephemeral dimensions of societal change. Even in eighteen months it was possible to discern the "circulation" of elites since elite status is, in itself, impermanent and, while it is perhaps the culminating status to be achieved in the sequence of Gondo spiralism, it is a status acquired by only a few and made manifest for but a brief span. African rural society, which has so rapidly undergone its great transformation, provides an apt field for the observation and analysis of elites in operation especially in those situations, such as the small township emerging in response to economic needs, where "because of social change or rapid social mobility, appropriate norms for social relationships have not been clearly defined."[27] Southall has characterized an elite as the growing edge of social activity;[28] we have called it the cutting edge of societal change.

Gondo has provided an exploratory case study in societal change in sub-Saharan Africa. The composite elements in the lives of its people have made us look back at their cultural heritage, framed within the grid of tribal organization and colonial overrule. They have made us consider the impact of a money economy and the introduction of cash crops upon an agricultural community, the creation of a peasantry. The interaction of this peasantry with an industrial economy, and the increasing openness of the society, have prompted us to look into the processes involved in polyethnic interaction and the growth of towns. Finally, perhaps, we have been led to understand something of the problem of maintaining community identity in the face of the universal process of increasing scale and complexity in human relations—a problem very real in the shrinking world of today.

Appendix A

abakungulu	(Luganda)	men of Kakunguru, Kakunguru's followers
aidieket	(Ateso)	moot, court, place of arbitration
aiwosa	(Ateso)	to accuse, call to court
ajon	(Ateso)	free millet beer
amalayat	(Ateso)	prostitute (pl. *amalayan*). From Swahili *malaya*
apapero	(Ateso)	girl friend, lover
apolon	(Ateso)	chief; "*lokapolon*, the big one, adult, the important one, the master, the boss, the elder, the chief" (Kiggen 1953:335)
apolon ka ateker	(Ateso)	clan head, area head
apolon ka eriga	(Ateso)	master of the hunt
apunya	(Ateso)	funeral feast
ateker	(Ateso)	clan (pl. *atekerin*)
atenus	(Ateso)	drum, dance
atutubet	(Ateso)	cluster
bao	(Swahili)	a (gaming) board
duka	(Swahili)	a shop (from the Arabic *dukkan*)
ecelet	(Ateso)	quarrel, uproar
eisenere	(Ateso)	a dialect group
eitai	(Ateso)	to work communally
eitela	(Ateso)	an administrative parish
ejie	(Ateso)	fight, combat
ekek	(Ateso)	a patrigroup

Glossary

emorimor	(Ateso)	coordinator (from *aimorimor*, v.t. to combine, amalgamate)
emuron	(Ateso)	doctor (witchdoctor); sorcerer
ere	(Ateso)	homestead
erony	(Ateso)	neighborhood, an administrative "village" or sub-parish (pl. *ireriya*)
esonde	(Ateso)	millet beer sold for cash
etem	(Ateso)	administrative sub-county, lit. "hearth"
etogo	(Ateso)	hut
gombolola	(Luganda)	administrative sub-county; *etem* in Ateso
kasanvu	(Luganda)	Central Government labor taxation
kiboko	(Swahili)	a (hippopotamus hide) whip
kondo	(Luganda)	night marauders, racketeers
luwalo	(Luganda)	compulsory unpaid labor for local chiefs
mlango	(Swahili)	a doorway
muluka	(Luganda)	an administrative parish, *eitela* (Ateso)
mulongole	(Luganda)	an administrative sub-parish, *erony* in Ateso
omukule	(Luganda)	chief, Big Man
porter	(English)	a wage laborer of any kind
shamba	(Swahili)	garden or field
ssaza	(Luganda)	an administrative county, *ebuku* in Ateso
waragi	(Luganda)	Nubian gin

Appendix B

Particulars of Respondent

No. in sample	*1*	*2*	*3*	*4*	*5*	*6*	*7*	*8*	*9*	*10*	*11*	*12*	*13*	*14*	*15*	*16*	*17*	*18*	*19*	*20*	*21*	*22*	*23*	*24*	*25*	*26*
Ward	2	5	1	4	4	6	6	6	5	2	1	6	2	1	1	5	2	5	6	4	5	6	2	6	3	4
Age class	2	2	2	2	3	3	3	3	4	4	4	6	6	5	6	6	6	4	3	2	2	4	5	2	2	2
Ethnicity	T	T	T	T	T	T	T	T	T	T	T	T	T	T	T	T	T	T	T	P	P	P	T	K	K	K
1. Ocen	×	×		×	×	×	×	×	×	×	×	×	×	×	×	×	×	×	×		×	×	×	×	×	×
2. Ekweru	×	×		×	×		×		×	×	×	×	×			×	×	×			×	×	×	×		×
3. Nakumusana		×		×						×			×			×	×	×					×	×	×	×
4. Elamu				×						×			×	×	×	×	×	×	×	×				×	×	
5. Emenu				×							×				×					×						×
6. Mulojja												×	×							×				×		×
7. Odera	×									×	×		×	×	×	×										
8. Akora				×		×						×						×			×		×			
9. Aringa	×		×							×			×	×	×	×	×						×	×		
10. Musana												×					×				×			×		
11. Opolot		×	×	×	×	×	×	×	×	×		×	×	×	×	×		×	×		×	×	×		×	×
12. Odico	×	×			×	×			×	×	×	×	×	×	×	×	×	×	×			×		×		×
13. Gawera		×				×	×	×	×										×	×	×					
14. Otoo		×				×										×			×		×		×			
15. Anyapo			×		×				×	×	×	×	×	×	×	×	×						×			
16. Otieno	×	×	×							×	×	×					×								×	
17. Ejau	×											×							×	×	×					×
18. Amir								×												×				×		
19. Sharif	×					×																			×	×
20. Ogot			×	×				×	×									×								
21. Ebelu		×						×											×						×	
22. Kintu								×																		

CONSERVATORS OR AUTHORITIES

Total votes cast: 226

The Big Man Inquiry

27	*28*	*29*	*30*	*31*	*32*	*33*	*34*	*35*	*36*	*37*	*38*	*39*	*40*	*41*	*42*	*43*	*44*	*45*	*46*	*47*	*48*	*49*	*50*	*51*	*52*	*53*	*54*	*55*	*56*	
3	6	3	3	3	3	5	6	6	3	6	6	6	6	4	6	6	6	6	5	6	5	6	6	6	6	1	6	6	6	
2	3	3	4	4	7	2	3	4	5	5	2	4	3	3	3	5	6	2	7	3	5	2	3	2	4	3	4	3	5	*Results of*
K	K	K	K	K	K	N	N	N	N	N	N	N	S	S	S	G	G	A	A	L	L	K'm	K'm	J	J	K'r	L'g	Ar	As	*Polling*
×	×		×	×	×	×	×	×	×	×	×	×	×		×	×	×	×	×	×	×	×	×	×	×	×	×	×		51
×	×			×	×	×		×	×		×	×	×	×	×	×		×	×				×	×	×	×	×	×		38
×	×		×	×	×		×	×	×	×	×		×	×	×	×	×	×				×	×		×			×		33
	×	×		×	×	×	×	×				×	×		×	×			×				×		×	×	×	×		29
×					×					×		×		×					×	×						×				14
×	×	×		×	×			×	×		×		×		×														×	15
		×				×									×	×										×				13
							×			×							×		×											10
		×																								×				11
×	×		×	×	×			×	×		×				×										×					12
	×	×	×	×	×	×	×	×	×	×	×		×	×	×	×	×	×	×	×	×	×	×	×	×	×	×		×	48
×	×		×		×	×	×	×	×	×	×	×	×	×	×	×						×		×	×	×	×	×	×	41
			×	×						×			×	×		×	×	×	×	×		×	×	×					×	21
				×		×	×	×	×	×		×				×			×		×				×			×		16
											×				×										×	×				17
×	×										×			×				×				×		×					×	16
			×					×		×				×													×	×		12
×	×	×				×	×					×	×	×														×		13
		×	×	×			×		×		×						×					×								13
																×	×	×				×	×	×	×					11
																		×				×	×	×			×			8
																							×	×			×			5
MEDIATORS OR INFLUENTIALS																													TOTAL	447

Total votes cast: 221

Notes

Introduction

1. M. Gluckman, "Inter-hierarchical roles," in M. Swartz (ed.), *Local Level Politics*, Chicago, 1968.

2. E. R. Wolf, "Aspects of group relations in a complex society: Mexico," *American Anthropologist*, LVIII (1956), 1065-78. C. Geertz, "The Javanese *Kijaji*," *Comparative Studies in Society and History*, 2 (1960), 228-49.

3. M. Sahlins, "Poor man, rich man, big man, chief," *Comparative Studies in Society and History*, V (1963), 285-303. J. Barnes, "African models in the New Guinea highlands," *Man*, 62 (1962), 5-9. A. Epstein, "Power, politics and leadership: some central African and Melanesian contrasts," in M. Swartz (ed.), *Local Level Politics*, Chicago, 1968. See, however, D. Oliver, *A Solomon Island Society*, Boston, 1955, Part III.

4. P. Worsley, "The kinship system of the Tallensi: a revaluation," *Journal of the Royal Anthropological Institute*, 85 (1955), 37-75; E. E. Evans-Pritchard, *The Nuer*, Oxford, 1940; *Kinship and Marriage among the Nuer*, Oxford, 1951.

5. I. Schapera, *Government and Politics in Tribal Societies*, London, 1956. F. Barth, *Political Leadership among Swat Pathans*, London, 1959.

6. T. J. Anton, "Power, pluralism and local politics," *Administrative Science Quarterly*, 7 (1963), 425-57. C. M. Bonjean, "Community leadership: a case study and conceptual refinement," *American Journal of Sociology*, 68 (1963), 672-81. R. A. Dahl, "The concept of power," *Behavioral Science*, 2 (1957), 201-15; "A critique of the ruling elite model," *American Political Science Review*, 52 (1958), 463-69; *Who Governs?*, New Haven, 1961. W. V. D'Antonio and H. J. Ehrlich (eds.), *Power and Democracy in America*, Notre Dame, 1961. F. Hunter, *Community Power Structure*, Chapel Hill, 1953. N. W. Polsby, *Community Power and Political Theory*, New Haven, 1963. P. H. Rossi, "Community Decision-making," *Administrative Science Quarterly*, 1 (1957), 415-

43. R. E. Wolfinger, "Reputation and reality in the study of community power," *American Sociological Review*, 25 (1960), 672-81. H. F. Kaufman, in "Towards an interactional conception of community," *Social Forces*, 38 (1959), 8–17, defines a community as a set of locality-oriented interactions: as goal-directed interaction processes engendered by the fact of people's common residence in a locality.

7. W. Watson, *Tribal Cohesion in a Money Economy*, Manchester, 1958, p. 193: ". . . insecurity of employment is one of the general conditions of labor in all underdeveloped countries; the men are unskilled, work for short periods, and present themselves in large numbers for employment . . . rights to the use of land are their formal security; they may be expelled from any job in the towns, but not from the land."

8. A. I. Richards, *Economic Development and Tribal Change*, Cambridge (1956), p. 168. "The methods by which the Ganda and other African tribes incorporate foreign elements have not been studied as fully as they should be in view of the enormous amount of movement of individual Africans. . . . Nor is this process of tribal admixture new. The history of Africa as we know it is a record of the continuous spread of different tribal or even kinship groups by a slow process of natural expansion and infiltration of other cultures as well as by more violent means. . . .Whenever individuals or groups of one culture try to penetrate another culture there is a problem of structural incorporation."

The name GONDO rather than BUGONDO, which appears on most maps and in most administrative records, is adopted here in order to avoid confusion with either Budongo or Buganda. Such usage conforms to the recent Teso practice of Ateso-izing English and Luganda place names. Gondo is a trading center under the direct control of the Teso Land Board (Teso Land Board General Notice No. 114 of 1963) and, as such, exemplifies the Type C African town which Middleton has recently added to Southall's dichotomy. A. W. Southall (ed.), *Social Change in Modern Africa*, London, 1961, distinguished traditional, homogeneous towns as Type A and new urban conglomerations with largely immigrant populations as Type B. J. Middleton, *The Effects of Economic Development on Traditional Political Systems in Africa South of the Sahara*, The Hague, 1966, pp. 31–33; "A third type of urban center (Type C) is the small trading and administrative center. These provide the main loci for the dissemination of external influence to the rural areas, and it is in them that the new elites and middle classes are largely recruited and that their members have relationships with those of their kind and neighbors who are not classed as elites or évolués. . . . Material on township (Type C) is scattered and slight."

9. L. Mair, "How small scale societies change" in J. Gould (ed.), *Penguin Survey of the Social Sciences 1965*, London, 1965.

10. Quoted in R. Frankenberg, *Communities in Britain*, Baltimore, 1966, p. 260. Cf. W. Watson, "Social mobility and social class in industrial communities," *Closed Systems and Open Minds*, Edinburgh, 1964: "The progressive ascent of specialists of different kinds through a series of positions in one or more hierarchical structures, and the concomitant residential mobility through a number of communities at one or more steps in this ascent, forms a characteristic combination of social and spatial mobility which I propose to call spiralism." See M. Stacey, *Tradition and Change: a Study of Banbury*, Oxford, 1960.

11. J. Barnes, "Networks and political processes" in M. Swartz (ed.), *Local Level Politics*, Chicago, 1968.

12. A. Etzioni, *The Active Society*, New York, 1968, pp. 47–48.

13. R. K. Merton, *Social Theory and Social Structure*, New York, 1949, p. 370.

14. *Ibid.*, p. 369.

15. *Ibid.*, p. 383.

16. E. Goffman, *The Presentation of Self in Everyday Life*, New York, 1959.

17. R. K. Merton, unpublished lecture notes, Columbia University, 1965–1967.

18. F. Barth, *Models of Social Organization*, London, 1966.

19. R. Firth, *Essays on Social Organization and Values*, London, 1964.

20. *Ibid.*, p. 61.

21. L. Mair, "How small scale societies change."

22. A. Mayer, "The significance of quasi-groups in the study of complex societies" in M. Banton (ed.), *The Social Anthropology of Complex Societies*, Edinburgh, 1966.

[283]

23. M. Ginsberg, *Sociology*, London, 1953, p. 40.

24. M. Mead, *Continuities in Cultural Evolution*, New Haven, 1964.

Chapter 1: Gondo Society

1. Geographical data on Teso District appear in G. S. Carter, *The Papyrus Swamps of Uganda*, Cambridge, n.d.; I. Langdale-Brown, H. A. Osmaston, and J. G. Wilson, *The Vegetation of Uganda and Its Bearing on Land Use*, Entebbe, 1964; D. N. McMaster, *A Subsistence Crop Geography of Uganda*, London, 1962; A. M. O'Connor, *An Economic Geography of East Africa*, New York, 1966.

2. J. W. King, "An historical note on Nile transport," *The Uganda Journal*, 30 (1966), 219–22.

3. TDA XCST/1.78/33-35, 78A, 78. *An index list to the archives at the office of the District Commissioner, Teso District* was compiled in 1960, and most of the files used at Soroti in 1966–1967 conformed to the system outlined in this index. A copy of the index may be found in the library of the Makerere Institute for Social Research, Makerere University College.

4. The linguistic classification followed is that of J. Greenberg, *The Languages of Africa*, Indiana, January 1963. See also I. Fodor, *The Problems in the Classification of the African Languages*, Budapest, 1969.

5. Ethnographic studies of Bantu-speaking groups include: (GANDA) L. Mair, *An African People in the Twentieth Century*, London, 1934; J. Roscoe, *The Baganda*, London, 1911; (KIGA) M. Edel, *The Chiga of Western Uganda*, Oxford, 1957; (NYORO) J. Beattie, *Bunyoro: an African Kingdom*, New York, 1960; J. Roscoe, *The Bakitara or Banyoro*, Cambridge, 1923; (HIMA) J. Roscoe, *The Banyankole*, Cambridge, 1923; (SOGA) L. Fallers, *Bantu Bureaucracy*, Chicago, 1956; (KENYI) J. Roscoe, *The Northern Bantu*, Cambridge, 1915; A. Kitching, *On the Backwaters of the Nile*, Cambridge, 1912.

6. The precolonial movement of peoples in this part of Uganda is attested to by G. Huntingford, *The Northern Nilo-Hamites*, London, 1953; D. Low, "The Northern Interior, 1840–84" in R. Oliver and G. Mathew (eds.), *History of East Africa*, Vol. I, Oxford, 1963; B. Ogot, *History of the Southern Luo*, Vol. I, Nairobi, 1967; A. I. Richards, *Economic Development and Tribal Changes*, Cam-

bridge, 1956; A. Southall, "The peopling of Africa—the linguistic and sociological evidence" in M. Posnansky (ed.), *Prelude to East African History*, London, 1966.

7. Ethnographic studies of Sudanic and Nilotic peoples include: (ACHOLI) F. K. Stirling, *The Acholi of Uganda*, London, 1960; (ALUR) A. Southall, *The Alur*, Cambridge, 1953; (LUGBARA) J. Middleton, *The Lugbara of Uganda*, New York, 1965; (LANGO) J. Driberg, *The Lango*, London 1923; (LUO) J. Crazzolara, The *Lwoo*, I-III, Verona, 1950, 1951, 1954. References to the Pagero (Jo-Kaweer) appear in Crazzalaro, 1950.

8. P. Gulliver, "The Karamojong cluster," *Africa*, 22 (1952), 1–22; J. Lawrance, "The Karamojong cluster—a note," *Africa*, 23 (1953), 244–49. Ethnographic studies include (KARAMOJONG) N. Dyson-Hudson, *Karimojong Politics*, Oxford, 1966; (TESO) J. Lawrance, *The Iteso*, London, 1957; A. Wright, "Notes on Iteso social organization," *The Uganda Journal*, 9 (1942), 57–80; P. and P. H. Gulliver, *The Central Nilo-Hamites*, Ethnographic Survey of Africa, London, 1953.

9. A study of Asians has been made by H. Morris, *The Indians in Uganda*, London, 1968.

10. E. Leach, *Political Systems of Highland Burma*, London, 1954.

11. L. R. Sharp, "People without politics" in V. Ray (ed.), *Systems of Political Control and Bureaucracy in Human Societies*, Seattle, 1958.

12. E. Leach, *Pul Eliya*, Cambridge, 1961; E. K. Gough, "Changing kinship usages in the setting of political and economic change among the Nayars of Malabar," *The Journal of the Royal Anthropological Institute of Great Britain and Ireland*, 82 (1952), 71–87.

13. F. Welbourn, *Religion and Politics in Uganda, 1952–1962*, Nairobi, 1965.

14. J. Elliott, *Report on an Investigation into Conditions Affecting Unskilled Labour, and the Supply Thereof, within the Protectorate*, Entebbe, 1937, pp. 7–8: "I had numerous opportunities of talking to some of the permanent labour employed at ginneries and on many occasions found that, although the men were permanently resident near the ginnery and very often called themselves members of the local tribe, they were, in actual fact, nothing of the sort."

15. Graduated taxation was introduced in 1956 and levied under

the provisions of the District Administration (District Councils) Ordinance 1955. The table in use in 1966 (mimeo: Instructions regarding tax assessment and composition of tax assessment committees in Teso District vide Local Administration Ordinance 1962, Part IX) recognized four grades of farmer:

"Grade IV. 50/-. This grade is for boys who are entered to pay tax for the first time at the age of eighteen.

"Grade III. 60/-. This grade for those who have no livestock but are strong enough to work to earn living.

"Grade II. 80/-. This grade is for men who own ploughs and also own a few number of cattle or livestock and bullocks for ploughing.

"Grade I. 100/-. This grade is for those men who are known in the area as progressive farmers and own a large number of livestock."

Incomes other than from farming fell under no strict guidelines, being classed simply as "wages, salaries and some business men" and tax was adjudged between 150 and 200 shillings.

16. Accounts of savanna agriculture include M. Haswell, *Economics of Agriculture in a Savannah Village*, London, 1953; and P. de Schlippe, *Shifting Cultivation in Africa*, London, 1956. Studies of Teso agriculture include E. Jones, "The Economics of Teso Agriculture," unpublished manuscript, Department of Agriculture, Entebbe, n. d.; D. Parsons, *The Systems of Agriculture Practised in Uganda: No. I, Introduction and Teso Systems*, Entebbe, 1960; T. Othieno, *An Economic Study of Peasant Farming in Two Areas of Bukedi District, Uganda*, M. A. Thesis (Agric.) , Makerere University College, 1966; P. Wilson and J. Watson, "Two surveys of Kasilang erony," *The Uganda Journal*, 20 (1956) , 182–97; P. Wilson, "An agricultural survey of Moruita erony, Teso," *The Uganda Journal*, 22 (1958) , 22–38.

17. C. Sauer, *Agricultural Origins and Dispersals*, New York, 1952.

18. A. Martin, *The Marketing of Minor Crops in Uganda*, London, 1963.

19. The politics of cotton marketing in Uganda is described by C. Ehrlich, "The Marketing of Cotton in Uganda, 1900–1950," unpublished doctoral dissertation, University of London, 1958; "Some Social and Economic Implications of Paternalism in Uganda," *Journal of African History*, 4 (1963) , 275–85.

20. This chronology is largely based on archival data. See also A.

Dunbar, *A History of Bunyoro-Kitara*, London, 1965; J. Gray, "Kakunguru in Bukedi," *The Uganda Journal*, 27 (1963), 31–59; R. Kirkpatrick, "Lake Choga and the surrounding country," *Geographical Journal*, 13 (1899), 453–64; A. Roberts, "The sub-imperialism of the Baganda," *Journal of African History*, 3 (1962), 435–50; A. Robertson, "Historical Aspects of Current Migration into Bugerere County, Buganda," unpublished manuscript, 1965; D. W. Robertson, *Historical Conditions Contributing to the Soga System of Land Tenure*, Entebbe, 1940; H. Thomas, "Capax Imperii—the story of Semei Kakunguru," *The Uganda Journal*, 6 (1939), 125–36; Lawrance, *The Iteso*.

Chapter 2: Political Institutions

1. TDA. VADM/3/1. (Kumi Station Diary, 1909)

2. Interviews with former chiefs (K. Abusi, Y. Akora, D. Alegan, M. Anyapo, E. Ocaet, Y. Oiko, Y. Okasu, P. Olinga, P. Omosing, A. Otigo), January–March, 1967.

3. TDA 1941. ADM/17. (Native Administration in the Eastern Province, Past Present and Future Policies—E. D. Tongue)

4. L. Mair, "Busoga local politics," *Journal of Commonwealth Political Studies*, Vol. 5, No. 2 (July 1967), 91–108.

5. See, however, G. Emwanu, "The reception of alien rule in Teso: 1896–1927," *The Uganda Journal*, 31 (1967), 171–82.

6. TDA. XADM/10/A. 1915. (Miscellaneous correspondence with Provincial Commissioner)

7. TDA. VADM/7/1. 1953. (The council system in Teso—notes for members of the District Team—J. Lawrance)

8. TDA. ADM/20/4/Pt. II. (Letter from K. Abosi to District Commissioner, July 22, 1958)

9. TDA. VADM/3/6. 1941. (Station Diary, September 1935– February 1938)

10. F. Burke, *Local Government and Politics in Uganda*, Syracuse, 1964, pp. 144–45.

11. There is no published reference to the office of *emorimor* in Teso. However, on the eve of the London Conference prior to Ugandan independence, the Teso District Council voted that the

title "Secretary-General of Teso" should be replaced by the "traditional" title *emorimor*. Through the years various other titles had also been suggested for this office, support for each reflecting local and dialectal differences in the district. Although on this occasion (Minute 61 of 1962) *emorimor* was adopted by a vote of 30 to 29, it does not appear to have been used subsequently.

12. R. Peagram, *A Report on the General Election to the Legislative Council of the Uganda Protectorate Held in March 1961*, Entebbe, 1961, p. 4.

13. R. Peagram, *A Report on the General Elections to the National Assembly of Uganda Held on the 25th April, 1962*, Entebbe, 1962, p. 5.

14. *Commission of Inquiry into the Management of the Teso District Council, March 1958*, Entebbe, 1958; *Memorandum by the Protectorate Government on the Report of the Commission of Inquiry into the Management of the Teso District Council*, Entebbe, 1958; *Uganda Argus*, July 6, 1958; TDA. ADM 20 (District Council, General correspondence: L. Okol to Chairman. Nov. 24, 1950; Ecaak to District Commissioner, March 4, 1957); Burke, *Local Government and Politics in Uganda*; L. Mair, "Review of local government and politics in Uganda," *Africa*, 34 (1964), 377; TDA. ADM 20/Pt. II (Letter Permanent Secretary, Ministry of Regional Administration to Secretary General, Sept. 6, 1962); TDA. ADM 21/1/0 (Teso Land Board minutes—letter Clan leaders to Secretary General, March 20, 1964; Letter from six councillors to Minister of Regional Administration, Nov. 24, 1962).

15. P. Worsley, *The Trumpet Shall Sound* (2nd, Augmented edition), New York, 1968, pp. 277–79; J. Vincent, "Anthropology and political development" in C. Leys (ed.), *Politics and Change in Developing Countries*, Cambridge, 1969, pp. 42–43.

16. O. Doctorow, "Group structure and authority," *American Anthropologist*, 65 (1963), 312–22.

17. R. Bierstedt, "An analysis of social power," *American Sociological Review*, 15 (1950), 730–38.

18. N. B. Ryder, in "The cohort as a concept in the study of social change," *American Sociological Review*, 30 (1965), 8–17, defines a cohort as "the aggregate of individuals (within some population definition) who experienced the same event within the same time interval. . . . Conceptually the cohort resembles most the ethnic

group: membership is determined at birth, and often has considerable capacity to explain variance, but need not imply that the category is an organized group."

Chapter 3: Land and Labor: The Historical Dimension

1. P. Powesland, in *Economic Policy and Labour* (East African Studies, No. 10), Entebbe, 1957, provides the national framework for the observations that follow. See especially p. 15, and S. Olivier, *White Capital and Coloured Labour*, London, 1929, p. 56.

2. TDA. VADM/IJ/1–2 (Administrative tour books, Serere County, 1914–27); XLAN/2 (Township plots); XMUN/1/31A, 55 (Small townships).

3. Interviews with chiefs, 1967; XLAB/1/264 (Native porters, Masters and Servants Ordinance, 1914); XLAB3/110/13 (Marine Kioga fuel cutting, 1913–22); XLAB/3/155/13 (Accidents to workmen in ginneries, 1913–22).

4. Powesland, *Economic Policy and Labour*, pp. 6, 18, 28, 37.

5. TDA. VADM/IJ/1. (Serere County tour book)

6. TDA. XAGR/4. (Famine reports; cultivation of food crops)

7. C. Ehrlich, "Some social and economic implications of paternalism in Uganda," *Journal of African History*, 4 (1963), 275–85.

8. TDA. VADM/IJ/1–2. (Tour book entries on Gondo in Serere County reports)

9. Entebbe archives.

10. *Uganda Herald*, October 12, 1912. Elsewhere, the same writer contributes a revealing sidelight on labor relations in the ginnery at this time: "Civilized countries need not think that they have the monopoly in labor disputes and strikes: for here among the semi-savages of darkest Africa, such incidents are not uncommon. But here is a very simple remedy which, when threatened to be applied, often nips the strike in the bud: I refer to the *kiboko*." The kiboko is a whip made from the hide of a hippopotamus.

11. TDA. XADM/10/A. 1912. (Miscellaneous correspondence with Provincial Commissioner: No. 549/A/148)

12. TDA. VADM/IJ/1. (Serere County Tour Book)

13. TDA. XMUN/1.30. (Letter District Medical Officer, Soroti to District Commissioner, Teso, on alterations to minor townships)

14. The original plan is among the Entebbe archives.

15. TDA. XCST/1, 78A. 1911b. (Census of Serere County, 1911). By the Control of Settlement Bye-law, 1951, a native of the district is "any African born in the District, or is cultivating land on date of this bye-law, or has lived for 3 consecutive years, or whose father is a native of the district." A settler means "a person of a tribe other than Teso who enters Teso District for the purpose of settling there." This Bye-law was approved by Crown Law Office, Nov. 14, 1950, TDA. ADM 20 (District Council General Correspondence).

16. No detailed account is given here of the Ganda since, unlike most of those settled in Serere, the Gondo residents were either fishermen or ginnery workers. Elsewhere in the county the Ganda elite has suffered status reversal to a politically significant degree.

17. TDA VADM/IJ/1; Entebbe archives.

18. J. S. Furnivall, in *Colonial Policy and Practice in the Netherlands East Indies,* Cambridge, 1948, considered one of the most marked characteristics of the plural society to be that the union of differing racial elements was not voluntary but was imposed by a colonial power or by the force of economic circumstance. Recent anthropological discussions of the model appear in H. Morris, *The Indians in Uganda,* London, 1968, and L. Kuper and M. G. Smith (eds.) , *Pluralism in Africa,* Berkeley and Los Angeles, 1969.

19. Morris, *The Indians in Uganda,* pp. 161–79; C. Ehrlich, "The Marketing of Cotton in Uganda, 1900–1950," unpublished doctoral dissertation, University of London, 1958. Critiques of the model appear in M. Freedman, "The growth of a plural society in Malaya," *Pacific Affairs,* 33 (1960) , 158–68; H. Morris, "Some aspects of the concept Plural Society," *Man,* new series, 2 (1967) , 169–84; J. Rex, "The plural society in sociological theory," *British Journal of Sociology,* 10 (1959) , 114–24; M. G. Smith, *The Plural Society in the British West Indies,* Berkeley and Los Angeles, 1965.

20. Furnivall, *Colonial Policy and Practice in the Netherlands East Indies.*

21. Kuper and Smith in *Pluralism in Africa,* pp. 7–22, suggest that cultural pluralism may provide an ideology of domination or of conflict in a struggle for power between different groups, the significance which each attaches to cultural differences varying with changes in the structure of their relationship with one another and, more particularly, with changes in relative power. This is applicable

both to an analysis of race relations in Gondo and to an understanding of the situations in which ethnicity is politicized. Charles B. Hagan, in "The group in political science" in R. Young (ed.), *Approaches to the Study of Politics*, Northwestern, 1958, p. 50, recognized three dimensions to group relations: (1) sizes of the groups; (2) intensity of their interaction; and (3) their organizational cohesion and leadership. In this way, the ethnic group organization of the Acholi and Luo, for example, can be seen to depend upon the numbers involved and to change over time. This point is elaborated in Chapters 4 and 7, and underlies the historical perspective of this present chapter since it is clear that tendencies toward group action cannot be fully described through cultural patterns. Intervening variables must be sought and referred back to the conditions which engendered and maintained them.

22. T D A. V A D M/I J/2. (Memorandum: Abantu abakola mikibuga Bugondo okupasa from Parish Chief to District Commissioner)

23. T D A. X M I L/3/9. (Repatriation of ex-KAR soldiers, 1919–22).

24. Powesland, *Economic Policy and Labour*, pp. 24–26, 31, 37. According to the *Annual Report of the Director of Public Works*, Entebbe, 1923, p. 10, at this time the Teso cultivator received 60/- from cotton, and the monthly wage of the unskilled laborer was 9–10/-.

25. Powesland, *Economic Policy and Labour*, p. 56.

26. J. Beattie, "Democratization in Bunyoro: the impact of democratic institutions on a traditional African kingdom," *Civilizations*, 11 (1961), 8–18.

Chapter 4: Ecology and Community

1. C. Arensberg and S. Kimball, *Culture and Community*, New York, 1965, p. 3.

2. Strip cropping was introduced with the plough into Teso in 1909, a 3-yard unploughed washtop being left between uncultivated plots. A District Council resolution stipulates that no one shall cultivate a field more than 35 yards by 140 yards in area. In agricultural statistics this is considered one acre (D. Parsons, *The Systems of Agriculture Practiced in Uganda: No. I, Introduction and Teso Systems*, Entebbe, 1960, p. 15.) This unit of cultivation is a garden; an acreage half as large is a plot. In carrying out a sur-

vey of landholding in the parish, the results were most usefully expressed in terms of gardens and plots, both translated into units or acres. The average seasonal cultivation is 4 gardens and 3 plots, some double-cropped, or 5.5 units or acres per adult male homestead owner. The largest holding in the parish was 21 acres. The actual land area cultivated in Teso in 1956–1957 was in the nature of 1.61 acres per head of population, or 6.1 units per taxpayer (*ibid.,* p. 31). Six farms studied in 1957–1958 ranged in size from 2.84 to 13.11 acres (E. Jones, "The Economics of Teso Agriculture," unpublished manuscript, Department of Agriculture, Entebbe, n. d.) ; the Serere County farm, considered "average," is 6.82 acres. The Gondo average, being slightly lower than this, would appear to reflect alternative sources of income rather than land shortage since there were large areas uncleared in Aojabule, Kabola, and Opucet. An important variable in the amount of land cleared is, of course, the availability of labor and ploughs; cultivation is related to these political facilities, as shown in Chapter 9.

3. R. K. Merton, *Social Theory and Social Structure,* New York, 1949, p. 385: "The individual moves more or less continuously through a sequence of statuses and associated roles, each phase of which does not greatly differ from the one which has gone before. Although his 'official' (socially acknowledged) transfer into a new status may seem to be sudden, more often than not this is only because the informal antecedent preparation has gone unnoticed. There is less discontinuity in status-sequences than might appear on the social surface, with its celebrative *rite de passage* and legally enacted changes in status." Of all forms of land rights, only land ownership receives such social acknowledgment in Gondo.

4. R. Redfield, *The Primitive World and Its Transformations,* Ithaca, New York, 1953, pp. 33–34.

5. S. Silverman, "Patronage and community-nation relationships in central Italy," *Ethnology,* 4 (1965) , 172–89.

Chapter 5: Kinship, Marriage, and Property Relations

1. A. Wright, "Notes on Iteso social organization," *The Uganda Journal,* 9 (1942) , 57–80, describes the "traditional" societal organization of the Teso: age classes, initiation, clans, and *itemwan,* criticizing Kennedy's resurrection of clan elders in the belief that they had a political role. J. Lawrance, *The Iteso,* London, 1957,

contains descriptive chapters on kinship, territorial and age-system groupings as well as a section on birth, marriage, and death, and useful descriptions of material culture and administrative history. F. Burke, in *Local Government and Politics in Uganda,* Syracuse, 1964, discusses confusions over *ateker* (clan) and provides comparative data on two Usuku villages.

2. J. Beattie, "Democratization in Bunyoro: the impact of democratic institutions on a traditional African kingdom," *Civilizations,* 11 (1961), 11.

3. J. Vincent, "Teso society in transformation: Colonial penetration in Teso District and its contemporary significance" in J. Coleman, L. Cliffe, and M. Doornbos (eds.), *Symposium on Penetration* (in press).

4. A case study of gerontocratic privilege with respect to the co-operative marketing of cotton in Gondo appears in J. Vincent, "Local cooperatives and parochial politics in Uganda," *The Journal of Commonwealth Political Studies,* 8 (1970) 3–17.

5. A. I. Richards, *Economic Development and Tribal Change,* Cambridge, 1956, p. 174: "Foreigners remain on the outskirts of social life unless they can marry into the landowning classes or build up groups of their own tribesmen and possibly land of their own. They cannot, and do not, play a main part in village affairs." (p. 179) "There is currently no infiltration of leadership roles."

6. J. Van Velsen, unpublished manuscript, Makerere Institute of Social Research.

7. M. Gluckman, "Kinship and marriage among the Lozi of Northern Rhodesia and the Zulu of Natal" in A. Radcliffe-Brown and E. Evans-Pritchard (eds.), *African Systems of Kinship and Marriage,* Oxford, 1950; M. Fortes, "Introduction" in J. Goody (ed.), *The Development Cycle in Domestic Groups,* Cambridge, 1958.

8. Fortes, "Introduction" in J. Goody (ed.), *The Development Cycle in Domestic Groups,* p. 2: "The process of social reproduction, in broad terms, includes all those institutional mechanisms and customary activities and norms which serve to maintain, replenish and transmit the *social capital* from generation to generation. . . . The nodal mechanism is well known. In all human societies, the workshop, so to speak, of social reproduction, is the domestic group. It is this group which must remain in operation over a stretch of

time long enough to rear offspring to the stage of physical and social reproductivity if a society is to maintain itself. This is a cyclical process. The domestic group goes through a cycle of development analogous to the growth cycle of a living organism. The group as a unit retains the same form, but its members, and the activities which unite them, go through a regular sequence of changes during the cycle which culminates in the dissolution of the original unit and its replacement by one or more units of the same kind. . . . A significant feature of the development cycle of the domestic group is that it is at one and the same time *a process within* the internal field (the domestic) *and a movement* governed by its relations to the external field (politico-jural)." Italics supplied.

L. Despres, in *Cultural Pluralism and National Politics in British Guiana,* New York, 1967, pp. 74–86, finds a sharp contrast between the development cycles of East Indians and Afro-Guianese. In Gondo, apart from Asians, Hima, and Luo, emphasis must be placed on similarities.

9. C. Arensberg and S. Kimball, *Culture and Community,* New York, 1965, p. 17.

10. P. Rigby, *The Gogo of Central Tanganyika,* unpublished doctoral dissertation, University of Cambridge, 1964, p. 6, and *Cattle and Kinship among the Gogo,* Ithaca, 1969.

11. See Wright, "Notes on Iteso social organization," p. 5: "The etem . . . consisted of a group of inter-marrying lineages (ekek. pl. ikekia) who maintained agnatic distinctions by the use of the kindred or clan names (ateker) among the men and by the observance of various taboos (eital, pl. itale) among the women."

12. The set of two-letter abbreviations introduced by G. Murdock, "Bifurcate merging: a test of five theories," *American Anthropologist,* 49 (1947) , 56–68, is followed. Thus Fa stands for father, mo for mother, o for older, y for younger, etc. To these are added h/c for head of cattle, and h/g for head of goats. The East African shilling, made up of 100 cents, was, in 1966, equivalent to 14 cents in U.S. currency.

Chapter 6: Core Families

1. J. Goody, "The mother's brother and the sister's son in West Africa," *The Journal of the Royal Anthropological Institute of Great Britain and Ireland,* 89 (1953) , 61-88.

2. Neither name appears in the Uganda census, and the Gondo enumerator of the 1948 census declares that he put them down as Nyoro. Pagero are most certainly the people Crazzolara, in *The Lwoo*, I-III, Verona, 1950, calls Jo-Pawiir. He suggests "a valuable witness to the eastward expansion of old Pawiir is the presence of the Jo-Lwoo pocket in southern Kaberamaido north west of Lake Kyoga. They call themselves Jo-Pawiir (the Jo-Wear, or Jo-Kaweer of the Lango). . . . Looking for good hunting grounds they came to Bululu which the Banyala had abandoned migrating to Bugerere. From Bululu the Jo-Pawiiri eventually . . . crossed Lake Kyoga to Kaberamaido and Kumam country, which latter was mainly a hunting ground. It was in Bululu that they changed their traditional hide clothing for barkcloth which they obtained from the Banyala in return for chickens." Most of the Pagero claim to have come from Kaweri Island from whence they were "cleared" by the administration at the beginning of the century.

3. These clusters are also units of peer group sociability, of constant daily interaction and intimate knowledge of family affairs. Within the *atutubet* each homestead in turn provides millet beer for the evening's drinking. H. Gans, *The Urban Villagers*, New York, 1962, p. 75: "Sociability becomes a routinized gathering of a relatively unchanging peer group of family members and friends."

4. The distinction would be expressed only to an outsider; it is not a basis for social interaction or discrimination as, for example, the cleavage between "traditional" and "non-traditional" in Banbury as described by M. Stacey, *Tradition and Change: a Study of Banbury*, London and Oxford, 1960.

Chapter 7: Immigrants

1. G. Simmel, "The stranger" in K. H. Wolff (ed.), *The Sociology of Georg Simmel*, New York, 1950, p. 403.

2. L. Fallers, "The stranger: a note," *Comparative Studies in Society and History*, 4 (1962), 335.

3. Nyoro in Gondo participate fully in agricultural activities. As early as 1913 it was recorded, TDA. VADM/IJ/1 (Serere County tour book) : "For a great many years past the Banyoro have established themselves on the shores of Lake Chioga, and have freely mixed up with the Bakedi."

4. *Teso District Annual Report*, 1954.

Chapter 8: Outsiders

1. R. Dunning, "Ethnic relations and the marginal man in Canada," *Human Organization*, 18 (1959), 117–22.

2. E. Leach, *Political Systems of Highland Burma*, London, 1954, p. 8.

3. H. Maine, *Village Communities in the East and West*, London, 1876, p. 127.

4. D. Stenning, in "Preliminary Observations on the Balokole Movement Particularly among the Bahima in Ankole District," Conference Paper, East African Institute of Social Research, 1958, describes the history of the movement.

5. T D A. A D M 21/1H/16/2. (Minutes of the Natural Resources Committee.)

6. This study was undertaken at the request of Dr. E. A. Brett, who, along with Professor M. Crawford Young, was carrying out an inquiry into cooperative organization in Uganda in 1967. The original report, which also included material relating to the Teso Cooperative Union with its headquarters at Soroti, was presented at a Cooperative Seminar held at Makerere University College, Kampala, on August 11, 1967.

Chapter 9: The Politics of Agriculture

1. F. Barth, *Models of Social Organization*, London, 1966, p. 4: "A clear concept of transaction leads us to a recognition of a very fundamental social process: the process which results where parties in the course of their interactions systematically try to assure that the value gained for them is greater or equal to the value lost."

2. C. Hagan, "The group in political science" in R. Young (ed.), *Approaches to the Study of Politics*, p. 49.

3. Barth, *Models of Social Organization*, p. 4.

4. The most important political facility is not simply legitimate claims to the labor of others but the power to muster it at the exact moment it is required in spite of the costs to those aligned. M. Haswell, *Economics of Agriculture in a Savannah Village*, London, 1953.

[296]

5. The actor's model presents *eitai* as "traditional" kin-based work parties. They may have been once, but are certainly so no longer.

6. Unlike the Mambwe community studied by W. Watson, in *Tribal Cohesion in a Money Economy*, Manchester, 1958.

7. The different sociological patterns underlying the command of work groups and the sharing of ploughs reflect the different set of transactions involved in the process of maintaining a fundamental relation between the structuring of internal and external relations for the neighborhood. In a study of social change and economic development of Gondo and the wider community (in the course of preparation) each neighborhood is characterized by its external relations as well as by internally structured transactions. On the basis of differences in the nature and complexity of both, a distinction may be made between more or less developed neighborhoods throughout the wider community, and this may be related to administrative penetration and the widening opportunities for change.

Chapter 10: Crisis, Violence, and Arbitration

1. R. Bierstedt, "An analysis of social power," *American Sociological Review*, 15 (1950), 736.

2. A neglected feature of the inquiry is whether increased violence and drink result from the increased cultivation of millet as the crop that follows cotton (introduced in 1907) in the rotation.

3. This observation would support the conclusions of Herbert Weiss, *Political Protest in the Congo*, Princeton, New Jersey, 1967, pp. 291–97, that local leadership has been a neglected factor in the study of nationalism and the politics of protest in tropical Africa. Compare Aristide Zolberg, "The structure of political conflict in the new states of tropical Africa," *American Political Science Review*, LXII (March 1968), 70–87.

Chapter 11: The Elite

1. My usage of the term "strategic elite" differs from that of Suzanne Keller, *Beyond the Ruling Class*, New York, 1963, who uses the term to indicate an elite made up of the leading members of certain specialized elites.

2. E. Bott, *Family and Social Network*, London, 1957.

3. Anthropologists would not accept G. Myrdal's assessment that there is no more objective way of determining status than by taking the evaluative measures of the people themselves (*An American Dilemma*, New York, 1944). A sociological model is derived from the observer's model taken in conjunction with the actor's model.

4. See p. 64. Ocen's wife died in January, 1969 (W. Ekwaru—personal communication).

5. F. Barth, *Models of Social Organization*, London, 1966, pp. 6–7.

6. G. and M. Wilson, *The Analysis of Social Change*, Cambridge, 1945, pp. 30–31: "Communities are areas and periods of common life of more or less intensity. . . . The boundaries of community are the boundaries of many-sided relationships; extra-communal relations are one-sided and tenuous."

7. S. Nadel, "The concept of social elites," *International Social Science Bulletin*, 8 (1956), 413–24.

8. M. Gluckman, *Politics, Law and Ritual in Tribal Society*, Oxford, 1965.

9. Nadel, "The concept of social elites."

10. E. Chapple and C. Arensberg, "Measuring Human Relations," *Genetic and Psychology Monographs*, 22 (1942).

11. According to the instructions circulated by the District administration, clan leaders as well as the parish chief could speak out on behalf of parishioners. This was not known to those I spoke to in Gondo in 1967.

12. Nadel, "The concept of social elites."

13. *Ibid.*

14. E. Wolf, "Aspects of group relations in a complex society: Mexico," *American Anthropologist*, LVIII (1956), 1065–78.

15. Nadel, "The concept of social elites."

16. C. E. Black, *The Dynamics of Modernization*, New York, 1966, p. 60.

Conclusion

1. C. Coon, *Caravan*, New York, 1951.

2. J. Furnivall, *Colonial Policy and Practice in the Netherlands East Indies*, Cambridge, 1948.

3. G. and M. Wilson, *The Analysis of Social Change*, Cambridge, 1945, F. Bailey, "Two villages in Orissa (India)," in M. Gluckman (ed.), *Closed Systems and Open Minds*, Edinburgh and London, 1964; M. Gluckman, *The Judicial Process among the Barotse of Northern Rhodesia*, Manchester, 1955.

4. M. Fortes, "Ritual and office in tribal society," in M. Gluckman (ed.), *Essays on the Ritual of Social Relations*, Manchester, 1962, p. 54.

5. J. Middleton, *The Effects of Economic Development on Traditional Political Systems in Africa South of the Sahara*, The Hague, 1966, p. 33.

6. L. Fallers, "Political sociology and the anthropological study of African politics," *Archives européennes sociologiques*, 4 (1963), 329.

7. J. Vincent, "Teso society in transformation: Colonial penetration in Teso District and its contemporary significance" in J. Coleman, L. Cliffe, and M. Doornbos (eds.), *Symposium on Penetration* (in press).

8. TDA. XNAF/5. (District council, 1919–48); ADM 20 (General correspondence).

9. E. Colson, *The Makah Indians*, Minnesota, 1954.

10. J. Helm (ed.), *Essays on the Problem of Tribe*, Washington, 1968.

11. A. Epstein, *Politics in an Urban African Community*, Manchester, 1958.

12. A. Radcliffe-Brown, "Introduction" to J. Embree, *Suye Mura*, Chicago, 1939, p. xvii.

13. S. Nadel, *The Foundations of Social Anthropology*, London, 1951; E. Leach, *Political Systems of Highland Burma*, London, 1954, p. 11.

14. Contrary to L. Fallers, "Are African cultivators to be called peasants?," *Current Anthropology*, 2 (1961).

15. D. Stenning, *Savannah Nomads*, Oxford, 1954; P. Gulliver, *The Family Herds*, London, 1955; N. Dyson-Hudson, *Karimojong Politics*, Oxford, 1966.

16. J. Vincent, "Teso society in transformation . . ."

17. R. Murphy, "Social change and acculturation," *Transactions of the New York Academy of Sciences*, Series 2, 26 (1964), 7.

18. Both the Kenya and Tanzania governments set up commissions of inquiry in 1967, and their reports were placed before their respective legislative assemblies in mid-1969.

19. C. Arensberg and S. Kimball, *Culture and Community*, New York, 1965, p. 304.

20. O. Handlin, "Peasant origins," in G. Dalton (ed.), *Tribal and Peasant Economies*, New York, 1967; *The Uprooted*, New York, 1951.

21. H. Maine, *Village Communities in the East and West*. London, 1876, p. 126.

22. E. Peters, "Aspects of rank and status among Muslims in a Lebanese village," in J. Pitt-Rivers (ed.), *Mediterranean Countrymen*, Paris, 1963, p. 171.

23. L. Wylie, "Demographic change in Roussillon" in *ibid.*, p. 236.

24. *Ibid.*, p. 17.

25. F. Barth, *The Role of the Entrepreneur in Social Change in Northern Norway*, Bergen, 1963, p. 10.

26. Handlin, "Peasant origins," p. 656.

27. P. Lloyd, "Introduction," *The New Elites of Tropical Africa*, London, 1966, p. 50.

28. A. Southall, "The concept of elites and their formation in Uganda," in *ibid.*, p. 334.

Index

[301]

INDEX